The Chief Information Officer's Body of Knowledge

People, Process, and Technology

DEAN LANE

WILEY

John Wiley & Sons, Inc.

Published by John Wiley & Sons, Inc., Hoboken, New Jersey.
Published simultaneously in Canada.

For general information on our other products and services or for technical support, please contact our Customer Care Department within the United States at (800) 762-2974, outside the United States at (317) 572-3993 or fax (317) 572-4002.

Wiley also publishes its books in a variety of electronic formats. Some content that appears in print may not be available in electronic books. For more information about Wiley products, visit our web site at www.wiley.com.

Library of Congress Cataloging-in-Publication Data:
Lane, Dean.
  Chief information officer's body of knowledge: people, process, and technology/Dean Lane.
    p. cm.
  Includes index.
  ISBN 978-1-118-04325-7 (hardback); ISBN 978-1-118-11378-3 (ebk);
  ISBN 978-1-118-11379-0 (ebk); ISBN 978-1-118-11380-6 (ebk)
 1. Information technology–Management. 2. Chief information officers. I. Title.
  HD30.2.L363 2011
  658.4'038–dc22

                                                            2011014257

Printed in the United States of America

10 9 8 7 6 5 4 3 2 1

This book is dedicated to Debbie—my wife, my life, the best thing about me!

Contents

PART TWO: PROCESS

Chapter 19: Project Reviews

Subbu Murthy

Chapter 19: Project Reviews — **187**

Chapter 20: Compliance

Gary Kelly

Chapter 20: Compliance — **195**

Chapter 21: Service Management

Himanshu Shah

Chapter 21: Service Management — **203**

Chapter 22: Balancing IT's Workload

David Blumhorst

Chapter 22: Balancing IT's Workload — **217**

Chapter 23: Outsourcing and Offshoring

Jeff Richards

Chapter 23: Outsourcing and Offshoring — **227**

Preface

I N THE EVER-CHANGING WORLD of technology, executives are increasingly busy, faced with multiple decisions to make, and fast. There is no doubt that executives are smart people, who have a deep understanding of their businesses, but their demanding schedules do not allow for painful details of everything that comes across their desks. So, while it might seem elementary, one of the most effective ways to communicate with executives is through *Big Animal Pictures*.

An easy way to understand the Big Animal Pictures concept is to think of the popular Little Golden Books. Each page has a big picture; for example, on one page, there is a picture of an elephant, and at the bottom of the page, there is an enlarged letter E, followed by the rest of the word. Nothing else appears on the page. Children learn quickly with little details, and so does everyone else. When we make presentations in this form, our audience will stay right with us, and they will ask questions about the details in which they are interested, so be prepared. Using the same elephant example, if someone asks, "What is that large tubular item protruding from the front of the elephant?" we must be prepared to explain that this is the elephant's trunk, and it is used to pick up food and water.

In orchestrating the writing and editing of this book, each of the contributors has presented an overview of his or her topic. Although it would be easy to write volumes on each of the topics presented, the authors have narrowed the discussion to present you with Big Animal Pictures. In the next few pages, I do the same with some overarching words of wisdom about what makes a great chief information officer (CIO) candidate.

Ten years ago, a major topic of discussion was that business was becoming increasingly more difficult, on all fronts. Corporations were focusing on their short-term business as enterprise-wide cost pressures were increasing, and so was competition. Consequently, CIOs were tasked with tightly coupling (*aligning*) what the information technology (IT) department does with how the business performs. This alignment issue was not a new one; it had been around for 10 years prior to the new millennium and stemmed from the need to have the systems more closely mirror the real-world manner in which a business attains its goals.

The consulting advice we gave to CIOs was to focus their efforts where they would be most effective and have the greatest impact. This required that they provide executive leadership, build organizational capabilities, and demonstrate through metrics that they were delivering value for the IT dollar by enabling the business.

You are probably thinking this sounds familiar and very relevant for today's IT executive. In my organization, CIOs are recognized as front-line business executives who just happen to have an IT background; we strive to help them become CEOs of their IT departments. They have the same collection of pressures as any other business executive, and it is their responsibility to oversee the IT foundations that will provide for long-term business successes. With this model as my experience, there are times I read a CIO job description and cannot resist rolling my eyes. The skill set required by a single CIO ranges from the ability to communicate with the board of directors, to hands-on ability to configure an off-the-shelf piece of software, to expertise in a programming language. Whoever writes these position descriptions is not looking for a CIO; they are looking to minimize costs.

To assist both CIOs and the hiring managers of CIOs, I would like to present, in David Letterman fashion, the "top ten" characteristics that should be sought in a CIO. We already understand the technology. The following pyramid is in a hierarchy of importance.

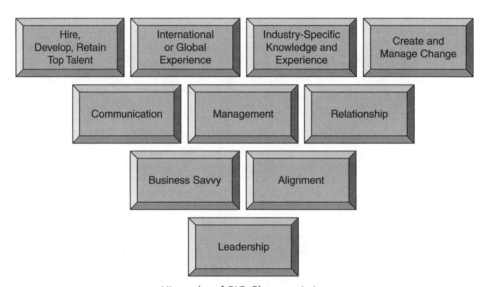

Hierarchy of CIO Characteristics

10. **Hire, develop, and retain high-quality IT professionals.** This critical ability is often forgotten when considering what makes a great CIO, even though numerous surveys show that CEOs consider this task to be high on their list of priorities. When I assist clients in hiring CIOs, I am almost always the one to emphasize the importance of a candidate's ability to attract, grow, groom, and hold on to excellent employees. And, of course, if the CIO candidate possesses these attributes it is a definite plus.

9. **International or global experience.** I have been offshoring since 1983 . . . prior to the fever of offshoring. At that time, most companies would not have put this item on this list. Today, however, most companies (from all continents) seek international customers. The Internet and the commonality of cross-border acquisitions have raised the bar so that CIOs are expected to have knowledge of

other cultures and an understanding of doing business in foreign markets. Companies are seeking CIOs with the experience of interacting with global teams and knowledge of the differences that exist when conducting business in other parts of the world.

8. **Knowledge of and experience in a specific industry.** A very common request is that candidate CIOs be from the same industry as the company performing the search (e.g., banking, retailing, insurance, hospitality, etc.). In some cases, this makes perfect sense. But this should not be a barrier to hiring a good candidate who has alternative experience in industries with analogous business models. Wise companies take the route of conducting CIO candidate searches that require the position be filled with someone from another industry. This practice provides the company the ability to bring in new ideas and thinking from a sector of the economy with a different orthodoxy.

7. **Ability to create and manage change.** This is a very common and important requirement, since most companies are hiring a CIO to implement some type of change. Changing the posture of the IT function from an operational need to a strategic element is the highest priority here. The expectation is improvement in both IT planning and execution. The ability to create change in the corporation's operating and business processes, for both efficiency and competitiveness, is also commonly sought. Business process reengineering and continuous process improvement are often on the minds of many CEOs. This is especially so in tougher economic conditions.

6. **Communication skills.** The ability to intelligently articulate a strategy, an idea, a thought, or a feeling, and to do so in a clear and appropriate manner, is an absolute must. That is not to say that a candidate needs to be an intellectual; as a matter of fact, it is preferred that you speak plainly. The apex of this aspect of communicating is the ability to tell a story and keep the audience's attention. Add in great listening skills as well. My father once told me, "You were born with two ears and only one mouth, so make sure you listen twice as much as you speak." Strong abilities to negotiate, persuade, and resolve conflicts are important parts of communication. All of these facets must be available within the written word, one-to-one verbal communications, group skills, and public speaking.

5. **Management skills.** An aptitude for directing and supervising people is the first required management skill. Proficiency in monitoring projects, resources, budgets, vendors, and other business partners should also be on the palette. To excel as a manager, one is expected to have a track record for building teams and to be able to motivate people in good and bad times and serve as a coach or mentor when necessary. Setting priorities and delivering on time and on budget are always seen as key requirements for CIOs who are considered to be outstanding.

4. **Relationship skills.** Today a majority of CIOs report to chief financial officers (CFOs). This puts the CIO in an interesting position from the standpoint of interacting with other C-level executives. CEOs and chief operating officers (COOs) are seeking good functional connections and a high level of trust and rapport between the CIO and other C-level officers, but reporting structures can complicate this for the CIO and often are the reason for failure. Excellent CIOs will

have superior interpersonal skills and establish strong bonds with the C-level and board members alike.

3. **Business savvy.** CIOs must demonstrate to others their understanding of the manner in which the organization conducts business. When a CIO does not possess this attribute, it is visible and can often lead to "phone guy" status. (The "phone guy" label depicts a CIO as only being asked for his or her involvement when there is an issue with the CEO's cell phone, and portrays a diminished role that is not strategic). CIOs must have the capacity to develop knowledge of the industry in which they are serving and the company's business strategy. Additionally CIOs must know how the company operates, its value proposition, who the competitors are, and what market position the company holds. This information enables the CIO to assist the organization in making progress and, ultimately, meeting its goals. Often a foundation in the principles of accounting and finance are sought when the CIO reports to the CFO. However, if the CIO reports to the CEO or COO, other disciplines (e.g., supply chain management, marketing, sales, and distribution) are seen as an advantage. The reality of the matter is that CIOs touch all of these areas in the performance of their duties, so some knowledge in all these areas is necessary to succeed and therefore required by senior management.

2. **Alignment.** Too often enterprises gain "alignment" in the following fashion: The CEO, the other C-levels, the CIO, and all significant others go to a resort for a weekend. Saturday morning is a working session that begins early and concludes with an on-site lunch. Saturday afternoon is an organized activity with significant others, followed by dinner. Sunday is golf or tennis, and Monday morning the company is aligned. This may be true for all of Monday, but as the weeks and months roll by, business conditions change, and the alignment fades. Alignment is a process that IT has been doing internally (within IT) almost since its inception. Business reviews, statusing, prioritizing, and deprioritizing are a few of the alignment components. CIOs typically know about alignment but have rarely had the opportunity to perform true alignment practices.

And the number-one requirement for the position of CIO is:

1. **Leadership.** This quality is listed in almost every search specification, regardless of whether it is for a CIO. Evaluation of this characteristic is very subjective because there are so many different forms and styles of leadership, but a CIO's resume and experience must indicate that he or she is a true leader. Describing the candidate as visionary, inspirational, supportive, or any of the other terms associated with leadership only indicates style. What matters here is whether this person can serve as a role model and whether others will follow his or her lead. Leadership is clearly the most important characteristic one can have . . . CIO or not!

All of the CIOs who have contributed to the writing of this book score highly when evaluated for these 10 attributes. What you are about to read is based on their personal experience. As all CIOs know, the best reference source to determine if a piece of hardware is worthy, or if a software application is bug-free, or if a vendor provides good service, is to discuss with a CIO peer group. That is what makes this book valuable.

Introduction

"It is not the strongest of the species that survives, nor the most intelligent, but the one most responsive to change."

—Charles Darwin

The Chief Information Officer's Body of Knowledge: People, Process, and Technology, written by experienced IT professionals, tells how the CIO and information professional might better manage IT budgets, projects, people, and overall IT operations. It is a compendium of how to manage both IT operations and one's career growth, balancing innovation opportunities and day-to-day operations with resource constraints. Most important, this book speaks to business leadership as a necessary quality of the successful CIO, since IT operations are the essential means for operational and competitive change.

In this introduction, I quote various chapter authors. I read the manuscript with a highlighter and pen in hand. When I returned to the text to begin writing, I found I had highlighted every chapter and so many key messages that I reluctantly selected only a few to quote. My apologies to the other authors but my intent is to give the reader a taste of this comprehensive book and a look inside the ideas, strategies, and operations of nearly 30 experienced information professionals.

In the preface, Dean Lane enumerates, "in David Letterman fashion," the "Top Ten" characteristics one should look for in a CIO. These characteristics are well worth reading by any business executive. *Number one is leadership.* Leadership is built on all the other essential characteristics: developing talent, global experience, creating and managing change, communication and management, relationship skills, business savvy, and aligning IT operations with ever-changing business goals and strategies.

Leadership flows from knowledge. It is one of those intangible qualities that is measured and quantified in the business world by financial results. Pamela Vaughan, CIO of Ariat, tells us elevation of IT's role within the organization will happen "when IT can report that we spent x and delivered y for an overall return of z." "IT portfolio management provides a decision-making framework" for discerning value-enhancing projects from low value-added and redundant ones.

In recent years, the CIO was faced with the formidable task of managing complex operations while cutting costs and streamlining operations. At the same time, CIOs worldwide faced an ever-increasingly innovative marketplace. Bystanders lost ground. We live in an age where every enterprise is information-dependent. And the world of information technology does not stand still in good times or bad times. Somehow, the more imaginative and better-managed IT operations find a way to balance innovation and cost management. That takes unusual talent.

In 2010, Gartner released a worldwide CIO survey. Some 1,586 CIOs participated in the study. While the reports found that budget cuts due to the global recession set back IT resources to 1995 levels, the list of issues and challenges facing the CIO were growing. The CIOs' top technology priorities included such areas as visualization, cloud computing, Web 2.0, networking and voice communications, mobile computing, and security. Those priorities were matched by their top business priorities, which included process improvements, reducing enterprise costs, increasing use of information analytics, improving enterprise workforce effectiveness, and creating new products and services.[1] Each and every one of the stated priorities is a significant resource challenge.

Tim Campos, CIO of Facebook, points out that "the resources allocated to the IT department are finite, yet the demands on the IT organization can at times appear infinite. It is a challenge that separates the mediocre from the exceptional IT organization. The secret to addressing this challenge is to strategically align your organization to the business."

The information age has given IT many tools to deal with business, market, and customer changes. IT is the arterial system of all modern-day commerce. Yet, many CIOs tell me that they spend much of their time educating and convincing their managements to allocate appropriate resources and to invest ahead of the issues and market demands. And those issues and demands are increasing. It is little wonder that the CIO, who is at the center of it all, is expected to be a strong leader as well as a strong manager of people, projects, and budgets.

Robert Slepin, CIO of Lifemasters Supported SelfCare, tells us that the "CIO sets the example for the IT organization. In fact, a CIO is a role model for the whole company, because one's influence extends far beyond the boundaries of the organization chart."

Managing change means dealing with the many shapes and forms of change while defining priorities and where to focus. But few CIOs have the luxury of dealing with one issue or program at a time. He or she must juggle multiple programs and issues at the same time while keeping up with what's happening in the technology and marketplace. For the CIO, staying current is not merely a "when I have time" event. It is a necessity. Dealing with normal daily processes and incremental changes is the norm. However, the CIO is expected to have his or her hands on the tiller through good and bad cycles, "normal" change and disruptive change. And in today's open-access world, disruptive changes seem to be happening with increased frequency.

In the first decade of this new century, we witnessed an unprecedented pace and reach of information technology: the expansion of global markets, Internet growth, expanding use and application of smartphones and tablets, the rise of social networks, mobility applications such as location-based services, demands for operational integration, the rapid development of "the cloud" as a basket of universally accessible services, the rising challenge of unstructured data, and more. Despite the struggling global economy, the pace of technological change is not slowing down. It is accelerating. And, if there is one defining criterion for a CIO, it is the ability to manage change.

We may well be at yet another inflection point in the evolution of "personal" computing. This inflection is not about bits and bytes, but rather about the growth of the global online consumer. Vast numbers of the world's population now have access not only to information but also to new media-driven experiences that will surely bring unexpected changes to the marketplace. Smartphones, for example, are growing at nearly 50 percent per year and will reach well over 500 million units shipped worldwide in 2012. Gartner predicts "by 2014, over 3 billion of the world's adult population will be able to transact electronically via mobile or Internet technology. Emerging economies will see rapidly rising mobile and Internet adoption through 2014. At the same time, advances in mobile payment, commerce and banking are making it easier to electronically transact via mobile or PC Internet. Combining these two trends creates a situation in which a significant majority of the world's adult population will be able to electronically transact by 2014."[2]

But the devices themselves are less valuable than the services that will flow through them. Interacting with diverse global populations with different needs and wants will stimulate the automation of IT services. In this new information-prolific and connected world, external forces more than internal forces are directly and indirectly shaping the nature of the CIO's work.

Social media is a good example. It seemed to have fallen from the sky overnight. And it did. Facebook, launched in 2004, reached 600 million users by the end of 2010, while Twitter, founded in 2006, reported on their fifth year of business over 100 million users, growing at 300,000 new accounts per day. Five years after opening its doors, YouTube was getting 2 billion views per day localized in 23 countries and 24 languages. According to royal.pingdom.com, 107 trillion e-mail messages were sent in 2010. These statistics are mind-numbing at first, but then one has to consider that they were all built on Internet platforms that enable rapid and global diffusion of content.

Globally, Internet access continues to expand, reaching over 2 billion people with an incredible 445 percent growth rate from 2000 to 2010. By 2015, it is expected that another 1 billion people will connect. Most of new Internet growth is coming from outside North America, with Asian markets showing the largest growth.[3]

We often look at the company or the application that is creating the numbers or user phenomenon but the actual effect will be a change in markets and consumer behaviors in the emerging markets. It is reasonable to predict that by tracking growth of the Internet and Internet access devices, social media will continue to have a huge impact on consumer and business cultures.

Already we have seen evidence of the power of the new social media. Facebook is credited with helping organize public protests against an oppressive government that had been in power for some 30 years. Yet, less than 10 percent of Egypt's population are Facebook subscribers. When digital technologies that allow consumers to connect reach the marketplace, they are rapidly adopted. And as a result, habits and cultures change.

This is but one more application of communications that the CIO must address in the coming years. For social media is growing too fast and spreading too wide across the globe to be ignored. CIOs are experimenting, and some are deploying applications inside and outside the enterprise. Gartner estimates that "in the next two years, 30 percent of the leading companies will extend the goals of their online activities to the design of enhanced service processes, such as social CRM."[4] Gartner predicts that by 2014, 90 percent of organizations will support corporate applications on personal devices. But, there are issues not the least of which are privacy and security.

Change often has a downside, particularly for those who are not prepared. We are seeing incidents where the trust consumers have developed for online services can be challenged. The incidents of hackers gaining access to sensitive customer data are increasing every year. Disruptions in online access now make for front-page headlines.

For example, recent news such the Sony PlayStation Network database breach cannot help but set every CIO scurrying to review and adjust current processes and safeguards. In early 2011, Sony PlayStation, a global, trusted brand, had over 100 million customer records illegally breached, forcing Sony to shut down its network for two weeks. This was the second largest data breach in U.S. history.

According to a vice president at Sony, "The forensic teams were able to confirm that intruders had used very sophisticated and aggressive techniques to obtain unauthorized access, hide their presence from system administrators and escalate privileges inside the servers."[5] Adding to the surreptitious and complex nature of such unlawful activities, Bloomberg News reported, "The hacker used Amazon's Elastic Computer Cloud, or EC2, service to attack Sony's online entertainment systems. . . . The intruder, who used a bogus name to set up an account that's now disabled, didn't hack into Amazon's servers."[6]

But customers are less concerned about where the fault lies; they *expect* continuous and secure access to their videos and games. Loss of revenue is certain but regaining the trust of users can take years. As Ted Leavitt, former marketing professor at Harvard, said, "with a service, you don't know what you don't get until you don't get it." This is but one example of the direct link between the CIO's operations and a company's brand or reputation. I firmly believe that the CIO is *the key player*, not only in sustaining a quality brand but also building and sustaining long-term customer loyalty. The lesson: Information is power but information technology is vulnerable.

Managing change, of course, means different things to different people depending on the responsibilities one has for assuring business continuity. It has much to do with migrating to new platforms and systems as well as looking out beyond the horizon.

Some years ago, I read a report by The Conference Board concerning the nature of technology and market change. I recall one statement in the report, "the future of business will be different in ultimately unpredictable ways." Technology is by and large predictable. In any given field, tracking patents and scientific and technical papers give indication of future change. What is not easily predictable is the consumer's response to the implementations of technology. My conclusion to this lack of visibility is that "businesses must be prepared for the eventuality of anything."[7]

One has to conclude that the CIO's job is managing change. It requires people skills but it also requires knowing how to apply technology to address change. It requires real-time information technology to create closed-loop, producer-consumer relationships by applying such tools as customer relationship management, sales force management systems, logistics, business intelligence (BI), analytics, and every connection or transaction that ends up benefiting the customer and the business. Because these systems automate end-to-end services, they are the most economical way to achieve profitable and competitive growth. And when they work, customers are satisfied.

As global competition increases and marketing costs rise, information technology provides new and better tools to understand the market, competition, and the customer.

More than a simple display of content, BI helps marketers and managers make better decisions.

During the past 40 years that I've spent in technology marketing I witnessed the adoption by consumers and the enterprise of the most common tools, processes, and services that are now part of our daily lives. I am particularly cognizant of the changes that the new information tools brought about in organizational structures and processes and in particular, marketing.

As I view it, we live in a world where computers and the network do most of the marketing work, from data gathering and analysis to customized messaging, product ordering, tracking, and billing to customer care and help desk. Throughout the value chain, the marketing function has disappeared into a network of relationships and responsibilities between man and machine. All the traditional components of marketing—product definition, lead qualification, prospect creation and tracking, logistics, pricing, forecasting, market analysis and segmentation, research, advertising, customer service, and management—are all now applications residing on platforms that are globally connected throughout the enterprise.

Michael Skaff, CIO of the San Francisco Symphony, tells us in Chapter 10, "accelerating change in consumer purchasing behavior reflects this new (consumer) cultural norm, and it has had far-reaching effects on business." Skaff goes on to say that e-commerce, once a novelty, has had enormous impact on the global economy. As evidence, he points out that online advertising surpassed print advertising in 2010.

It has become increasingly clear that IT now touches every customer and that because of this, it has the potential to influence and significantly impact the producer-consumer relationship.

I see the CIO as the keeper of the corporate brand. Marketing people love to talk about "brand" and "branding." Building brand leadership takes time, for the consumer must develop *trust* in the product, service, or relationship. Like the brake pedal on our automobiles, we have come to assume that information systems and tools can be trusted. Brakes on a car are obvious, but for most consumers, the complexities of the technology are hidden from view. But the expectation is the same: Action or inquiry demands immediate response.

A brand, by definition, must have a history of a relationship between the consumer and the product or service brand. And because a brand is also a perception, it changes and adapts to cultural and market changes. A one-time event does not create a brand relationship. Where are those customer histories generated, updated, transactions confirmed and assured, tracked, analyzed, segmented, and serviced in the twenty-first century enterprise? IT systems keep tabs on consumer behavior as transactions take place. It may take longer for many marketing organizations to react than it does for IT or the BI system to present consumer brand behavior using visualization tools in living color. I am not proposing that IT replace marketing but rather I am emphasizing the fact that today's marketing cannot function without an IT foundation. BI was once the direct responsibility of the marketing function as well. Today, it is being automated and the results distributed to all decision makers in the organization.

All of the above components add up to what we might well call brand management.

IS THE CIO READY FOR THIS NEW WORLD?

"Help—my IT department is overloaded. There is an ever-present 'base demand' placed on IT from within and outside the IT organization. That demand is 'Keeping the Lights On.' This type of work is mostly invisible outside of IT—unless, of course, something goes terribly awry," says David Blumhorst, vice president of professional services at Daptiv Inc.

The old assembly-line management process is rapidly fading into the sunset as networks and information systems reach across boundaries, changing the way work is done. Job descriptions are also changing. The CIO and the information professional have a great deal of responsibility. Keeping the lights on across the globe 24/7 is a daunting responsibility. Not the least part of which is that the CIO must continually trade off cost management with opportunity costs.

It would also appear that the CIO's most time-consuming task is project cost management. Sam Chughtai, director of risk management at Microsoft, points out that "52.7 percent of projects will overrun their original cost estimate by 189 percent. . . . Big projects fail at an astonishing rate, causing a multitude of brand value, market share compromise, reputational impact, and regulatory compliance risks."

On the other side of the coin, IT costs are becoming a large percentage of business capital costs. As such, IT has come to be taken for granted and too often is seen as a necessary cost rather than an opportunity for innovation and market leadership.

An article in the *Conference Board Review*, "Embracing Ambiguity," addresses the general issue of prediction, decision, and problems that arise:

> Problems really crop up after you make your bet. As with many senior leaders, your training and instinct tell you to look outward, determine what is likely to happen, and create a strategy designed to take advantage of or protect you from your 'prediction.' The problem? On one hand, you have been taught that leaders stay the course—they make a decision and stick with it. On the other, high degrees of uncertainty require course shifts; adaptability is the name of the game. This is the paradox of commitment—of balancing conflicting priorities.[8]

In today's event-filled, complex, real-time, IT-dependent enterprise, the CIO must surely feel besieged from all sides. Pressed by the constant operational demands, market changes, competitive pressures, customer issues, ever-changing new technologies and applications, upgrades, budget management and constraints, competition, and a myriad of internal and external pressure points, it is little wonder that the CIO must continually upgrade his or her own knowledge base.

This book is not about radical change. It is about fine-tuning an area of business that has always been on the leading edge of change. For the CIO and information professional today, keeping current, staying aware of technological and market change, and self-educating most frequently come from professional collaboration and personal, hands-on experience. Fortunately, the IT professionals who contributed to this work have generously shared their experiences and body of knowledge for the benefit of the CIO profession.

—Regis McKenna

Regis McKenna founded his own marketing strategy firm in 1970 and retired from active consulting in 2000. His early clients included Apple, Intel, Genentech, Electronic Arts, AOL, and many others. He and his firm also consulted to HP, IBM, SAP, Oracle, and other IT companies. McKenna is included in the San Jose Mercury News's Millennium 100 *as one of the 100 people who made Silicon Valley what it is today. McKenna has written and lectured extensively on the social and market effects of technological change advancing innovations in marketing theories and practices. He has written five books on marketing including* Real Time: Preparing for the Age of the Never Satisfied Customer *(Harvard Business School Press, 1997) and* Total Access: Giving Customers What They Want in an Anytime, Anywhere World *(Harvard Business School Press, 2002). He was a general partner of Kleiner Perkins Caufield in the late 1980s and early 1990s. McKenna was the seed investor and board member of WebLogic, which was sold to BEA in 1998; a co-founder of Broadware, a high-availability video server company that was sold to Cisco in 2007; and most recently an investor and member of the board of Golden Gate Software, which was sold to Oracle in 2009. He continues to advise start-up companies and sometimes invest.*

 NOTES

1. www.gartner.com/it/page.jsp?id=1283413, January 19, 2010.
2. www.gartner.com/it/page.jsp?id=1278413, January 13, 2010.
3. www.internetworldstats.com/stats.htm.
4. www.gartner.com/it/page.jsp?id=1570814, March 3, 2011.
5. www.pcmag.com/article2/0,2817,2385397,00.asp, May 14, 2011.
6. www.bloomberg.com/news/2011-05-15/sony-attack-shows-amazon-s-cloud-service-lures-hackers-at-pennies-an-hour.html, May 16, 2011.
7. Regis McKenna, *Real Time: Preparing for the Age of the Never Satisfied Customer* (Boston: Harvard Business School Press, 2002).
8. Peter C. Caird, David L. Dotlich, and Stephen H. Rhinesmith, "Embracing Ambiguity," *The Conference Board Review*, Summer 2009.

PART ONE

People

CHAPTER ONE

Collaboration and Teamwork

Robert Slepin

IMAGINE FOR A MOMENT a professional sports team walking onto the field of an athletic competition. Its team members are confused about the strategy for the game and who is playing what role. During the game, communication and coordination errors occur. Not surprisingly, the team loses. Now consider this same team suffers from a systemic failure to effectively learn from its mistakes. It consistently fails to recognize the root causes of its performance problems and invest adequately in improvements necessary to achieve better outcomes. This chronically losing team, unable to effectively and efficiently harness its individual talents as a cohesive unit, loses again and again to far better prepared competitors. Not a pretty picture—and yet this scenario can be observed in businesses and information technology (IT) organizations where words such as collaboration and teamwork are inscribed onto corporate values cards but do not consistently come alive in day-to-day actions. The good news is there are actions a chief information officer (CIO) can take to help the company and the information technology (IT) organization achieve higher performance by creating a culture of collaboration and teamwork.

In this chapter, we discuss warning signs and underlying causes, issues, risks, and opportunities for cultivating a culture of teamwork and collaboration consistent with a high-performing IT organization, including:

- Signs, symptoms, and root causes of teamwork and collaboration problems
- The role and importance of the CIO in modeling the way

- How the entire IT leadership team is critical to teamwork
- How to develop effective teamwork skills throughout IT
- How to recruit for people skills
- How to set clear direction
- How to communicate effectively

SIGNS, SYMPTOMS, AND ROOT CAUSES

Problems with collaboration and teamwork reveal themselves in various ways. But a major red flag is an infestation of organizational silos. These are individual functional areas, or departments, operating too independently—to the detriment of critical business processes that, by their nature, must cross functional boundaries. Well-intended but isolated employees operating in silos focus on achieving their individual unit's goals at the expense of other internal groups and ultimately the company's customers and share-holders. As the functions consume people's time and other corporate resources to accomplish the tasks du jour, not necessarily in alignment with the priorities of other areas, tensions inevitably arise. When these tensions erupt in an unhealthy way, such as overheated arguments, passive-aggressive avoidance, or other inappropriate behavior, the spirit of collaboration across groups suffers. This can easily send the organization into a dysfunctional cycle, eroding the capability of functional units to work together as a cross-functional team in an optimally productive way.

Silos can exist within IT and across the organization at companies large and small, for-profit and not-for-profit, at the local, regional, and headquarters levels. Amid these silos, teamwork still can exist—and when it does, it is great—but it might be present only in pockets or for fleeting moments. For example, it might be evident within the software development team but not the operations group. It might exist for a period of time during a company crisis or during a mission-critical project bringing together people of different disciplines to achieve a clearly defined goal by a given date.

Detecting the presence of silos is simple. Listen to what IT employees say about their work environment. They might complain about constantly being bombarded by an endless stream of projects, requests, and issues thrown over the wall by business customers or colleagues from other IT areas. Employees also might point to conflicting priorities and not having enough resources to get all their work done. Poor requirements or constantly changing requirements are frequent complaints of IT organizations but can also be a sign of chronic issues in IT's ability to partner with the business. Territorial behavior—us versus them—and absence of trust across team boundaries are other signs of silos.

Issues with collaboration and teamwork may be caused by having the wrong people on the team or the right people in the wrong positions. Other possible root causes include leadership, skills development, recruiting, clarity, and communication.

MODELING THE WAY

As a CIO, you set an example for the IT organization. In fact, you are a role model for the whole company, because your influence extends far beyond the boundaries of the organization chart. Every word you speak in public or private, every action taken, every message written in e-mail, and every blog entry will be scrutinized closely by others not only on the IT team but also around the company and even possibly by external stakeholders such as suppliers, auditors, and customers. Facing intense scrutiny is common for leaders from all walks of life, whether corporate executives, politicians, religious leaders, or star athletes.

Given an ever-present corporate magnifying glass, CIOs should consider what example they are setting in interactions with bosses, peers, direct reports, customers, and employees. Reflect on your day-to-day behaviors and their consistency with values of teamwork and collaboration. Look in the mirror, and solicit candid, unvarnished feedback from trusted colleagues. Participate in a 360-degree review. Objectively compare your leadership skills with those of a respected peer or other executive within the company or elsewhere. Examine your strengths and weaknesses of character, leadership style, and interpersonal communications, and identify one or several personal improvement goals for the next 12 months. Determine specific, time-phased actions to drive improvement, and follow through: Take the planned actions, achieve results, evaluate outcomes, and consider the value from further improvement in a particular dimension of performance.

An orientation to continual self-improvement is well worth the investment of time and energy. The example you set is among the most powerful tools in influencing the IT organization to achieve peak performance in satisfying IT's customers. Conversely, if your actions do not mirror the values and principles of a collaborative culture, your performance as a leader is, simply put, unacceptable—and the efficiency and effectiveness of the IT team will suffer.

 ## THE IT LEADERSHIP TEAM IS CRITICAL TO SUCCESS

Besides modeling teamwork and collaboration themselves, CIOs ultimately are accountable also for the outcomes, actions, and behavior of the IT management team. If a CIO's direct reports behave badly, this can have a negative ripple effect down through the ranks of their respective organizations as well as across functions. Given the scope and magnitude of the influence of these senior leaders, among the most important tasks of the CIO is selecting the right people for these key positions. These heads of such functional areas as applications, infrastructure, and project management office (PMO) will make—or break—the success of the overall IT operation.

If the senior IT leaders cannot get along with each other and their customers, then Houston, we have a problem. The majority of IT work in most companies demands that people work together toward a common goal, whether it is sustaining day-to-day operational processes or executing projects large and small. For many activities, IT employees must possess more than sharp technical and business skills; interpersonal communications skills also are critical to lubricate relationships and achieve efficient coordination within and across teams.

Newly hired or promoted CIOs who have inherited senior managers behaving badly would be wise not to let these behavioral issues fester. They must confront the situation head-on. These senior managers must either step up their performance or move on to some other, more suitable role.

As a CIO, you should hold each manager accountable to the values, principles, and standards of the organization and their job role. Where there are gaps between actual and desired performance, openly but privately discuss these issues in a candid, clear dialog with management. This is very likely more than a one-time conversation; the dialog should be a routine part of weekly interactions with the manager until there no longer is an issue to discuss. Coach and mentor employees on their interpersonal skills as you would with any other areas where employees need help with performance. Offer formal training, where appropriate. Recognize and reward signs of improvement; clearly point out trouble spots. If the manager does not respond quickly to coaching and counseling, consult with your human resources (HR) partner and take other steps in keeping with the company's policies and procedures related to progressive discipline. At the end of the day, if employees, regardless of their level, still are not performing up to par after being given an opportunity to improve, either terminate them or move them into positions where they can be successful. Ignoring the issue or hoping it will go away is unacceptable.

The farther down in the organization one goes, the greater the risks to accountability. Except in the smallest IT organizations, CIOs do not have direct oversight of every employee. As a CIO, you naturally rely on the IT management team to lead their respective functions effectively. Your direct reports must hold all the managers and everyone else in the IT organization accountable for performance, including being good team players.

You are only as strong as your weakest link. If there are people in your organization whose subpar interpersonal skills are creating unhealthy friction, they are negatively affecting their coworkers and causing errors, rework, delays, failed projects, service disruptions, and so on.

One risk to this chain of accountability is that managers may believe that some of their people are so important to the organization, due to their rare knowledge or special technical skills, that they should be immune from the norms of good teamwork that apply to everyone else. It is okay for them to be lone rangers and behave badly. But when you net out the pros and cons, you typically will find that the damage a person does in not cooperating as a team member outweighs the benefits he or she creates. The return on investment is negative.

Another risk is that of seeing yourself as savior: "Give me enough time, and I will work with this person and help him improve his interpersonal communications or team leadership skills." In the meantime, month after month passes by, and the person continues spreading poison unabated into the business environment, destroying employee morale, productivity, and output results. Customer service and satisfaction suffers; your entire business literally can be harmed by not taking action swiftly enough in a situation like this.

Some managers feel that they must observe all the evidence of poor behavior with their own eyes before drawing any conclusions about a performance issue and taking action to deal with it. They will not trust the observations of others, no matter how clearly articulated. This unwillingness to consider all available evidence, whether directly observed or not, delays the inevitable. It is a form of paralysis analysis.

Timeliness of action is important. Ideally, leaders want to catch people doing things right so that they can offer sincere praise, recognition, and rewards in a timely manner. But when there are serious problems, effective managers want to find those, too, and fast, and deal with them appropriately. Personnel issues are not like wine; the effects of these problems do not improve with age. These situations do not usually resolve on their own.

 ## DEVELOPING TEAMING SKILLS THROUGHOUT IT

Besides focusing on improving your own skills as a collaborative leader, as CIO, you also are responsible for providing the company with the complete set of skills required to execute IT work aligned with business objectives. This means supporting employees in developing their skills, too. Training employees is not only about making people technically better as technology architects, software developers, network engineers, or systems administrators. It also includes improving their business and interpersonal skills.

One effective strategy is to require employees to annually self-assess their skills and create and implement an individualized development plan to drive self-improvement. This strategy can produce excellent results for a modest investment of time and resources. As part of the annual IT operating plan, establish a written goal that 100 percent of employees have an individual development plan. Make it clear that each individual's plan should include specific, measurable, actionable, realistic, time-phased objectives and the corresponding tasks for attaining those objectives. Hold managers at every level accountable to review, comment on, and sign off on their employees' plans and to monitor progress throughout the year, as part of their ongoing review and discussions with each team member about the entire set of objectives related to the individual's job function and priorities for the year.

Although training is important, management monitoring of performance and one-on-one coaching also are critical tools for improving employee performance. Teamwork problems may not necessarily be caused by gaps in interpersonal communications skills. There may be other root causes at play that should be explored between manager and employee. Deficiencies in business or technical skills, knowledge, or confidence could be at the heart of an employee's performance problems, which might surface as a problem communicating or getting along with others. For instance, a project manager who consistently does a poor job in running meetings can wreak havoc, destroying team efficiency and causing tremendous frustration. This project manager might need basic training or coaching in meeting management: when it is appropriate to call a meeting, creating an agenda, sticking to an agenda, managing difficult people during a meeting, ending a meeting with action items, and using action item logs and follow-up actions to hold people accountable in between meetings. Project managers who routinely schedule status meetings with no agenda involving large groups of people for hours on end may believe they are promoting teamwork when in fact they are frustrating their project team members and robbing the organization of precious productivity.

RECRUITING FOR PEOPLE SKILLS

Make people skills a priority in talent appraisal when recruiting and hiring new employees. One good practice in use among many organizations today is the behavioral interviewing technique. Work with your HR business partner to integrate behavioral interviewing into your standard recruiting process. Train IT management and staff in the process; interview for the presence of skills that are consistent with teamwork and collaboration. After each interview, each participant should write up her observations, conclusions, and recommendations regarding a candidate as input to the hiring manager's evaluation and decision. This front-end attention to screening for people skills will increase the odds of hiring individuals who are ready, willing, and able to work with others as part of a team—saving you downstream headaches of dealing with personnel-related problems that can damage your organization by draining productivity, harming employee morale, increasing cost, hurting quality, and dissatisfying customers.

 ## SETTING CLEAR DIRECTION

Leaders who are unclear in communicating priorities, roles, and assignments will likely (although perhaps unwittingly) send employees off into the wrong direction. Confused, employees will spin their wheels and waste time. Faced with too many goals or a lack of clarity, employees may feel overwhelmed and unable to cope with the sheer volume or ambiguity of work expectations. Marching off into opposite directions, employees may run into barriers across the organization in securing IT and business resources needed to complete their tasks. With priorities colliding, tensions will naturally emerge, stifling collaboration and teamwork and hurting productivity. Of course, some measure of conflict is completely natural and even desirable. In any organization, there can be multiple demands simultaneously competing for the attention of a finite human resource pool. A complete absence of conflict might be a sign of some other serious problem. But a great deal of dysfunctional conflict can be avoided through increased clarity and consistency in establishing expectations and aligning resources efficiently and effectively to priorities.

To clarify business priorities, it is important to document them in writing, share the documented priorities with the appropriate employee audiences, and provide specific guidance regarding relative ordering or weights of priorities. When priorities are clear, employees can make better decisions about what to work on day to day. This can improve timeliness and efficiency in resolving critical operational issues, keeping projects moving, and improving customer responsiveness and service. Clear prioritization can empower employees on or close to the front line to make appropriate decisions and resolve more issues on their own, avoiding unnecessary time lags and costly escalations to higher levels of management.

When employees are unclear about their roles and responsibilities and how their roles relate to other people in their groups or other areas, teamwork efficiency is at risk, as people waste time arguing about who is responsible for what. It is worth spending time writing out job descriptions in consultation with your employees, discussing the content of each role and how it relates to others.

Organization charts are good tools to visually describe on a single page who is responsible for what. A management-only chart can not only show who reports to whom and who owns what function, but can also include a paragraph of text or bullet points that flesh out the key responsibilities of each functional area.

Tables of responsibilities, or RACI charts (an acronym that stands for *r*esponsible, *a*ccountable, *c*onsulted, *i*nformed), are excellent, simple tools for going beyond a traditional organization chart and further describing roles and responsibilities across an organization, whether company wide, within IT only, or for a particular functional area or project team. There can be more than one R, C, or I on a chart—but only one person should be accountable. This makes the ultimate accountability completely clear.

In a matrix, list on the left axis each of the responsibilities or tasks. Across the top, list the names or job titles of the people involved in the organization, team, or process. At the intersection of each row and column, list whether someone is responsible, account-able, must be consulted, or must be informed, or leave the cell blank if none of these applies. This simple technique of documenting roles and responsibilities is very powerful in clarifying who is responsible for what—and should be a living document to which people can refer from time to time to refresh memories, to orient new people into the organization, and to manage changes to responsibilities over time as the organization structure, process, and/or people change.

A good tool for being clear with employees about priorities is the employee performance review process. When goals, objectives, recognition, and rewards, such as performance appraisal ratings, salary increases, and bonuses, are tied to results produced by silos or individuals within silos, remember that you get what you pay for. Rewarding only silo work may constrain achievement of results to those which silos can produce on their own. To encourage more cross-functional teamwork in support of a critical end-to-end process spanning multiple silos, engineer the rewards system to align with the desired behaviors and outcomes. For example, weight an employee's goals for the year with 50 percent of the review tied to team performance and 50 percent related to individual performance.

A variation is to alter the percentage split based on level in the organization. Senior executives might have 90 percent of their review tied to team goals; middle managers, 50 percent; and individual contributors, 25 percent. This is a good topic for discussion with your HR partner and is an issue that goes beyond the IT area. This is an item for attention at the senior executive level. Creating consistency across the company is important to developing a supportive environment for all the cross-functional processes and to drive high performance toward achievement of corporate goals and objectives.

Informal and formal public recognition of outstanding team performance also will send a powerful signal to the organization. Conversely, if management talks about teamwork but publicly praises or formally rewards only individual performance, leaders are sending mixed messages and employees will surely notice.

One company had an annual all-company recognition program consisting of a handful of awards for outstanding leadership, values in action, and operational performance. The program overall was very well received and effectively administered. But the rules called for nominations of individuals only, not teams. In some cases, employees asked if they could nominate teams that produced outstanding results. The answer was no because they did not meet the program criterion.

Best-practice governance, quality, and management frameworks, such as COBiT, ITIL, CMMI, and ISO, when properly deployed, require focused attention on clarity of accountability and excellent teamwork to work effectively. These frameworks can increase value and reduce risk in IT delivery, improving IT/business alignment and customer satisfaction. Some CIOs might be averse to the idea of implementing these kinds of frameworks, believing that they are too process-heavy. Although there are implementation risks, many aspects of these frameworks, when adapted and applied effectively and efficiently to a given IT organization's situation, can be incredibly powerful in improving cross-functional teamwork and organization-wide performance.

These frameworks build on the RACI concept and expand it further in clarifying the what, how, and who of the process. They provide specific, detailed guidance based on the experience of many other IT organizations across a wide array of commonly encountered IT processes.

It is not necessary to implement all of a framework to benefit from it. Nor is it necessary to start at point A and go in order to point Z. Approaches can vary based on the unique business environment and still be successful.

Speaking of important IT processes, requirements management should be evaluated as part of a review of opportunities for performance improvement. Chronically poor requirements are a common problem and can cause a great deal of friction between the business and IT and lead to costly project failures, waste, and rework. Although the business is responsible for providing good requirements, IT is accountable for the requirements management process that extends across functional boundaries and affects the cost, time, scope, risk, and quality of what IT produces.

 ## COMMUNICATING EFFECTIVELY

Communication is vital to collaboration and teamwork. It would be ideal if all the employees of a company or all the members of a project team were literally sitting in a single room. For a small start-up, this scenario might be practical. But for most companies, situating everyone in a single space is a tall order. A management challenge is to develop and maintain a sense of everyone sitting together in one room regardless of how large and distributed the company becomes. Certain strategies, tools, and practices have been demonstrated to be effective in creating a sense of community despite barriers of time zone, team size, space, language, and culture.

Leverage technology for improving communication and coordination among employees. Conference calls using voice and interactive Web technology are effective, inexpensive tools for improving collaboration across geographic sites. Consider using intranet, wikis, blogs, text, and other Web 2.0 and social media tools.

Standardize on an internal, secure communications tool for chatting, asynchronous or real-time group dialogs, and making visible real-time presence information. Presence can identify whether a user is on- or off-line, at their computer actively working or temporarily away for the computer (including how many minutes they have been away). Employees can note whether they are busy or not and turn on or off a do-not-disturb symbol. The tool makes it easy to quickly strike up an online, real-time chat between two people or even a team of three or more. PC desktop screens and files can also easily be shared.

Deploy video-conferencing. This technology is not new, but it is usually confined to boardrooms and possibly some conference rooms. If there is a business case and bandwidth is cheap enough, move to desktop video-conferencing. Eventually this capability will be ubiquitous.

Low-tech communications, such as department, management, team, and project meetings, are ways to foster efficient teamwork. Meet with the entire IT department once a month for an hour to provide the team with regular updates on key items worth their attention, such as progress against annual goals and objectives; risk areas needing the team's support; public recognition for exceptional performance of teams and individuals; and questions and answers for key issues on employees' minds. Attendance should be mandatory.

For smaller-size management and work-group meetings, a go-round session where each person has some time to speak is good, but be careful about managing this process. This is not a time for people to go on and on about every activity in their respective area; regurgitating this level of detail is unnecessary, unhelpful, and a time waster. Put a strict time limit on each person's update, perhaps two to three minutes, and ask everyone to focus comments on specific issues, such as key recent accomplishments, upcoming milestones, and—most important—critical issues or risks where help from other team members is needed. One manager focuses his team meetings on what he calls "blocking issues."

Collaborate with IT managers and staff to devise a communications strategy for the department as a whole to support daily operations and again on a project-specific basis to support project related needs. These plans should consider all stakeholders and identify who will send what message to whom when using what medium. Seek help from a corporate communications professional from within your company or, if the function does not exist internally, from outside.

SUMMARY

High-performance IT organizations must have the resources and capabilities for, and consistently demonstrate in practice, high levels of teamwork and collaboration within IT and across the company. Moreover, collaboration can extend beyond the firm's boundaries into the realm of key external stakeholders, such as customers and suppliers. Risks to effective, efficient teamwork and collaboration are readily identifiable and can be eliminated or mitigated. CIOs can easily recognize signs of trouble, such as presence of silos, poor teamwork behaviors, distrust, dysfunctional processes with hand-off problems, and confusion about priorities and roles. As CIO, you must serve as a role model and hold direct reports accountable for strongly supporting a vision of a high-performance team throughout the organization in their day-to-day actions as leaders. Leadership can raise the bar for all IT staff by recruiting top talent with people skills and helping employees improve performance through training, professional development, monitoring, and coaching. Leaders also can foster improved teamwork and outcomes by being totally clear about who needs to do what, when, and why, whether for run-the-business operational processes or IT projects. Finally, leaders can create and implement communications plans that will promote a sense of community regardless of how large the organization grows and how diverse the employee population becomes culturally or geographically. Good practices in creating and nurturing teamwork and collaboration exist. CIOs can either reinvent the wheel, or they can learn from and apply proven practices in their organizations, creating increased value to their key stakeholders and customers.

2

Recruiting Best Practices

Walter Bacon

I N TIMES OF ECONOMIC growth and in recessions, identifying, attracting, and securing top IT talent poses a challenge to most organizations, whether they are a start-up, Fortune 500, or the fastest-growing Internet company in Silicon Valley. Why? In this chapter, we address these three aspects of recruiting with a handful of best practices. Some of the principles will be familiar; others might offer you an "aha" moment and provide you with a few tactics to add to your already established methodology. Either way, often we need to be reminded of the basics and the importance of not skipping steps in the recruiting process. When we forget the simple steps and rush the process, we can find ourselves painfully short staffed and perplexed as to why. This chapter is a reminder to slow down and cover your bases when it comes to building out your teams with top IT talent.

Best practices for recruiting top IT talent need to be looked at from two perspectives and addressed accordingly. The two perspectives are proactive efforts versus reactive efforts, or strategic versus tactical. Proactive efforts and strategies are what you do to prepare and ready your team for recruiting success. Reactive efforts, of course, are what you do when time is running out and you need the talent *now*! Both strategic and tactical game plans are needed to succeed in recruiting.

Let us first remind ourselves of the many steps a search can take us through as it continues to challenge us in greater degree. Our goal will be to keep searches to a short, efficient, and successful process rather than becoming all-consuming drains of our resources.

- **Phase 1: Internal Recruiter.** You first rely on your internal recruiter to deliver wonderfully accurate and qualified candidates to you in a timely manner. You feel fortunate because there is no finder's fee and the cost of the contract recruiter is not hitting your IT budget either. (*But to your disappointment, the internal recruiter is not delivering candidates or is giving you stacks of unqualified resumes.*)

- **Phase 2: Friends and Family.** You send out an e-mail to your past associates, friends, and family, looking for a highly recommended referral to come your way. (*But unfortunately your contacts seem to be preoccupied with their own work, or they send you their down-and-out associates who are desperate for work but have none of the skills you need.*)

- **Phase 3: Online Communities.** You start reaching out to your online technology communities and posting your requirements with user groups, hoping to cast a wider net and attract at least a few candidates. (*You do attract some candidates, but they seem to be off the mark or from the other side of the country in need of a generous relocation package.*)

- **Phase 4: Outside Recruiting Partner.** You send an urgent request to your favorite outside recruiter, hoping he will deliver top talent to you immediately, since after all, you will be paying a respectable finder's fee. (*But the recruiter lets you know that the requirement you have designed is a hybrid of skills and cannot be readily found in one person. Or, if they can, you will need to pay 30 percent more than you have budgeted and someone at that level would not be interested in the role or the career path you have to offer. You are thinking to yourself, "The person who left the vacancy had all the right skills, and we were not paying her top dollar. Why can't we find a replacement at the same cost?")*

- **Phase 5: Tweaking the Job.** You finally notify your favorite outside recruiter that you are willing to engage a contractor who can perform the primary role while you revisit the "must-haves" of the job description, your budget, and the existing or potential skills of your current team. (*However, your favorite recruiter, although he has delivered excellent candidates in the past, seems to be failing on this particular search. Two weeks have passed with no success.*)

- **Phase 6: Multiple Outside Recruiting Partners.** You ask a few peers whom they use for recruiting, you engage additional recruiters, and among the two or three individuals trying to fill the job, you finally get some qualified candidates in the door. (*However, the candidates are not excited about your opportunity. They do not accept the offer, and you are back to square one.*)

- **Phase 7: Revise Your Strategy.** You ask your trusted partners why the candidates did not accept your offers, and you get insight into their perceptions of you, your team, your company, and the overall career opportunity. With the help of your partners, you tune up your overall story, your interviewing game plan, and your selling abilities. Shortly thereafter, you have secured your new hire, and your team is running on all cylinders.

Let us agree that none of these phases is bad or can be avoided altogether. Instead, let us consider some proactive and reactive best practices in recruiting so we can avoid trudging through *all* the phases for *every* search. With a little foresight, recruiting can be done with speed, accuracy, and efficiency. And hitting the bull's-eye (with fewer shots) will become the norm for you and your team.

INTERNAL RECRUITERS

Internal recruiters include those who are located at your company, regardless of their employment status, and whose compensation is not purely commissionable. This would encompass full-time employees, contract recruiters, or onsite managed staffing services. There are some positives to using internal recruiters. They are a shared resource with a minimal, if any, cost to your IT budget. They are on-site, and you can easily go back and forth to them daily, helping them to better understand your needs and wants. They have a more intimate understanding of your business and the personalities and culture in which the candidates will need to fit. They tend to migrate around to different companies in the same territory, which allows them to collect a pretty good personal network of candidates. And they do have access to your enterprise applicant tracking system, which probably contains plenty of qualified talent from previous searches.

However, some factors make this relationship less than ideal, especially for producing IT candidates. They usually report to the human resources department, whose main concern is recruiting "revenue-generating" roles as compared to "operations" roles such as IT. When it comes to priorities, they typically focus on recruiting engineers, product development, sales, marketing, and executive roles first. This leaves your IT jobs on the back burner. Internal recruiters are also keenly focused on demonstrating their own positive return on investment (ROI) so they will be reengaged for future hiring surges. This causes them to focus on slam-dunk requirements and some revenue-generating roles first so they can pay for themselves immediately and stay on the engagement. They tend to build networks of individual contributors in support of the product development side of the company instead of building the network of IT directors and IT managers you need as you expand your group. They get paid whether they fill your roles or not. They cannot afford to proactively build networks of the talent you anticipate needing because they must focus on filling the urgent, core technology roles first. Often they are spread so thin that they do not take the time to read between the lines of a resume to discern if the applicant might have the right DNA, even though the resume does not scream with all the right buzzwords. I have often heard of hiring managers reviewing stacks of candidates rejected by internal recruiters and finding three to four hidden gems worth interviewing who eventually got the job. If the candidate you need is not actively applying to the recruiter's corporate job posting and the skills you need are not readily available on the popular candidate web sites, typically internal recruiters do not call competitors directly to proactively shake the bushes for passively interested talent, even though these are among the best candidates to pursue.

So for the most part, internal recruiters will not go the extra mile to find you the best and brightest talent for your IT positions or put your needs at the top of their priority list.

To offset this dim reality, you should at least become very friendly with the internal recruiters before you have an urgent deadline. If you have aggressive hiring plans, you should get a dedicated recruiter for your team. However, be sure to maintain realistic expectations about the limited quality of recruiting you will receive from internal recruiters. Do not expect miracles, and do not put all your eggs in one basket.

 ## NETWORKING

You need to do something today for your recruiting success tomorrow. If you do not get results from internal recruiters, a good next step would be to look for a highly recommended, low-cost or no-fee referral. If you do not lay the groundwork for quality referrals today, you will not have them tomorrow when it is crunch time. In reality, your past associates are trustworthy and will respond to your e-mails, but they probably do not have access to the specific talent you want for the critical role you have. Have you reached out to your personal network in the past and been bombarded with candidates who were not even close to what you needed? Perhaps your first thought was "I need a bigger network."

How do you proactively build a network? A few areas you need to focus on are:

- **Find peers from similar profile companies.** Are you a software-as-a-service company with 500 to 1,000 employees? You should know of a handful of similar companies, maybe not your direct competitors, but companies with technology stacks similar to yours. How do you make yourself aware of these companies? What is your path to an introduction? Just ask for one. Figure out on LinkedIn who you might want to know and look for any connections you may have to them. Ask your connection to introduce you, and then invite your new contact to lunch or coffee.
- **Identify and attend groups with other CIOs, vice presidents (VPs), and IT directors.** Why will this help? You will get to know leaders who have seen quality candidates come and go from their own teams, perhaps consultants or full-time staff who left for other opportunities. By networking, you will also get a feel for which skills are in short supply. You can start asking around now for what you will need tomorrow. Or with the advice of your peers, you can adjust your technology strategy to avoid impossible or hard-to-find skills. Ask a trusted outside sales professional or recruiting partner to connect you with a few CIOs, VPs, or directors. Sales representatives are a great source for finding potentially valuable peer relationships.
- **Give referrals.** When someone else asks you for referrals, take a minute to think of someone for them. This will come back around to you when you have a need in the future.
- **Stay on good terms with everyone you used to work with on past teams, and add them as connections on LinkedIn.** Create your own group or join alumni groups from previous employers, and always keep track of where your best

teammates have gone. By making them a connection on LinkedIn, you can avoid losing track of your best performers.

■ **Join relevant groups on LinkedIn, Meetup, or Yahoo groups and get involved.** Post some comments or questions. Start making yourself visible to a community related to the technologies you use or plan to implement. Have your team join groups according to their individual skills. For instance, there are Linux groups, Cisco groups, SAP groups, and so on. If you can imagine it, there is a group for it online. If your team members become active in these groups, it will not be difficult to ask for referrals and post jobs when it is recruiting crunch time. Another advantage with community outreach is that you can proactively let people know what type of skills you expect to need and passively identify them ahead of time. If some of your connections have the time, bring them over to your office for lunch to get a feel for your team or meet them at the neighborhood lunch spot. Take the time to build community and engage that community. Slowly you will develop a broad network of relevant talent.

One thing you should not do is post false jobs to collect new resumes. Doing so wastes everyone's time, and word will get around.

 ## PARTNERS

In this chapter, we refer to any outside recruiter, recruiting company, or search firm operating on commission as a "partner." Why do you need partners? What are the benefits? What are the pros and cons?

Let's start with the cons. It takes a while for partners to understand your style, your business, your culture, and your technology. So they might send some candidates off the mark at first. It takes some time to get to know each other. It may seem like partners are somewhat expensive, especially if you have not budgeted a finder's fee to fill vacancies left from unplanned attrition. Partners are motivated by *this* month's revenue so your job might not be top priority if they have an easier requirement to fill at another client they have worked with successfully before. Agencies can have their own underlying corporate agendas, such as trying to supply you with contractors only because recurring revenue is more valuable to their shareholders or owners. And sometimes they merely use clients to meet mandated activity quotas. Some can even be pushy, urging you to see their candidate today, insisting the person will be off the market tomorrow.

Let's look at the pros. Partners are paid well to fill your openings. They are motivated by commissions. They usually have specific expertise in an organizational layer or skills silo across a specific geographical market. A partner might focus only on IT operations positions or IT leadership positions in the Bay Area. The advantage to you is that the partner has been building a network of the candidates you need for years prior to the day you asked for their help. The chances of them having access to the skills you need is much higher than your one-off need presented to the internal recruiter who is working on 10 completely different roles, ranging from administrative, to sales, to engineering, to IT operations. Some tenured partners are fearless with no qualms about poaching the talent you need from other local companies. Partners can also get in front of the widest range of talent. It is very easy for them to meet a candidate at the candidate's own job site. I meet talent on a regular basis at their offices to avoid any real interruption to their workday. Internal recruiters can interface only with candidates willing to dress up and venture across town for a preliminary interview. Most busy candidates do not have the time for this, especially if they are gainfully employed. Candidates perceive partners as brokers of multiple and limitless opportunities. Candidates would rather work with an individual who can send them to any company of their choosing. The best candidates tend to maintain a few relationships with trusted brokers of opportunities, and they rarely reply to job postings but rather depend on a representative making a warm introduction for them. Because of this, only diligent outside recruiting partners are able to reach the entire candidate pool. Use partners, but not just any partner.

Often I meet with a new client who tells me a story of a horribly performing recruiting vendor. I ask what specifically the vendor was doing that was not working. It is usually the same five things:

1. They send low-quality resumes, way off the mark, not even close.
2. They do not understand what the hiring manager is asking for.
3. They are not listening, and they are doing exactly what the client told them not to do.
4. The candidates they send do not actually know what they claim to know on their resumes so the meetings end up wasting everyone's time.
5. They send candidates who do know the technology but cannot communicate effectively and whose people skills are horrible.

Why does this happen? I believe it is due to a lack of tenure and a lack of commitment to the search industry and their future in it. These are rookie mistakes and traits of people merely trying to keep their job rather than people trying to build a lasting, well-maintained reputation and a solid personal brand.

 SELECTING A PARTNER

Get referrals. Ask your community and your peers whom they use. Ask who blows their socks off with outstanding results. Who is efficient to work with and makes the recruiting process easy and enjoyable? That is what you are paying for—value.

Some things to evaluate when choosing a partner are:

▪ **The individual.** Work with people who know that the search industry is where they belong. These individuals should be committed to IT recruitment as a long-term career and business, not drifting from one commissionable job to the next. They should be obsessive about networking top IT talent and getting to know everyone of importance in the field they are in. They should have some years under their belt. Listening skills are key. Investigators, problem solvers, and analysts are more effective than smooth talkers. Inquisitive personalities continually probe and dig to discover what you really need and want for your business. They should be on the conservative side, underpromising and overdelivering.

- **The company.** The partner's company culture needs to be concerned first about the client, not the sale. When vendors try to push on you what they readily have available instead of taking a posture of service and trying to meet your needs and wants, there is going to be friction, wasted time, and wasted energy. The partner also needs to be strong financially and able to adapt to a client's changing engagement patterns. For instance, when the economic downturn hit in late 2008, most direct-hire and contract-to-hire recruiting abruptly stopped. Many of the smaller agencies and niche boutiques that placed only a few full-time employees per month and whose businesses relied solely on finder's fees were hit hardest and driven out of business. When things started to pick back up again, most of the client demand was for highly skilled technology consultants instead of full-time permanent new hires. Smaller companies could not accommodate these requests for consultants because they did not have the cash reserves needed to payroll the consultants prior to collecting client fees. Therefore, choose partners who are client-centric and who can weather economic storms and adapt to your changing needs.

- **One relationship to manage.** In order to minimize vendor management of 5 to 10 different recruiting relationships, it is much more efficient if the partner can support your talent needs across the board, no matter how high (C-level) or low, or how near (onshore), or far (offshore), or self-managed (direct hire) or outsourced (fixed-bid, project-based engagements). As you know, your organization will be faced with a broad range of IT talent needs and will migrate in and out of talent delivery models. Having a single vendor who can continue to engage with you as your needs change is a great value saving time, money, and headaches.

- **Back-office technology.** How often have you had a billing dispute or wanted a report generated and your vendor had to manually pull together the information and cut and paste it into a spreadsheet with a two-day turnaround? That is not acceptable these days. Industry-standard integrated systems make all the difference for auditing, evaluating trends, and reporting. Let's start with the customer relationship management (CRM). Your vendor should be able to track every meeting conducted with you and make it visible for other people within its company in one central system. Your conversations leading to engagements should not be in someone's notebook that was left in the trunk of a car. When your job order gets entered into the vendor's CRM, all the modifying criteria should be entered for the internal team to see. This would include required certifications, tenure, experience, interview methodology, acceptance of candidates on H-1B (foreign workers in specialty occupations) visas, acceptance of candidates in need of relocation, salary ranges, pay rate, and bill rate ranges. All these criteria should be searchable and recorded data for the internal teams to properly support you. Your partner must be able to generate client reports in an instant. Useful queries would include: Which candidates were submitted to specific jobs, what were the submission and interview dates, who interviewed them, what is the candidate's citizenship, and what is his or her employment status? There should also be a document management component to the CRM whereby all related recruiting documents can be stored electronically with the candidate's record. Is an electronic version of the resume attached to the candidate record? Who are their references? Is the completed reference check form attached? Regarding contractor time sheets and approvals, is it all online, and is that system tied into the billing system so the hours approved by you online are used to create the invoice you then receive? Can all this information be extracted and displayed in reports for you on demand?

- **National and international footprint.** How many times have you worked well with your local vendor up to a point, but now you are opening an office in another U.S. city and your current vendor does not have anyone there to support you? Now you are forced to bring on yet another vendor and billing relationship with different online systems. It is best to have national coverage with local representation in most cities where you might do business. A national footprint also offers the advantage of providing a steadily growing national database of candidates. Sometimes it is necessary to search the whole country for rare skills. If the vendor does not have a national footprint and database, this can greatly limit your success through that partner.

 ## WORKING EFFECTIVELY WITH YOUR PARTNER

Now that you have chosen a few partners, you should be aware of how to get superior results from them. What are the tricks to getting your partners to provide you with appropriate talent while saving you time and eliminating the common hassles associated with vendor relationships? How do you achieve effective recruiting without making it your secondary core competency? How can you turn over your requirements to your partner and be confident it is diligently working on filling them while you stay focused on running your IT organization?

- **Motivating the partners.** Offer a temporary exclusive on the search in return for a slight discount if you have a buffer of time before the new-hire deadline. When a partner knows it is the only company working on your job and it must deliver results within a few weeks, the whole office jumps into high gear to get your jobs filled. The partner wants to set the stage for future searches, knowing that if it can demonstrate success for you on this search and deliver on time, you will be more likely to keep the relationship exclusive once this confidence has been established.
- **Retainers.** Offer a retainer, even on positions that would normally be recruited on a contingency model. In most cases, retained search firm fees are broken into thirds with one-third to start, one-third upon delivery of short-listed candidates, and one-third upon placement. However, if you are offering a retainer on senior- and mid-level positions, you and your partner can create a variety of flexible fee arrangements. This raises the commitment level from the partner to a whole new level and ensures 100 percent focus on your requirements.

- **Knowledge transfer.** Start the search out properly. Sit down for an hour or so and hash out with your partner what you need and why. Help them understand your business and your existing team. Partners need to know:
  - Who your competitors are
  - What the ideal candidate's background would be
  - Which companies you have poached talent from before
  - What you expect from the person in the first 90 days
  - What the bonus structures are
  - Why someone would want to join your team and your company
  - What the candidate will learn and gain from coming aboard
  - What you look for when you screen a resume
  - Your management style

  Take the time to sell your partner on the opportunity as a whole and present the unique pros and cons of the role. Candidates will trust you more and choose to work with you if you clearly present the positives but disclose a few shortcomings as well. Doing this also will give you a little role-play selling session before trying to sell a live candidate.

- **Communication.** Agree on communication methods and standards prior to the search. Give solid and thorough feedback from the first submittal. The first one is most important. Immediately be clear on what you want to see differently so your partner does not waste time focused on the wrong priorities. If you give thorough feedback and guidance, the team will stay motivated and on task. It is very deflating for recruiters when you do not give feedback and they are pounding out the phone calls and screening candidates all while being slightly off the mark. By the time you finally let them know of the change in focus, they have spoken to 40 candidates and are hoarse in the throat. Do not let recruiters wear themselves out running in the wrong direction. Update them frequently of any changes or developments on your side.

- **Commitment.** Do not disrespect your partner's time by changing your mind frequently and putting requirements on hold, then activating them again then calling a fire drill, then . . . you get the point. Clients who do not know what they want and keep changing their minds get moved to the bottom of the recruiter's priority list.

  Caution: Partners can fire clients too. One reason you do not want to be on a partner's pain-to-do-business-with list is that, shortly thereafter, your company will get placed on the great-place-to-poach-talent-from list. You do *not* want that. I pursued and secured a working relationship with a major Silicon Valley software company whose managers could not bring themselves to communicate their interest in our candidates any sooner than two weeks after the initial submittal. Invariably, when they finally expressed interest in the candidates, they were already off the market and no longer available. This happened again and again until my entire team of recruiters refused to lift a finger to support this client. The lesson is to not be a pain to do business with by disrespecting people's time. That can come back to haunt you.

PLAN FOR FLEXIBILITY

Be open to various forms of engaging talent, such as contractors, contract-to-hire candidates, and permanent/direct-hire candidates. A huge challenge to working effectively with clients occurs when they have budgeted for a salaried person only at below-market rates. This is often the case because someone recently left a vacancy on the team and the CIO only has budget to replace that exact person at their existing salary. But the problem is the person had developed a unique skill set pertaining only to your company and the specific job. The person had become a hybrid entity who had grown and morphed into something that only your company breeds. When it is time to replace the person, you craft a three-in-one job description (three diverse skill categories in one person). You have a below-market salary for the new role because the previous person was hired three years ago as a mid-level technologist and developed the ability over time to do the job of three typical individuals. In reality, to replace this person, you need to hire a more senior and more expensive individual with all the skills, or you need to be more flexible. Dissect the role. Extract the most important skills and recruit primarily for those. Try to find someone with the potential to become what you created in the last person. Because doing this will still pose a recruiting challenge, you need to have set aside money to hire a consultant who may not be a perfect fit culturally but who will get the job done and keep the recently vacated IT function moving forward. My point is this: Do not beat your head against the wall trying to fill the exact shoes of the person who left. I have seen jobs go unfilled for unnecessarily long periods of time because of this lack of flexibility.

Understand the climate of the market. Especially during a recession, the best candidates are holding on to their jobs for security. You will have a hard time headhunting. But you might find some top talent on a temporary basis to get you through the valleys. Think of ways to maximize these individuals and fast forward some of your projects. Be able to change up your game plan.

 ENVISION YOUR IDEAL TEAM

Take the time to evaluate your team, your culture, your strengths and weaknesses. Define who it is you need and want as well as who will fit in. This often comes down to values and what motivates your team members, not just the technical skills they bring to the table. Recruiting a variety of personalities and demeanors has proven to be successful for my clients. If you only recruit clones of yourself, you create either too many headstrong individuals who must have it their way or the highway or you create a team with too many meek, agreeable individuals, and no one pushes things forward or challenges the status quo. Mix it up. What personalities are needed on your team, and why would it be good to add them? Do you have a few team members who are great at selling to the business? Do you have some who are highly analytical and can go back to their lab and come up with all the possible risks to the nth degree? Do you have some peacemakers and some negotiators? Do you have some visionaries? Do you have a skeptic and an optimist? How about a few who can spot every point of failure and some who just know there *must* be a solution to this problem? Regarding their level of motivation, do you want to have a few status-quo people who will stay in the same position for years? They can be valuable too. Or do you want aggressive overachievers? Do you need people who push themselves and their own development, constantly going beyond expectations? Do you need innovators? Do you require them to think first of the benefits to the business, then the team, then themselves? Do you want people whom you can personally develop and mentor, so you can take them with you as your career advances? In summary, know what you need and want before you start recruiting. In my experience, the personality is sometimes more important for team success than the depth of technical expertise.

 ## INTERPRETING RESUMES

There are a number of things to look for when reviewing resumes that can differ depending on your strategy. But for now let's assume you are looking for movers and shakers.

- **Progression.** Looking back to their earlier career and working toward the present, has the person had a logical career path? Has there been advancement? Look for someone who attacks a position as a challenge and a learning opportunity, then masters the position and advances to the next higher position. This tells you that the person is goal oriented, can focus like a laser beam, and is dedicated to the field she is in. If a person stays in the same position for 10 years and does not advance, that tells you he likes to be comfortable and probably is not the mover and shaker you are looking for. Another aspect of progression is staying in the same field versus jumping around. Jumping around from sales engineer to Java developer to systems analyst tells me the person does not really know what she wants and probably takes life as it comes at her instead of being in the driver's seat; she probably is not an expert at anything.

  Caution: If people show all the signs of being on a solid career trajectory, do not expect them to happily fit into your position if they have already mastered the role at another company unless you have a continuing career path for them. When the market heats up, they will probably leave.
- **Values.** In the resume, what people brag about will show you where their perceived self-value lies. Do they boast about the ability to handle the toughest deadlines or about innovation and discovery or solving problems enabling break-throughs for the team? Resumes reveal what their nature is and what they think was great about their past accomplishments. If they brag about being able to use a multitude of technologies or mastering cutting-edge tools to get the job done, you know you have the techno teammate whom you can turn loose on new tools to figure out and become the resident expert. Read their sentences and ask yourself what they are trying to say to readers. If you were not a techie, how would you interpret the underlying message?
- **Accomplishments.** Look for actual accomplishments. What did they personally create, produce, discover, implement, architect, change, eliminate, lead, write, and present? Look for all the action words.

- **Quantifiers.** Of equal importance to the action words are the quantifiers. For instance, what was the ROI achieved? By what percent did they reduce costs? What was the dollar amount of the budget they managed? How many team members did they recruit and lead? How many releases in what time frame? How much money did their solutions save the company? How many servers and data centers did they manage? How many data centers did they consolidate? How much did they negotiate in contract reductions? How many mergers and acquisitions did they manage? How many projects did they manage to completion? What dollar value were the projects?

- **Ownership of the result.** Most candidates produce results as part of a larger team, but resumes should not merely talk about team accomplishments. They should explain their individual accomplishments as part of the bigger picture. Resumes should disclose their role on the team and demonstrate that they executed their duties effectively. It should specify if they were, for example, the sole systems architect, the only network engineer on the team, or if they alone managed all incident response and resolution for the company.

- **Top performer.** Was the candidate the lead person? Did she have more responsibility than the others on the team? Was she the go-to person on the team? During times of downturn or layoff, was she the person that was indispensable and remained on the core team? Did the candidate advance quickly from individual contributor to team lead or to manager? As an individual contributor, did the person advance over time, being entrusted with more responsibility of more mission-critical systems, applications, and highly visible projects?

- **Out-of-the-box thinking.** Although it is good to see logical progression of roles, it is also good to see someone who did not just do what the role typically demands. Did the person go above and beyond by making additional contributions to the business? Does he have an eye for where he can add value and do so without being asked or told? Does he think in terms of what will help the team mission, not just his own job function? For example, I placed a Linux systems administrator at a start-up who quickly learned how to function as a MySQL database administrator (DBA) in addition to his own duties because the team did not have budget for another person. He stepped up to the challenge and felt like he was the one who gained most out of the experience. Shortly thereafter, I placed a senior DBA alongside him who willingly infused his expertise to the systems administrator, thus creating a backup DBA on the team. Both possessed out-of-the-box thinking and a commitment to the business that was not in the job description.

- **Believable list of skills.** If candidates list too many skills that are not typically found together, you might have an embellisher on your hands. How can you be a Websphere administrator, Oracle DBA, core Java developer, user interface designer, Ruby developer, server-side engineer, Cisco Certified Network Engineer, RedHat systems administrator, Windows systems administrator, *and* certified information systems security professional? If they do list a huge number of technologies, they should rate themselves in each in terms such as expert, advanced, proficient, familiar, or exposed to.

INTERVIEWING

Be organized, prepared, and more organized and more prepared. Get as much insight as possible regarding your candidate beforehand. Before you conduct a phone interview with anyone, have your internal recruiter or partner give you a full summary so you know what you are getting into and what you need to address in your interview. Have your partner do some initial, basic technical screening and provide you with the candidate's answers. Request a write-up that describes their personality, strengths, relevant experience, salary expectations, reason for wanting to leave their job, reason for being laid off, availability to start, and their competitive interviewing activity. You do not need to waste 30 minutes going over the basics. Instead, use your time to really test candidates on the technology they claim to know, to see how fast they can think on their feet and how well they communicate. Being organized for the in-person interview also requires having an interview plan. Figure out who is going to target which aspects of candidates' background you need to uncover. For instance, who will dig into the technical skills? Who will look at behavioral traits? Who will judge their problem-solving skills? Who will drill them on their resume to get a total picture of their career path and motivation? Who will do the selling, should you want a candidate person on your team immediately? In addition to your assigned interviewing agendas, you should all know and agree what your selling points are regarding your company and your team. If a candidate starts probing each interviewer and gets different responses to the same questions, that is not good. You all need to know your own reasons plus your team members' reasons for working there. As a team, agree on and communicate to each other the personality traits and skills you are looking for so you all appear to have a clear direction in mind. Too many interviewers go into the room and have a conversation, do most of the talking themselves, and end up not accomplishing anything except repeating the same few questions as the previous interviewer, plus rambling aimlessly. Get your team on the same page and execute the investigation. Decide what you can and cannot say to candidates ahead of time. An interview is an orchestration of your key players. So take the time to make it a performance.

Digging

Past behavior equals future behavior, right? Ask about occasions when candidates were in specific circumstances and how they handled them. Keep throwing scenarios out there until you are sure you know what candidates are made of. Ask why they moved from one company to the next. How did they find each job? Why did they choose each opportunity? What do they want? What are they looking for in their next opportunity? Why do they enjoy the role they are in? What made them choose their field of technology? What challenged them the most in this role and in previous roles? What was the most satisfying aspect of each job? How did they accomplish the things on their resume? How did they ensure a project was successful? This is polite and friendly interrogation. Be sure to assign certain groups of questions to each of your team members, so you do not overlap and ask the same things.

Your Gut

Have you ever heard a candidate say something that made you screech on the brakes in your mind? Take note of whatever it was and jot it down. Come back to it later in the discussion. Do not ignore anything that makes you feel uneasy. And do not forget to come back to it. Do not probe immediately; you want the person to get comfortable and trusting enough to open up to you as much as possible. But do not forget to come back to the issue. If your gut is telling you that this is the perfect candidate, try not to listen to it. Often candidates perfect the art of interviewing but bomb on the job. Use your gut mostly to uncover areas of caution and concern.

Tying Up Your Candidate's Time

There are good ways to tie up candidates and bad ways. You want to try to pack your interviews together to be respectful of candidates' valuable time. They had to take time off work to interview with your team. You do not want to make them come in to meet one person today, two tomorrow, and another the day after that. It will not happen, and candidates will push you off or accept an offer with an easier company to work with. Be organized and efficient. However, do recognize that candidates cannot take too many half days off work, and they will be exhausted after a four-hour interview session. It is best to keep them for two to four hours so they have time for travel and a meal, but not the opportunity to entertain another competitive interview or return to work. Then bring them back for another two to four hours the next week and so on. If you keep doing this until you hire them, you will keep them from entertaining other opportunities. Inevitably, other companies are trying to interview them too; lock them into your opportunity by committing them to the calendar. Most quality candidates do not want to burn a bridge by canceling on you. In this way you can funnel the candidates you truly want right into your opportunity and yours alone.

Etiquette, Respect, Composure

I once had a candidate fly in from out of town to interview with a CIO. The CIO maintained a strange, negative, elitist posture that turned off the candidate so much that he came out of the interview saying he would never work for that guy no matter what the pay. Why? The CIO's attitude was one of doubt and mistrust. He rudely challenged the candidate on everything on his resume as if it were all fabrication. The CIO came across as determined to uncover the lies and prove the candidate's deceptive nature. In another case, a manager implied to the candidate that she was lazy because she remained in her current position for several years without promotion. Another interviewer threw out random mathematical riddles to see what the person could solve on his feet, although the hypothetical situations had nothing to do with the challenges of the job at hand. Do not use the interview as an opportunity to abuse people just because they need a job and you are holding their future in your hands. If you must, tell them politely that they do not have what you are looking for and you would like to end the interview. Have human resources politely escort them out of the office, say some encouraging words, and wish them luck.

Believe it or not, once I presented a candidate to a hiring manager who told me, "That candidate was an &*%$*# when the roles were reversed and I was looking for a job five years ago. I think I'll pass." What goes around comes around. Do not be rude to candidates. You may find yourself interviewing for a job on their team in the near future.

Body Language

From the moment candidates walk into your, office take note. Are they slowly walking in, hunched over and depressed, or are they upright and positive? When they speak with you, are they locking their hands behind their head and leaning back in arrogance, or are they hunched over in their seat looking at you from under their eyebrows as if they have something to hide? Pay attention to body language. It tells a lot about people. Are they leaning forward when they speak and getting louder with a furrow in their brow, as if they might have anger issues? Do they constantly touch their nose and look up to their right, pulling the answers out of thin air? Or are they speaking with sincerity and composure with their hands in front of them, not trying to hide a thing? Is one hand supporting their chin or slightly covering their mouth for a long period of time? If so, you are probably talking too much and boring them. Get back to asking questions about candidates.

When to Sell

You want to start selling when—and only when—you have gotten candidates to divulge their entire picture. You need to know what motivates them. What emotionally has brought them to the table to speak with you? Is it frustration about compensation, responsibility, scope of assignment, or a crazy commute? Do they doubt the success of their current company, or did they just inherit a tyrannical new boss? Will their role be offshored, or do they simply have a friend who works at your company whom they enjoy working with? Is their spouse nagging them about being at a more stable company and leaving the start-up world? Or do they feel that they do not make a difference at their current company? Maybe they want the chance to learn the technologies that your company uses. What other opportunities do they have and why would they choose them over yours, or not? Which opportunity looks the best so far, and why? How do they feel about your opportunity? What do they like best about it, and why? What would cause them to *not* want your job? Before you sell, you must know everything, especially the stuff that might cause candidates to reject your offer.

 SELLING YOURSELF, YOUR TEAM, AND THE COMPANY

Once you have the whole picture, start addressing their list of interests and concerns one by one. Now you are selling! As you address each of their interests, get confirmation that you have satisfied the issue and keep moving. Do this conversationally, not like a robot, and not like a hard-core closer. Once you feel you have satisfied their concerns, go for a conditional close. It should go something like this: "Based on what we have talked about, if we were to offer you the position with the right pay scale and title, is there any reason you would not accept it?" If there is a reason, get back to selling. If there is not, start talking about total compensation and ask if they would accept the package you are describing. If so, lock in a time frame and a verbal closure: "I am going to have the offer written up. Can you come by tomorrow and pick it up? It will have a three-day expiration, so you can discuss it with your family and get back to us with your decision. Is there anything else we need to cover before you would feel excited to join the team?"

Once I had a candidate come back from an interview and tell me, "I will not be working at that company." I asked him to explain and he said, "One of the interviewers has a bleak picture of the company's future. Because the profit margins are so low, he does not know how they are going to survive."

You and your team need to know why your company is a great place to work and for what type of person. If one of the interviewers is dissatisfied with the company or planning on leaving soon, do not allow that to be conveyed during the interview. Just conduct the interview. Conversely, do not portray your company as flawless either. Be realistic and objective. Decide as a team what the pros and cons are about working there and what you are comfortable sharing with prospective candidates. You and your team all need to have the same general story. By being prepared, you demonstrate that you are a mature, organized, well-managed, and cohesive team. Team synergy sells candidates just as strongly as all the great things you say about yourselves. I have had candidates choose an opportunity based solely on the quality of the experience with the team throughout the interviewing process. People want to work for a team they can learn from and grow with and who will energize them on a daily basis. Be real, down to earth, and personable. Know why you all work there (individually and corporately), and be able to explain some if not all of the negatives and positives about the environment.

CHECKING CREDENTIALS

Ideally you will be hiring local candidates. Local IT communities are closely knit, and you probably know someone who knows the candidate you are interviewing. A trusted, personal reference is the best kind. If you do not know who might know this person, look the candidate up on LinkedIn to see if you are connected. Also check for whom you know who worked at the same company as your candidate. You can do this through LinkedIn's "reference check" feature. Reach out and ask the person a few pointed questions. Save the detailed questions for the references the candidate supplied.

In addition to the do-it-yourself-through-your-network method of checking someone's reputation, you should also get responses in writing from the candidate-supplied references from your recruiting partner. It is best to craft a form with approximately 10 questions. Stick to the form so you do not forget anything and you can move quickly, being respectful of the person's time. You can do these reference checks yourself, but it is quite a hassle catching people on the phone and you probably will need to try several times. Therefore, you might want to pass this duty to the recruiter and have the person write detailed responses for your files. I suggest sending an e-mail to the references with the subject line "Ten-minute reference request for Joe Candidate, can we speak today?" This way you can schedule a quick appointment instead of catching them off guard and having them hurry you off the phone with half-baked answers.

Competency Testing Tools

Several tests on the market check candidates' general knowledge in a given area. With the increase of tools, languages, and various technologies, there are more than 500 different tests specific to a technology and skill level, such as senior Oracle DBA. These tests can be helpful, but they each take an hour of the candidate's time and do not really tell you the whole picture regarding the person's expertise or lack thereof. I have found that tests are helpful when a client has been burned in the past by candidates who ace interviews but fail on the job. In such cases, I use the test tool as a double confirmation that the candidate is legitimate. When requiring candidates to take tests, you face the risk of losing them to another opportunity that does not mandate testing. Getting gainfully employed candidates to carve out an hour or two for a test is extremely difficult, especially when they have a family, a job, and a commute, and they want to be fresh and uninterrupted when they take the test. The interviews are grueling enough. As a rule of thumb, only require unemployed candidates to take the tests. Or use the tests after you and the candidate like each other enough to move forward. Then administer the test as a double verification and to add to the candidate's employment file. If you are working with a partner, the partner should provide unlimited tests for free (recruitment firms typically pay for an unlimited access account). If you are paying for the tests yourself, they cost $100 to $150 per test.

Closing

Rarely have any of my candidates rejected an offer from one of my clients. When this has occurred, it was due to a competitive offer providing just a few more of the candidate's wish list items than my client could. How can you ensure a similar success rate? Put simply, you should be interviewing only those candidates who fit within your budget, can make the trip to your office, and have a reason for wanting the job. If you engaged candidates in interviews knowing ahead of time that their salary expectations were $10,000 over your budget, and you have determined through the interview process that they really are worth the extra $10,000, do not shortchange them at the final hour. Having said that, here are some tips:

- **Know what candidates want, need, and will accept before you craft a document that does not appeal to them.** Are they looking for advancement in title? Are they looking for a pay raise? Do they want a certain career path? If so, you may want to insert verbiage such as "Based on performance and business circumstances, candidate will be given opportunity for advancement to manager [for example] in six months." Do they want their home Internet, cell phone, or mileage reimbursed when driving to different company locations? Do they want to telecommute one day per week or come in early and leave early? What bonus structure will motivate them the most? Include a full explanation of the company benefits, 401k, and paid time off.

- **Add an expiration date to your offer.** I have seen companies make offers to candidates and not include an expiration date. Then they wait two weeks for the person to respond, but there is no response. If candidates are delaying the acceptance of your offer, all they are doing is leveraging your offer to get additional and better offers. People do not need more than three days to decide on a job. They need to talk it over with the family and sleep on it. And that is it.

- **Use conditional closings throughout the interview process and prior to the offer.** As mentioned earlier, conditional closing involves questions to the candidate such as: "Based on what you know about the opportunity, our team, and the company, if the compensation was in line with your expectations, is there any reason that you would not accept an offer?" (Yes, you must state it in "negative" form.) If there is a reason, you need to find it and address it before crafting your offer. And once you have addressed the reason, ask the question again until the person says, "No, there is no reason I would not accept this offer." Just to be sure, probe for additional scenarios candidates may be keeping to themselves by asking: "Are you entertaining any other opportunities that also meet your career objectives?" If the answer is yes, ask; "What do you like better about this one versus that one?" Continue the process until you have discovered the complete picture. If you find out candidates have five interviews scheduled and they insist on attending each one before they can decide, do not make the offer yet. You do not want them to go to competitive interviews with an offer in hand. Simply let them know you are willing to make a very appealing offer and you sincerely want them on your team. Lock in another appointment to meet with them after their other interviews. At this point you may have to compete with their offer or you may not. The other interviews may have been dead ends. But I repeat, you do not want to send your favorite candidate over to the competition with an offer in hand to use as leverage. When candidates have no obstructions or encumbrances, then make your offer and time-stamp it, so they do not have time to shop for a better one.

- **Outsource "the close."** Use your partner as a negotiator, mediator, and a third party between you and the candidate. It is much easier to have your partner do all the probing and conditional closing along the way. That way you can focus your energy solely on determining if you really want the candidate, leaving the rest of the art of closing to your partner, who does this effectively every day for numerous clients. This method also works best because the partner has developed a trusting bond with the candidate from the day she picked up the phone and described the job to the candidate. Therefore, the candidate will be more honest and up front with the partner about the situation and state of mind than with the hiring manager. And the candidate will often be more willing to compromise at the offering table because he feels comfortable and wants to consummate the relationship. I have seen hiring managers lose candidates by trying to do all the communicating directly. Both parties need a mediator who can filter and distill the communications from the other party. This method also keeps both of you from showing your degree of desperation. If communication is one step removed, it stays objective and efficient.

SUMMARY

Avoid prolonged and painful recruiting campaigns by being strategic and tactical. Utilize all your tools, and do so proactively, not just reactively. Foster relationships with your internal recruiters (but don't put all your eggs in one basket). Stay connected to friends and associates through LinkedIn. Otherwise, you will lose track of valuable resources for talent, reference checks, and a general pulse on the market. Get active with online groups and Meetups (but do so habitually, in advance of your recruiting needs). Be very selective about whom you use as an outside recruiter. Think long term with performance, flexibility, and business stability in mind. Learn how to motivate your outside recruiters for optimal results. Create buffers in your budget to mitigate against unexpected attrition and the use of consultants. Get clear with your team regarding the skills and personalities you seek to recruit. Have a tight game plan for interviews. In advance, discuss with each other how you will present your company and the opportunity, and who will interview for which skills and personality traits. Do not sell prematurely. When you do sell, decide who will do the selling. Outsourcing the sales process to your recruiter/partner can be most effective since recruiters close candidates regularly and may have a more open and frank relationship with candidates.

Most of these best practices may already be familiar to you. The chapter has explained how and why you should use these practices to make your searches go smoothly and efficiently. If you do find yourself under a tight recruiting deadline, use the tools described in this chapter to kick your searches into high gear with a successful and quick conclusion every time.

CHAPTER THREE

Career Pathing

Retaining and Developing Your Best and Brightest

Art Klein

C AREER PATHING PROGRAMS ARE critical tools that can boost morale, improve productivity, and help IT leaders grow and retain top talent. They give staff members a sense of purpose. In addition, these programs can also serve as a way for an IT executive to stand out as a leader of people and build his or her personal brand. This chapter discusses the relevance of career pathing and presents a model that can be used by an IT executive to define what type of career-pathing program best serves individual personal needs and the corresponding corporate culture.

 INTRODUCTION: THE CHALLENGE OF IT STAFFING

One of the great understated challenges IT leaders face is that of talent management. Although the topic frequently ranks high in executive surveys as a point of concern, it often takes a backseat to the urgent day-to-day issues IT leaders confront. Today's IT executives grapple with the challenges of balancing the interface with business partners, reprioritization of a constantly changing portfolio of projects, maintenance of operational continuity, and the drive to reduce operational costs across an entire enterprise. However, behind every successful leader is a team of contributors and managers who make it all happen and deliver the actual technical services. Although the statement "People are our greatest assets" may be overused and sounds contrived, it could not be any truer.

It is interesting to observe how much focus is placed on recruiting as opposed to retaining current resources. Where recruiting is typically a dedicated function that is part of an overall human resources (HR) program or team, retention is a responsibility that is often considered a part of administrative management. Retention, like many other management functions, becomes something that is addressed on an as-needed basis. Unfortunately, when retention becomes a visible issue, it usually is too late. Late-breaking interventions may help keep a key contributor from walking out the door with no transition plan, but more often it delays rather than reverses an employee's decision to resign. Rarely is the key person on the verge of resignation converted into a recommitted, passionate, long-term contributor.

When you factor in the events that follow the departure of a key staff member, the price of poor staff retention becomes visible. Consider all the different costs: the time invested in initiating the hiring process; the productivity lost in the weeks or months after resignation; the creation of a replacement position; the interview and hiring process. These are just a few of the more pronounced costs that come with the need to replace a departing key contributor. This chain of events concludes only after adequate training has resulted in the new team member being able to contribute effectively. When added up, the cost of recruiting is high, whether it is through placement fees or the efforts of the internal recruiting department.

A key component to staff retention is the concept of *career pathing*. According to BusinessDictionary.com, career pathing can be defined as a "sequence of jobs along which one may be promoted within an organization or progresses in one's career."

From the management perspective, career pathing can be considered the process of implementing a structure and program to steer staff through the sequence of jobs described in the definition. The practical application of career pathing can be considered the creation of a framework that provides a clear road map for staff members so they can see how their career may be able to develop through a natural progression of roles with increased responsibilities and increased rewards.

Consider the experience of the large accounting firms, referred to as of late as the Big Four. These organizations in general have a well-socialized career progression. Their employees understand that as they grow and develop, if capable, they will advance. This progression through the ranks of associate, senior associate, manager, director, and, ultimately, partner is well understood. Although the names of titles may vary across the Big Four firms, the structure is the same. Their employees recognize, at a big-picture level, what shape their career progression can take.

 ## THE ROLE OF THE CIO

Clearly the concept of career pathing is not one that is limited to IT. Where an organization has employees, career pathing can have an impact. That said, the discipline of IT happens to be poised to benefit greatly from a well-defined career-pathing program.

IT professionals can be some of the most impactful contributors in an organization. Often it is the IT staff that invests the largest number of labor-hours per person to operational continuity across the enterprise. In technology-enabled businesses, systems are supported around the clock, high-risk changes are a regular occurrence, and a wide variety of sensitive data is retained. Under these circumstances, IT staff members are typically the watchmen, first responders, and problem solvers for the engines that drive entire enterprises. Unfortunately, the personalities of technical experts are not always the simplest to deal with. IT experts can be mercurial, fiercely independent, and ambiguous when it comes to describing their personal goals. The challenge is to create a structure and set of personnel programs that will keep high-caliber technical performers motivated to remain committed to the organization and also allow them to develop some of the key skills they will need to remain strategic resources in the future. When one considers the what's-in-it-for-me mentality of the rising Millennial generation as a factor, the importance of retaining and developing technical experts and the challenge it presents becomes very apparent. In a contracting market, where cold, hard cash may be not be a viable (or the best) retention tool, career pathing presents an opportunity not only to retain the talent but also to tool employees in ways that will serve the business and present them with the opportunity for growth in terms of both hard and soft skills.

Implementing a career-pathing program presents a unique opportunity for the technical leader as well. Leaders strive to define their individual personal brand—those things that make each leader unique and their teams unique. In a world where IT is considered more and more a commodity service, and where contributors question their future relevance, a leadership message crafted around career pathing can inspire, engender loyalty, and do great good for the employee. The mandate is not merely practical, it is moral as well. From a branding perspective, some very positive outcomes can be attached to rolling out a career-pathing program. Developing an effective career-pathing program can help leaders grow their teams, enabling them to stay at the cutting edge of an industry that is in the midst of transformation.

Creating and implementing a meaningful career-pathing system is not the same as installing a one-size-fits-all program. It is important that the approach be tailored to the nature of each individual technical team, the structure of the overall company, and, most important, the corporate culture. This chapter presents a framework that leaders can use to contemplate and craft a career-pathing program that is all their own, and tailored to their own organization. Although no two organizations are the same and no two programs are the same, it is interesting to note that all career-pathing programs most likely have similar elements.

 ## THE CAREER-PATHING SOLUTION SPACE: DEPTH, BREADTH, CLARITY, AND FLEXIBILITY

All career-pathing philosophies and programs have similar structural elements. The program must have a method and philosophy that governs how actual career paths are designed and what sort of growth takes place. In addition to this, the rollout of the program, including how it is presented and marketed, is very important. A program with robust structure and no communication strategy may be perceived as simply a training curriculum. Conversely, a well-messaged intention to provide career-pathing services with no physical program behind it may be seen as all talk—a program with no meat on the bone.

Placing these two very different elements on a sheet of paper, you can create a career-pathing solution space. Leaders looking to implement a program such as this can consider the expectations and the corporate culture under which they operate in order to find the balancing point on this space where a career-pathing program will fit best within the current organization. Figure 3.1 is a pictorial representation of this solution space.

The vertical arrow on Figure 3.1 represents the range of approaches that a career-pathing program can take: in other words, what the defined parts of the program are, and how the staff may choose a path and stay on it. Whatever the details are, in general, a career-pathing program is comprised of a blend of two different approaches. One is to tailor the program toward developing people in specific areas (*depth*) in order to develop a deep subject matter expertise in specific disciplines or roles. Alternatively, a program can be geared to give its participants a broad-stroke big-picture view (*breadth*) that shapes those engaged into generalists who have a knowledge base that is more holistic and enterprise-wide.

Career-pathing programs are fundamentally people-based and staff-centric. How these programs are framed, rolled out, and presented to both staff and management is as relevant to their success as are their actual contents. Some very real human resource issues need to be addressed when implementing a training or career-pathing program. As an IT leader, it is important to be mindful of explicit or implicit contracts that are presented to the staff around training dollars and time. The horizontal arrow in Figure 3.1 conveys a range of approaches communication may take. On the left side it

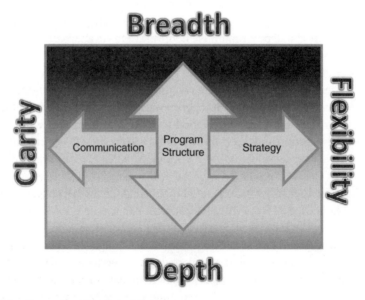

FIGURE 3.1 Career-Pathing Solution Space

represents a well-documented, structured, and formalized program (*clarity*). The right side of this arrow represents a program presented in a conceptual manner and designed such that business needs and company conditions may dramatically change (or curtail) this program with little or no lead time (*flexibility*).

How do you develop a program that balances depth and breadth? How can a program attain the right level of clarity while still providing flexibility? The answers lie in understanding your staff and your style to find where on this solution space you, as a leader and the owner of this program, are most comfortable. Most important, the answer lies in understanding the organization and developing a program that will dovetail with its structure and philosophy. Before addressing the issue of understanding the organization, we discuss each of these four concepts—depth, breadth, clarity, and flexibility—in more detail.

Depth: Career Tracks

Career-pathing programs that are centered around depth often have very specific and clear end states. Completion of the career path will culminate in an expertise or personal mastery of a specific discipline. One of the first questions asked of depth-centric programs is: What are the end goals? In other words, how are these career tracks defined, and how many of them are there? How do you want the team to grow and develop? A good place for this process of defining paths to start is to determine if technical versus managerial tracks are appropriate.

This is a very important question to answer. Frequently, IT staff members make the assumption that their only growth path is into the work of traditional administrative management. This can result in a managerial team that does not necessarily have the skills or demeanor for a position that may have very different objectives and measurements. It may result in the most technically gifted people on a team being called on to abandon their greatest skill sets and the roles they truly love. For example, the resident security guru may not be the best person to conduct performance reviews or contribute to the budgeting process. However, perhaps with succession planning and the right financial and soft skills training program, this person may truly transform from a technical leader to a leader of people. Creating distinct technical and management career paths will allow staff to self-select their paths, take an active role in their career development, and give management a good window into their individual aspirations and goals, which in turn may keep morale high within the IT department.

Other natural breaks in functional roles tend to follow those present in organizational structures. An IT department that has well-defined and segregated teams may have a like number of different career paths that can be created and clearly defined. As an example, if an IT organization has a development group, an operations group, and a project management office, the structure lends itself to three well-defined career paths. Other potential career paths can follow technical disciplines from the perspective of operational functions (e.g., security management) or technology platforms (e.g., Windows, UNIX, networking). The variety of career paths that can be carved out is virtually limitless. However, it is essential that these paths overlay well with the organization's functions and structure and also that they are presented in such a way that technical staff members can both understand and affiliate themselves with one or more of these paths.

This concept may seem somewhat obvious. Most leaders instinctively look across their teams to learn who is developing, growing, and on the road to promotion and also to determine which team members are progressing slower, stagnating, or perhaps in a position outside their skill set. Most leaders can envision the career potential of each member of their team. As intuitive as that piece of management is, the importance of the word "pathing" should not be underestimated. Leaders have a responsibility to literally create, define, and signpost actual paths. Doing this enables staff members to clearly see the road that they are responsible to both select and walk down. Without the clarity of documented paths or processes, staff members may mistake a leader with an eye for talent for one who is playing favorites. Declaring and carving out paths allows the executive to use a measuring stick of sorts, as opposed to simply knowing talent when he or she sees it.

Breadth: Rotational Strategies

Developing a career-pathing program that has depth is one element in an effective program. An alternative approach can be considered in combination with depth or as a completely different strategy to program design: an approach based on *breadth*. In some circumstances both people and organizations thrive on variety, and understanding the greater perspective of a business or even the discipline of IT is of great value. In these organizations, a career-pathing program that has a breadth-based component can have great impact.

One way to design a breadth-based career-pathing program is to apply rotations across a collection of functions. Rotations may be isolated internally to the IT department or across an entire company into business or other operational functions. Rotational programs are often seen in large corporations as a path available to those being groomed for executive positions. Think of the leadership programs where top performers or strategic recruits are placed in a series of several multimonth rotations across an organization to gain the bigger picture. Part of what makes these rotational programs such compelling examples is that many large companies use this breadth approach in combination with the depth concepts described earlier. For rotational models to work on their own, there must be a deep commitment to breaking organizational barriers. In much the same way, a purely depth-based career-pathing model works only for the most structured and centralized companies.

With a breadth-based program comes a cost that must be considered and accepted. As individuals shift roles and responsibilities through a rotational system, there is a period of time where new roles are being learned, knowledge transfer takes place, and overall adjustments are made to accommodate for incoming team members. Undeniably, productivity may drop shortly before and after points of rotation. Understanding and popularizing this productivity hit and the offsetting strategic gain are very important parts of gaining buy-in and sponsorship for a rotation program with peers at the executive level. Steps can be taken to manage this risk and control the impact that cross-training has on productivity. Placing well-considered boundaries around rotational programs can contain both the risks and the productivity hits. Carefully consider what the most appropriate duration for rotations is. For example, if the time anticipated to get up to speed in a job function is one month, structuring a program that has six-month rotations will help ensure that the organization realizes the return on the one-month investment. A program that has practitioners rotate out of teams when they have just begun to understand and contribute will not be meaningful to the organization or to the staff in rotation. Another compensating measure that can be put in place is a staggered system, so rotations do not all commence at the same time. This method allows more individuals to rotate concurrently and smoothes out the total learning curve of the rotating staff. Establishing thresholds as to the number of rotations based on team size, business demand, and talent depth is also a very important control to consider implementing.

Clarity: Framing Your Career-Pathing Philosophy

It is as important to consider how a career-pathing program is presented to staff, as a good structural model is vital. Career-pathing programs must be messaged so as not to be construed as free training that is transportable to another company. The best starting point for determining the right way to roll out a career-pathing program is to look at the overall management philosophy and communication style of the organization.

Some organizations have well-understood formal training programs. The concept of a formal, curriculum-based system given the shorthand name "Company U" has been embraced across organizations of all sizes. The idea of a structure that feels similar to higher education, one where staff members can design and build a curriculum of sorts, can empower staff members and allow a greater level of self-motivated development. When designing a career-pathing program, understanding the current training and development programs already in place at an organization can allow for smoother integration and leverage of existing processes. If training programs follow a calendar or schedule, it is important to time the career-pathing program so that it dovetails well with the training calendar. If there already is a rotational program in place for executives or high-performing staff, constructing a program with a level of similarity gives a new program the gravitas and brand of a well-established program.

The level of formality of career pathing should be consistent with the overall formality of the learning and education features of the company. In cases where training is not delivered with a cohesive and overarching brand and structure, it may be wise to tailor a program so that it is presented in a similarly informal manner. It certainly is key to have a strategy and plan in place, but if presentation of a formal strategy would appear profoundly different from other training programs, keeping the structural documents internal may make the program easier for a HR department to support and easier for staff members to understand within the company's framework.

One important question to answer is how to ensure that a career-pathing program is selective and invests in personnel who in turn are invested in the organization. Again, it is important to look for consistency and a level of harmony with programs already in place but also to consider designing some form of application or sponsorship process, whether formal or informal. This allows the potential participants to be understood and evaluated in a consistent and objective manner. It also reaffirms that this is an opportunity that an executive can award and give, as opposed to a program that is simply there for anyone to take regardless of qualifications or commitment. It may be appropriate to consider some level of "handcuffs" that state that participation in a program such as this is based on a two-year commitment to either the department or possibly the company. You should work with the HR department on this sensitive matter, as likely a program such as this cannot be designed with any financial repercussions in the event of an individual's resignation, the way in which many tuition reimbursement programs operate. That being said, a nonbinding letter of intent is something that many professionals take seriously and sign with an appropriate level of commitment.

Flexibility: Management Overrides

One aspect to a program of this nature that is often neglected is how to embed in its design and rollout a degree of flexibility. The recent economic downturn reminds us that growth is cyclic and that in challenging times, organizational structures are changed, discretionary spending is reduced, and often nonessential programs are contracted or eliminated. This is one of the many reasons that a level of flexibility at the point of program design and rollout can be helpful. Organizations may feel unable to break their commitment to a program, even when conditions may make changing it appropriate and beneficial to them. Specific circumstances that may warrant the reexamination of a career-pathing program are corporate acquisitions (either being acquired or making an acquisition), leadership changes, significant changes in headcount, business demands, and addition or removal of products or business lines. Management should not be cornered into maintaining a program. Sufficient flexibility must be in place to allow for changes to any overall career-pathing program.

Although it may be impossible to avoid disappointment, conflicts, or disputes based on changes that ultimately may need to be made to a career-pathing program, some proactive steps can be taken to manage expectations. The ability of management to override decisions and make adjustments at will based on changing conditions is often undervocalized. It is often implicit that strategies and programs are subject to change without notice. However, in many cases, it is not well understood where these management prerogatives end and an employee's inherent rights begin.

Similar to the notion of clarity discussed earlier, the messaging for flexibility must be driven by the structure of the overarching HR department and the nature of the relationship between employees and the HR function. It will likely be your responsibility as leader to close any gaps between the existing protocols and the degree of flexibility you need to declare. Expressing flexibility and prerogative does not always manifest itself in formal communications or policies. In more entrepreneurial and policy-light organizations, spoken word may be the more effective vehicle. Choosing the method of messaging is as important as choosing the actual message, and will impact how you are perceived as a leader.

The content of your message should be based on the unique enterprise conditions and climate. Usually key messages are tailored to maximize flexibility in program implementation and direction. Applicants should understand that career-pathing programs are not totally self-directed. A talented staff member may not be able to carve out a career path that suits his or her personal agenda. Take the opportunity, when it presents itself, to reiterate that the career-pathing program may be subject to change without notice, but do not turn the message into an ominous statement. The right of management to override and modify programs is often underemphasized with staff. In fact, it is often forgotten that making these sorts of changes is part of what management is supposed to do. Keeping this concept front of mind with staff may make changes that are made understood and hopefully supported by staff, and can keep the inevitable water cooler conversations away from the perception of broken commitments and focused more on business and market conditions.

FINDING YOUR PLACE IN THE SOLUTION SPACE

In this chapter, we have discussed four different concepts that drive the structure of a career-pathing program: depth, breadth, clarity, and flexibility. It is how a leader applies these core concepts to career pathing that makes his or her program one of a kind and tailored both to the individual leader and the organization. These four concepts define the solution space presented earlier in Figure 3.1.

Although breadth and depth are two opposite perspectives, the question of program structure is certainly not a binary choice of depth versus breadth. A program's structure is a combination of attributes that in total will place a program somewhere on this continuum. In fact, most programs will have elements of both breadth and depth. It is not unheard of to have rotational programs on top of a structure that has very clear promotion paths up specific functions and disciplines. This is even truer in the context of communication strategy. Often career-pathing programs have many different elements: distinct job families; an overarching review and training program; mentorship; formal rotations across departments; and so on. There may be isolated parts of a career-pathing program that are well served with formal branding as a distinct program and benefit. One example is a clear definition of two promotion paths—one that culminates with managing directors who lead teams of people and another that produces technical directors who serve as the most senior individual contributors and experts. Other aspects may be better implemented at the management level and not presented to staff as a benefit. (An example is the allocation a fixed amount of training dollars per employee.) Figure 3.2 presents some potential aspects of an organization that may pull a career-pathing program in one direction or another on the solution space.

Generally speaking, every career-pathing program will have some of each of the four elements within it. One place to start structuring a program is to look at Figure 3.2 and to determine where on this space a career-pathing program may be most impactful. Then, with a rough idea of the tone of the program, you may start to build out the elements. Do not be afraid to shift and readjust the starting point in the career-pathing space. Use the reference of the solution space to ensure that the program is taking a deliberate shape and is not simply a collection of tools and components that are available. Figure 3.3 is a visual example of a pilot career-pathing program that is

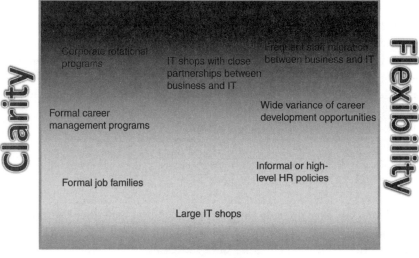

FIGURE 3.2   Company Structures that Impact Program Design

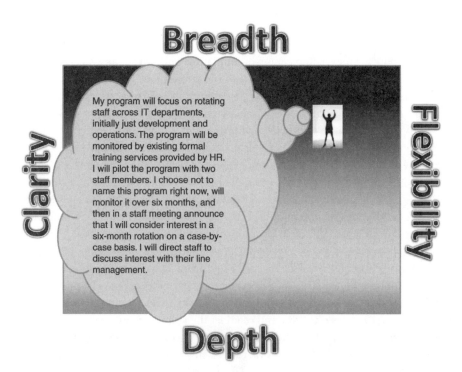

FIGURE 3.3   A Career-Pathing Program Is Born

positioned on the solution space and some of the elements that a leader may decide to base the program on as this planning process starts to gel.

CONCLUSION

In many ways, the issues that surround people are far more challenging than technical problems. It is the responsibility of the chief information officer or senior technical leader to apply both people and technology skills to solve business problems and to deliver business relevance. Managers are driven to lead often because these challenges fascinate them and mastery of this skill is part of their own personal career-pathing program. Arming staff with skills and incentivizing them with growth, challenge, and visibility is a great opportunity. It presents the chance to change the way a technology team is perceived, internally and externally, and to deliver a service to staff in lieu of pure monetary compensation. In many ways, it is much more valuable than simply dollars and cents. With the right planning and monitoring, a career-pathing program can change your employees' lives, as it simultaneously elevates the skills of your technology team. There can be no better legacy for a leader.

4

Why Provide Professional Development to IT Professionals?

John Moran, PhD

I N SOME WAYS THE question in the chapter title is an oxymoron. The rapidly changing nature of hardware, software, and responsibilities of any IT professional forces each of us to "develop professionally." In other words, if we want to stay employed, we must keep up with the current technology and the shifting responsibilities of IT positions. Most IT professionals welcome the chance to explore new possibilities and seek psychological success through lateral or spiral career moves. They continually seek opportunities to learn new things and see their career as a series of learning cycles.

When I started in the "computer industry," I was programming in assembly language and FORTRAN. The information system of the day was the IBM 360, used mainly for back-office financial record keeping. Very few people, if anyone, had even heard the term "chief information officer." Along with many other computing industry veterans, I stayed employed by learning and growing professionally and personally as we moved from the mainframe era to minicomputers with distributed processing and UNIX, to the world of personal computers and servers. While most of the organizations that employed us would never have called our collective learning experience "professional development" that indeed is what it was.

In today's global marketplace, the objective of IT organizations is to provide businesses with access to the trusted information that is needed to evaluate performance, make informed decisions, and respond quickly to new requirements; therefore, the position requirements for IT professionals are becoming more demanding in multiple dimensions, and there is a shift in emphasis from a traditional, central information systems organization toward a more decentralized, end user–focused business orienta-tion. IT professionals are also instrumental in helping tomorrow's leading businesses create more adaptable and responsive organizations. By supporting social networks and real-time collaboration, they are enabling closer ties with partners and customers and supporting today's highly dispersed workforce. This workforce needs instant, anytime access to people and information, business-grade social software, and better team-based decision making. The responsibilities have become increasingly critical to the effective operations of organizations and are far more complex and ill-defined than ever before. These more demanding position requirements increase the need for IT professional development. A few examples illustrate the point:

- Transitioning from individual contributor to supervisor/manager
- Integrating and productively using virtualization
- Managing global workforces with diverse cultures
- Providing productive collaboration systems across the organization
- Managing security for the organization's information
- Managing outsourcing and cloud computing

Each of these examples requires (or required) learning on the part of the IT organization management and staff to evaluate, plan, and execute. That learning is their professional development, and it is essential for their organization to receive value from their investment in IT.

Now that we have responded to the *why* professional development for IT, let's take a look at *what* it means for IT personnel.

TYPES OF PROFESSIONAL DEVELOPMENT

There are two basic classifications of professional development: formal and informal.

Formal Professional Development

The phrase "formal professional development" refers to organized instructional activities that take place in educational or training institutions and often lead to a degree, certification, or credit. For example, I teach in an information systems master's degree program at the University of Nevada. Many universities offer similar programs. Many of my students state that the work toward the degree broadens their perspective on the relationships and ways IT provides value to the business and how they can use that knowledge in furthering their careers. As an example, one student worked for a global manufacturing organization. In his final project, he presented several specific ways his company could improve processes and efficiency through using IT more effectively.

Additionally, there are several certificate programs, such as those offered by the Institute for Certification of Computing Professionals for Certified Computing Professional (CCP) and Associate Computing Professional (ACP). Certificates can be sought in many areas, such as security and networking. Certificate programs usually provide IT professionals with focused and in-depth learning experiences in a specific technological area. Many companies provide financial and reduced work hours for IT professionals to participate in these formal learning programs.

As CEOs want CIOs to lead innovation and promote change by employing technology to drive the kinds of business transformation that supports corporate objectives, enables new business models, and exploits new opportunities, a few CIOs and IT professionals are taking a time-out and returning to universities to acquire increased business and/or technology degrees. This formal education also opens the possibility of moving beyond the CIO position, perhaps into the chief operating officer or CEO roles. For more information on formal professional development, contact your local university or the Information Technology Association of America.

Informal Professional Development

The phrase "informal professional development" refers to activities initiated by people in work settings that result in the development of their professional knowledge and skills and can be either planned or unplanned and structured or unstructured. Examples of informal learning include talking and sharing resources with others, attending seminars and conferences, reading trade publications, searching the Internet, and experimenting with new techniques or tools.[1] As IT continues to do more with less, job demands concurrently increase the need to acquire new job knowledge and skills yet decrease the amount of time available for learning. Due to these factors, it is highly likely that IT professionals rely heavily on informal learning as a means of developing the knowledge and skills they need to perform their jobs. Even in difficult financial times, sending employees to conferences or trade shows provides good returns in professional development and employee satisfaction.[2] CIOs can also hold brown-bag lunches with open agendas to facilitate discussion on future technology directions and the impact that employees see for their own future. A CIO's example of professional learning becomes part of the expectations for other IT professionals and forms an integral part of the culture of the organization. Drawing on experience and helping to produce new knowledge can be as compelling as consuming preexisting knowledge. In fact, one process feeds the other. Being involved as a learner and a participant provides openings to new knowledge and broadens the agenda for thought and action. In important ways, such activities link individual professional learning to collegial and communal learning.

Another method of providing professional learning is to work with other departments outside the IT organization. For example, have the marketing department present its uses of information or have finance share some of its processes. This cross-functional exchange can act as learning experiences for all involved and build better relationships throughout the company.

In most informal learning, there is an element of collaboration or knowledge sharing. Promoting informal learning among IT professionals to create virtual communities is a way to facilitate collaboration.

Knowledge sharing focuses on the facilitation of sharing among a number of participants. One very successful form of knowledge sharing and professional development is a

FIGURE 4.1 Community of Practice

knowledge network, often referred to as a community of practice, as shown in Figure 4.1. Usually, the reason for bringing the members of the network together is a specific shared practice. These networks are driven by the need to address a specific concern (purpose-driven) and by the availability of expertise to address it (expertise-based). In many cases, an intermediary plays the role of the coordinator of the network's processes and knowledge flows and provides the necessary governing rules and controls for the efficient operation of the community.[3]

Knowledge sharing and collaborative forms of learning require the development of stable relationships and trust between the members. The actionable knowledge gained from the interaction of community members has to be diffused across organizational borders by allowing people to access the learning content in order for the organization to derive benefits and specific changes. The duty of the intermediary is to support the process of learning that leads to active interaction between member organizations that in turn guarantees efficient sharing of knowledge and exchanging experiences. Moreover, the intermediary should design and facilitate the knowledge exchange by identifying and bringing together all the knowledge elements that cover a recognized learning opportunity.[4]

Knowledge sharing through knowledge networks, such as communities of practice, encourages professional development and allows participants to share information from many other forms of informal learning. In the knowledge-based economy, sustaining enterprise development and retaining competitive advantage necessitates that firms focus on their knowledge assets. Doing so is very difficult when an organization functions as a closed system. Importing knowledge flows from sources lying outside the organizational boundaries and harnessing the knowledge assets within interorganizational networks is critical in the knowledge economy.

RECOMMENDATIONS FOR THE CIO AND OTHER EXECUTIVES

The issues for professional development today extend beyond mere support for the IT professional's acquisition of new skills or knowledge. Professional development today also means providing occasions for employees to reflect critically on their practice and to fashion new knowledge and beliefs about their professional practice and personal careers. Professional development:[5]

- Must be grounded in inquiry, reflection, and experimentation that are participant-driven
- Must be collaborative, involving a sharing of knowledge in communities of practice
- Must be connected to and derived from the professionals' work
- Must be sustained, ongoing, intensive, and supported by modeling, coaching, and the collective solving of specific problems of practice
- Must be connected to other aspects of business and technology changes

IT professionals learn by doing, reading, and reflecting; by collaborating with others; by looking closely at their work; and by sharing what they see. This kind of learning enables IT professionals to make the leap from theory to accomplished practice. To understand deeply, professionals must learn about, see, and experience successful learning-centered practices.

Greater amounts of unencumbered time need to be built into an IT professional's workday. Simply increasing unencumbered time may not be sufficient to foster informal learning in the workplace, however. Structure over free time is also a critical element in informal learning.

CIO and executive modeling and coaching assist in building mind-sets and behaviors such as lifelong learning, flexibility, adaptability, self-awareness, and networking and career planning, and help build career assets and thus support ongoing employability and long-term career success. They also offer a good fit with the shift toward more transactional employment relationships.

CONCLUSION

As career patterns continue to evolve, the ability to adapt and change will be critical to individual career success as well as to organizational performance. Career management at an individual level will need to focus more on the development of attitudes and behaviors supportive of employability, such as job mobility and a future career orientation, than on formal career planning. At an organizational level, the shift to an employability mind-set can be supported by providing opportunities for career-enhancing activities, such as job rotations, short-term projects, and internal and external networking. Today, career management and employability may be considered primarily an individual responsibility, yet organizations have much to gain by encouraging more flexible attitudes and behaviors and helping prepare their employees for the future.[6]

NOTES

1. M. C. Lohman, "A Survey of Factors Influencing the Engagement of Information Technology Professionals in Informal Learning Activities," *Information Technology, Learning, and Performance Journal* 25, No. 1 (2009).
2. Ibid.
3. G. Mentzas, D. Apostolou, K. Kafentzis, and P. Georgolios, "Inter-organizational Networks for Knowledge Sharing and Trading," *Information Technology Management* 7 (2006): 259–276.
4. Ibid.
5. L. Darling-Hammond and M. W. McLaughlin, "Policies that Support Professional Development in an Era of Reform," *Phi Delta Kappan* 76, No. 8 (1995).
6. M. Clarke, "Plodders, Pragmatists, Visionaries and Opportunists: Career Patterns and Employability," *Career Development International* 14, No. 1 (2009).

CHAPTER FIVE

Skill Building for the IT Professional

Training, Training Plans, and Maintaining Skills

Rossella Derickson

T HE C-LEVEL OFFICER'S PERSPECTIVE encompasses the entire enterprise, so it is not surprising that the CIO role has shifted from technology "guru" to business strategist. In addition, the successful CIO must demonstrate mastery in planning, budgeting, and forecasting. This mastery includes effectively determining the skills needed by the CIO's team to successfully execute enterprise goals and initiatives.

Although IT professionals share responsibility for maintaining current their skills, successful CIOs will include staff development in their own organizational goals. Two key benefits of this objective are employee effectiveness and staff retention. Investment in employee training produces more valuable and skilled contributors, and staff development fosters increased retention of valuable employees.[1]

CIO Magazine's 2008 "State of the CIO" report[2] found that 56 percent of surveyed CIOs said long-term strategic thinking and planning is the executive leadership skill most critical in their current role, followed by collaboration and influence (47 percent); and expertise running IT (39 percent). The rate of change among the responding CIOs dictates the need to be proactive in bringing solutions to their organizations rather than waiting for business units to present their needs to IT.

Regardless of the initial capabilities of the CIO's team, a plan for continuous IT training will increase the skill base of the IT workforce. During periods of intense competition for skilled IT professionals, investment in professional development is rewarded with higher levels of employee satisfaction and loyalty.

DEVELOPING THE TRAINING PLAN

The CIO's plan for IT organizational skill development includes occupational requirements, needs analysis, training cost and budget development, training source identification, training delivery, and ongoing skills assessment. Each of these training plan elements is discussed in the next sections.

Technical Requirements

The IT professional is expected to possess the necessary technical skills and to collaborate effectively with people to achieve enterprise objectives. The IT function can encompass relationships with customers, vendors, suppliers, and internal staff. A typical IT professional's job description spans a broad set of capabilities from technology procurement/tracking, to troubleshooting technology problems, to enterprise system implementation while maintaining excellent working relationships across functions. Fortunately "leaping tall buildings in a single bound" is not expected, too.

Enterprise-wide tools necessary to automate enterprise functions, such as customer service, purchasing, human resources, finance, sales, and marketing, depend on IT implementation and maintenance. The IT team will also enable enterprise tools for ecommerce, manufacturing, and distribution, among other functions. Software, hardware, and automated procedures that affect servers, data storage equipment, networks, telephony, web sites, desktop computers, laptop computers, portable devices, and so on are integral to enterprise business operations.

On the technical side, training has changed significantly over the years. IT professionals rarely attend training programs at IT vendor sites for one- to three-day training sessions. A decade ago, an individual might have attended a three-day course on a Microsoft Windows update. Today's IT professional is expected to maintain skills currency using online training portals. IT employees are expected to keep technical skills up to date on the ever-changing hardware and software platforms.

Emotional Intelligence Requirements

A software or hardware engineer for a product development company can be an individual contributor working alone or on a small component development team. Enterprise IT professional counterparts are expected to possess excellent technical skills; they also must collaborate effectively with nontechnical enterprise professionals. These emotional intelligence skills are developed through on-the-job, trial-and-error methods with peers, bosses, and direct reports. This inefficient approach is unreliable; if it is unsuccessful, it can alienate the very people whom IT supports.

By employing a more proactive approach, a CIO can provide ongoing skill development for the team to increase the likelihood of its success. Unfortunately, training in the "softer" skills such as communication and teamwork skills sometimes is secondary to other IT organizational imperatives. By contrast, sales organizations recognize the direct impact of soft skills development on their results. They often provide ongoing training for their professionals in this skills arena on a quarterly and annual basis.

Needs Analysis

There are a few key steps a CIO can take to impart strong interpersonal skills among IT professionals. The first step is to assess key needs:

- What are your team's strengths? For example, do team members interface well with engineers but have difficulty with customers? Identify skill gaps in communication and rapport building, managing goals, dealing with conflict, and other key skills that result in collaborative problem solving.
- What are the priorities for your organization?
- What are the nice-to-have options?
- Evaluate prior training efforts. Identify which training initiatives have been effective and which have not yielded results.
- Who needs the training?
  - Organizations
  - Project teams
  - Departments
  - Key employees
- What skills are needed, and how will the skills be imparted?
- When will team members need the new skills?
- Where can the training be conducted?

Needs analysis also examines organizational goals, climate, and internal and external constraints. Training needs can be discerned through a series of focus group sessions, via surveys, or in one-on-one interviews.

Technical needs analysis happens on an ongoing basis. Online learning, virtual classrooms, and online certification exams comprise standard industry options for technical training. New employees' technical skills should be thoroughly evaluated during the hiring process. Although their resumes may cite certifications for Oracle, SAP, and/or Microsoft products, their demonstrable skills may not correspond with the certification. The convenience of online training and testing is a double-edged sword. An individual may master cognitive learning but lack corresponding hands-on capability. Delving deeper into technical questions during the hiring process has become mandatory.

Training Budget

In favorable economic times, large organizations invest 2 to 5 percent of salary budgets in training. Regardless of the budget available within your IT organization, the key is to allocate a portion of your budget for investment in your people. Determine the appropriate amount based on a comprehensive analysis of the knowledge and abilities required for your employees' success.

A comprehensive training budget would include the costs of deliverables indicated in Table 5.1.

Some employers offer tuition reimbursement for advanced university degrees. The investment can affect employee retention by either formal or informal agreements.

TABLE 5.1 Budgeting Items for Training

Initial Communication about the Training Program
Training delivery (e.g., classes, video tutorials, e-learning, course fees)
Training materials (workbooks, videos)
Staff time (including replacement time)
Instructor fees
Travel, lodging, or meal expenses required to participate
Ongoing training (maintenance)
Contingencies

Frank Papp, in the CIO Office of Lawrence Livermore National Laboratory (LNL), works in a high-matrix IT organization, so budgeting and planning are key factors in success. His team of 5 people is augmented by other program groups, sometimes reaching 125 people to support LNL's sophisticated weapons development initiatives.

To support the site, a solution rollout budget includes resources from many organizational departments, an endeavor that requires deft cooperation and thorough budget planning. Papp's team plays a lead role in developing a robust safety and security training program. As part of the training implementation, Papp organized a matrix team to maintain skills currency in cybersecurity to address any escalated issues.

Education and Training Sources

The CIO's selection of training options should consider the level of the targeted IT professionals. Senior people might welcome coaching and mentoring to fine-tune their skills. More junior people may need to develop key skills, such as conflict management or building cohesive teams. Table 5.2 shows a wide spectrum of options as well as their relative cost.

Walt Thinfen, CIO of Visioneer Corporation, a Xerox scanner licensing partner, has a budget line item labeled "Employee Morale" for offsite team- and skills-building activities. In addition, Thinfen uses a 10-10-10 coaching model in his weekly meetings with direct reports: 10 minutes for the employee, 10 minutes for him, and 10 minutes for proactive planning. The door is closed, and the employee receives uninterrupted time to discuss priorities, solve problems, and plan ahead. To maintain their IT teams' organizational skills, both Papp and Thinfen allocate budget for industry conferences, such as Oracle World.

In-House Training Design and Delivery

The CIO aligns specific goals with the purpose of the training. Examples of goals that require tailored training initiatives include:

- Design and implement a specific business improvement initiative (e.g., customer complaint reduction).
- Execute a significant change in direction or a new organizational directive.

TABLE 5.2 Training Options

Learning Category	Cost	Employee Level
Training for project management, relationship skill building, influencing, etc.	$	All
e-Learning, webinars	$	All depending on topic
Mandated training (health, safety, environment, etc.)	$	All
Human resource process: hiring, performance evaluations, corrective action		Managers
Coaching	$$	Executive, rising star manager, key contributor employee
University for advanced degree	$$$	Rising star manager, key contributor employee
Executive MBA, MA	$$$	Executive
Professional conferences	$	All
Technical seminar/Networking	$	Executives—to stay up to date with trends
Leadership training: on-site	$$	Managers
Leadership training: offsite (e.g., Center for Creative Leadership)	$$	Managers, executives

Legend: $ low cost; $$ medium cost; $$$ high cost

- Increase market competitiveness by exploiting new technology opportunities.
- Increase organizational productivity through interpersonal skills training and development.

Training delivery entails much more than presentation. Training delivery encompasses student registration, progress tracking systems, training materials production, equipment purchase and implementation, facilities management, and prepared instructors. A CIO will need to ensure that both budget and time are available for effective training.

Best practices to consider when creating and organizing a learning experience include:

- Conduct a pilot.
- Explain and discuss training program goals and training session outcomes with participants.
- Take time to discover students' motives (e.g., what prompted them to enroll).
- Ensure that the training content is relevant and appropriate for the audience's level of expertise.
- Include participant interaction, such as group discussion, case study analysis, and role-playing.

- Encourage participant interaction, such as asking questions, expressing points of concern, and contributing comments at appropriate and identified stages.
- When appropriate, utilize multimedia, such as video, to enhance learning.
- Bring in skilled facilitators of group and individual learning who communicate in ways that are appropriate to the workplace culture and target group.
- Address the specific competencies and outcomes to be achieved in the training design.

Commitment from both senior managers and employees is needed to embrace the opportunity for employees to grow and change.

Supplier/Offshore Partner Training

Developing a partnership approach, a CIO's team can collaborate with an IT supplier to build the skills necessary to integrate complex business processes. By investing in training in the early phases of an outsourcing partnership, the teams can more readily overcome integration issues.

Thinfen decided on an opposite approach—to bring IT services in customer support and technical support onshore. His team could create a rapid closed loop system to solve problems. A case in point is a product problem that was identified and resolved within four calls as individuals in IT, customer support, and engineering worked together as a team. Thinfen mentions that having an offshore team has a downside as there is a lack of "emotional attachment" to solving problems for the customer and corporate organization. Since Thinfen invests considerable time in coaching his team, keeping his team trained, he finds more reliable results with an onshore strategy.

Ongoing Assessment

Training can be costly, so the CIO can implement an assessment strategy to ensure the expected impact is achieved. However, the results from training may encompass factors that cannot be reflected in financial metrics.

Effective results assessment entails tracking relevant variables before and after training to verify improvement. For example, if the training was focused on internal customer service, the end result may be fewer complaints or complaints of lower severity. The results assessment should be directly related to the original training goals. Assessment criteria should include:

- **Curriculum effectiveness.** What worked well? What had the least impact on results?
- **Training delivery.** Even experts may need your help to become effective instructors for your organization. Be sure to monitor the class to evaluate training delivery effectiveness.
- **Solicit feedback from the participants.** Feedback will help you and the instructors refine the training delivery.

CONCLUSION

Training opportunities are available even when the budget is slashed. Thinfen, for example, tasked product champions with writing standard operating procedures and troubleshooting information guides for use as training materials. Senior IT personnel may serve as mentors to less experienced employees. Such techniques are even more important when budgets are reduced, because it is generally less costly to retain good employees than to replace them. When hiring is frozen, retention of good employees can determine whether the IT organization is humming along or whining along.

Optimally, a CIO invests in the professional development of the IT team. In review, a CIO identifies the training requirements, conducts an analysis of needs versus budget, sources a training plan, and implements across the organization.

In closing, spend time getting to know your employees. By understanding what motivates them, you can structure and enhance their job. According to Rich Freeman, an IT business and technology expert, "Helping employees expand their expertise pays a second dividend: IT departments composed of generalists often survive with fewer people, according to Gartner research, because they can redeploy current employees when new demands arise rather than add specialized roles or hire consultants."[3]

Skill building the IT professional is sound advice for CIOs who support and develop their staff.

NOTES

1. "IT Employee Retention: It's Not All about the Money," *Computer Economics*, August 2008, www.computereconomics.com/article.cfm?id=1385.
2. "The State of the CIO," *CIO Magazine* (2008), http://a1448.g.akamai.net/7/1448/25138/v0001/compworld.download.akamai.com/25137/cio/pdf/state_of_cio_08.pdf.
3. Rich Freeman, "8 Great Tips for Reducing Your IT Costs," Microsoft, 2009, www.microsoft.com/midsizebusiness/business-value/reduce-technology-cost.mspx.

CHAPTER SIX

Retain Your Talent by Creating a Fun, Engaging Culture

Baron Concors

WHETHER WE LIKE IT or not, CIOs are in a talent war. As we press for continuous improvement, we go to great lengths to find and grow great talent, hoping they are satisfied and stay for many years. As someone intelligent once said, "Hope is not a plan." The fact is that our high performers will be tempted by headhunters and better offers throughout their careers. In addition, there is no longer a dying commitment or loyalty to people or companies as there was in the past. Why is retention such a big deal? Well, let's start with the obvious financial impacts of turnover. There is a lot of debate about the average dollar amount it costs an organization for employee turnover, but we can agree on one thing: It is an unnecessary cost that can and should be avoided. There are also a number of intangible costs associated with turnover, and often these carry a larger impact than financial ones. Intangible costs include things such as increased workload of other employees, declining employee morale, and the loss of intellectual capital. With baby boomers leaving the workforce and an entrepreneurial group coming out of college, we have to constantly assess our workplace environment and understand what issues are top of mind for our teams. We must constantly adapt and grow our leadership styles to accommodate this changing workforce. Leadership is not just about setting a strategy, vision, and prioritizing work for your teams. More important, it is about winning the hearts and minds of your people in order to create an engaging, positive work environment where people feel empowered to speak their minds and bring their ideas forward. How do you create such an environment? Is there a class for management to teach how to win the hearts and minds of their people? Of course not. It all starts with forming the right culture that fosters the open communications and trust needed to get there.

Some key messages throughout this chapter have to be top of mind as we go forward. First, one of the hard realities of being an employer is this: People do not leave companies, they leave people. Yes, there are rare examples where this is not true, but I have read enough exit interviews in my career to know that a majority of people leave because they do not feel their manager cares about them. It is a simple truth: If people have a bad boss, it is going to be very difficult for them to be actively engaged and committed to an organization. Second, you need the right people and mind-set on your management team. Every manager in your group needs to believe that it is his or her responsibility to create the right culture to retain employees. Many managers believe employee retention is beyond their control because they think the only way to keep good people is to increase salaries or bonuses or grow other benefits. Do not let your managers off the hook with that excuse. Good leaders know that retention has little to do with money; it is more about respect, challenging work, recognition, and, most important, having an available boss who helps to grow and develop staff members throughout their careers. Great bosses spend time coaching, mentoring, and providing constructive feedback to their team members on a regular basis. In addition, managers should be great coaches and motivators. I want my leaders to have a teachable point of view and look for ways to promote their team's accomplishments. Bad bosses do not want their team members to bother them or often take days to answer their e-mails or phone calls.

Creating a great culture is a journey. It starts by clearly communicating values to your management team and setting expectations on what kind of behaviors you want leaders to exhibit. For example, in my organization, we do not have time for leaders who do not put their people first. People are the greatest asset we have, and as leaders, our job is to help them succeed and look for opportunities for them to grow and develop. I am always concerned when I go through our annual employee survey and see troubling comments about individual managers. For example, I have seen comments from team members such as "My manager only gives me feedback once a year during my performance review," or "My boss says not to bring him problems, only solutions," or "My manager doesn't have staff meetings." What kind of manager says "Don't bring me problems?" It is our job as leaders to support our teams and help them overcome whatever roadblocks are in their way.

When I coach new managers, I often like to point out the power of their new role. I ask them: "When the folks on your team go home each night and sit at the dinner table with their family, what do you think they talk about?" The manager usually thinks for a while and says, "Probably work and how their day went." I reply, "That's true, but you know what they are really talking about? You, their manager, and how you acted that day or how you treated them. Do you want them to sit around the dinner table with their family and talk about what a jerk you were to them in the office?" Sometimes this is a big revelation for new managers. They do not always comprehend that everything they say and do can have such a profound impact on their team members.

Do not get me wrong—creating this kind of engaging culture is not easy. It begins with taking an honest assessment of your current corporate culture. There are symptoms you can look for to determine whether your culture has opportunity for improvement. For example, do you find that when you speak in front of your team, no one seems to want to ask any questions or voice any opinions? Do you rarely have people in your office proposing an innovative idea or a better way to do things? If these are true, you likely have some fear in your group. Fear is the root of all evil when trying to form a great culture. When people feel fear, they do not speak their mind due to feeling ridiculed or punished in some way. Another symptom of culture issues is what I call the "hierarchy blues." This occurs when no one feels comfortable communicating unless it goes sequentially up the chain first. This situation results in a culture where employees are never allowed to talk to their manager's boss unless they talk to their manager first. This issue gets in the way of open, honest two-way communications. You must look for ways to make it clear to people that they can walk into your office or speak with you whenever they want. Why? Because this is a sure sign you care about their thoughts and you are available to help them. Finally, when people do decide to start voicing ideas and opinions, make sure you never ridicule them, or else you will never get open, honest communications in your culture.

Just how do we go about creating an engaging culture where people feel committed and engaged? Well, there is no checklist, project plan, or map that describes how to successfully change a culture. Changing a culture is somewhat like moving a mountain—especially if the culture you are trying to change has been in existence for many years. It is accomplished by doing what you think is right and connecting with the people on your teams. I can only offer guidance and advice on how I have done this, and I am always looking for ways to improve. If I see a group with culture issues, I try to influence change by practicing what I call the six Rs: *respect, reset* expectations, *relate* to your people, *remove* hierarchies, *recognize,* and *relax.*

 ## SHOW RESPECT

The basis of any great corporate culture is respect. Showing respect is the foundation for trust, commitment, and integrity. I am sure you, as a leader, are aware that everyone is watching your actions and words. We cannot lose sight of that fact, and I am sure everyone reading this thinks they demonstrate respect for others at all times. However, a lot of people do not realize when they are showing disrespect.

How often has this happened: You are in a meeting with others and someone is talking, when suddenly someone pulls out a phone and starts looking at e-mail. Although this may seem like a minor act, what does it show? It shows that the person looking at the phone does not care what the person talking has to say. Now, I know that is not the intention of the person looking at the phone, but it is absolutely a sign of disrespect. Always show basic respect to everyone by practicing active listening: Focus on the person talking, and do not get distracted by electronic devices or sidebar conversations.

Another example is passing people in the halls at work. Do you always say good morning or hello, or are you busy looking at your BlackBerry as you walk down the hall? Again, although minor in nature, how significant an impact can an event such as passing people in the hall without acknowledging them have? You are the leader—recognize that it can have a major impact on the psyche of your team. They might even sit down for dinner with their family that night and say, "I guess the CIO doesn't like me. He passed me in the hall today and didn't even say hello."

A final note on respect: Do not be the boss who is hard to get ahold of or always too busy. You never know why someone on your team needs you to respond quickly—maybe someone in their family is sick, or they need to attend a meeting at school for their child. In all cases, it is important to be available and responsive to your team members. Pay attention to their wants and needs, even those things that seem small or insignificant to you. Those wants and needs clearly are important to them. If you want to keep your people, it is critical that you lend an ear to them whenever they need it and recognize the value in each person's unique talents.

 ## RESET EXPECTATIONS

It is always prudent to take the time to set clear expectations of your leaders and management team. The expectations I set for my team are clear:

1. People are our number-one priority.
2. We demonstrate accountability by doing what we say we are going to do.
3. I am here to knock down whatever barriers are facing you—just let me know.

Sometimes you have to get a little more granular with these expectations. I have been put in charge of organizations where I have had to make it clear that I expect my management team to have regular staff meetings and provide performance feedback to their employees once a quarter. These actions reinforce the core values by which you want your organization to operate. If you do not have these expectations, start immediately working with your group to define a vision and a purpose along with core values. Core values are at the heart of what you value as a leader—things such as integrity, innovation, trust, respect, accountability, and so on. Once you define these core values, they need to become a part of your everyday conversations and perform-ance assessments. Do not just create these things to put on a poster in the hall; live them and reinforce them so your teams understand they are important.

 ## RELATE TO YOUR PEOPLE

Ever worked for one of those bosses who always has a wall up and will not let you get to know him or her? It is not fun and not motivating. No one likes working for some stiff who is always in "work mode" and will not have fun or share anything about their personal life. Bosses who do not share a lot about their personal lives lose an opportunity to build rapport or relate to their people. For example, early in my career, I worked for a boss who shared little about his personal life. I often tried to open him up by initiating some dialogue. Every Monday, I would say, "Hey, Mike, how was your weekend?"

He would say, "It was okay," and he would walk into his office and shut his door. Now, as a lowly project manager, do you think that helped me relate to my boss? Of course not. I was taking the initiative to create conversation to get to know him better, and he obviously was not interested or thought I was not deserving of his time. I always talk to and treat my team at work just like my friends in my personal life. Some may think this is dangerous—to get personally connected to your team at work. However, I believe that is exactly what you should be trying to accomplish if you want to win their hearts and minds. Always be authentic and genuine with the people you work with; your culture will improve as a result of it.

 ## REMOVE HIERARCHIES

Do not let your culture and work get stifled by a command and control structure. Anyone should feel like they can talk to anyone at any time without consequences. This type of behavior will not only speed up things in your organization but will also allow healthy conflict where people can feel they are empowered to speak their mind and bring forward new ideas. I cannot tell you how many times I have worked with companies where we have endless meetings sitting around for hours on end looking at a single slide in PowerPoint presentation. Why? Because everyone is worried about how a certain vice president or C-level executive is going to react to every single sentence in the presentation. Do not let your culture be driven by this type of behavior. It slows things down and stifles innovation. Let everyone know that your door is open and you want to hear people's issues and concerns. Getting these issues on the table early prevents people from getting frustrated and prevents morale from turning negative.

 ## RECOGNIZE

I know many people reading this have formal recognition programs in place. You know, the kind where your group gets together once a month or quarter and hands out the plaque or award to recognize someone on the team. This type of recognition is important, but there is an even more important type of recognition—it is something I call spontaneous recognition.

Spontaneous recognition is very powerful because it is not as calculated as your scheduled recognition program. This type of recognition is when you see something that deserves recognition and you take action immediately. You walk down the hall to the person's cubicle/office, or you take the time to send a handwritten note thanking the person for his efforts. Keep in mind that it is important to be specific and direct in your feedback. Do not use general statements, such as "thank you" or "nice job." It is better to say something like: "I like how you showed a sense of urgency when dealing with that problem, and I appreciate your tremendous work ethic." Tell people exactly why you liked what they did; doing so lets them know you truly appreciate the effort they put forward.

Imagine someone on your team getting a call at home one night from you thanking her for something she did at work that day. Imagine someone getting a handwritten note from you mailed to his home, recognizing him for an achievement. This type of spontaneous recognition has a big impact on people; they realize you took the time to actually hand-write a note or personally call them. They will be very grateful that you took the time to show you care, and they will be more engaged as a result of it. You will start to win their hearts.

RELAX

This may be the most important topic in this chapter: Relax. Have fun. There is no reason you cannot work hard and have fun at the same time. When your team sees you having fun, they will have fun. It is okay not to be in "work mode" 24/7; let loose sometimes with your team. Also, it is important to laugh at yourself; that lets everyone know you do not take yourself too seriously. When your team members are having fun, trust me: They are less likely to leave for another company.

SUMMARY

Most people reading this have been through a culture change, are in the middle of creating change now, or are planning for change in the future. Know that people will resist change. It is human nature. Some of your managers might not even embrace the change despite your coaching and counseling. You will have to decide how you will handle those cases, but understand that one bad person can create enough turmoil in an organization to ruin the culture.

People will not believe that you want them to be honest and that you want to hear their ideas. Show your team that they can trust you by delivering on your promises and doing what you say you are going to do. Be transparent. Be real and genuine. Take the time to talk to everyone and get to know your team members on a personal level.

The rewards will be worth the effort; creating a fun, engaging culture will not only result in a better retention rate of your talent, but will also make the office a more enjoyable place to work on a daily basis. Morale will improve, and people will become more open and collaborative, which will result in the ultimate reward: high-performing teams delivering exceptional results.

7

The CIO Career Guide

Mark Wayman

MY NAME IS Mark Wayman; however, my friends call me the Godfather of Las Vegas. After 20 years of corporate life and 3 years at a start-up, I set up my own company doing what I do best: helping people. In my case, that means placing highly compensated executives in the gaming and high-tech industries. My executive placement business allows me to follow my passion: helping and serving others.

This chapter is written for executives in transition. And CIOs always seem to be in transition—either unemployed or unhappily employed and trying to find a new job. As a matter of fact, of all the C-level executives I represent, CIOs are the most transient. This chapter is based on my 20 years as a corporate executive and 5 years as the owner of an executive talent firm. I place approximately 50 executives annually, primarily at the C and vice president level, with an average annual compensation of $200,000+.

The goal of this chapter is to educate you on how to be part of the top 5 percent, the candidates in high demand that Fortune 500 companies search for. In the search business, these candidates are called the A players.

YOU'RE FIRED!

Every executive will be terminated or laid off at least once in his or her career. For many, it will happen multiple times. And when you are on the street with no job prospects, it may not be the end of the world, but you certainly feel like you can see the end of the world from where you are standing. Before you do any bridge jumping, let's look at a few statistics and philosophies.

Statistics

- The average executive career is four years. That means you can expect to change jobs 5 to 10 times over the course of your career.
- The average executive career at the C level (CEO, CFO, CIO, etc.) is two years.
- 50 percent of employees are unhappy with their job.
- 75 percent of employees would change jobs if given a chance.

Philosophies

- **The company is all about the company.** The company is "for profit." Decisions are made for the best interest of the company. They may or may not be in the best interest of the employee. Do not take it personally.
- **Do not define your identity through your job.** This is really important. If you define yourself through your job, being terminated can be devastating. It is just a job, and there will always be more jobs. Jobs are a means to an end.
- **Success takes hard work.** There is no return without investment. Success takes hard work.
- **The secret.** There is no secret. The real secret to success is hard work, relationships, perseverance, and never giving up.

 ## HELP WANTED

There are always jobs for talented executives. Even in the worst economy, there are jobs for talented people. That stated, finding that next opportunity can be hard work. You have to hustle, stay active, and work your personal and professional networks. Over 80 percent of career opportunities are found through your network. If you hustle, if you stay active, you *will* get a job! You will be among the 5 percent who worked hard while the other 95 percent were watching TV.

Whether you get a particular job or not has zero to do with your worth, so do not get discouraged. Maybe you are a great candidate, but another candidate was just a little closer fit for the client.

Over the past 12 months, the most common stumbling block for candidates has been *unrealistic expectations*. This is being written in early 2011, and we are experiencing the worst economy of our lifetimes. So why are candidates expecting a 25 percent increase in base salary and 50 percent bonuses? If you are going to seek a new career opportunity, be aware of the economic realities and set your expectations accordingly.

Your chances of getting hired through an online job posting or newspaper ad are slim to none. An online job posting can generate as many as 500 resumes. About 495 are not qualified, and it is obvious that 200 did not even read the posting. The resumes are typically passed to a human resources generalist who sorts through the stack of resumes looking for keywords. Job postings and ads are for candidates in the

$50,000 salary range. CIOs find their jobs through two sources: personal networking and executive placement firms.

Executive talent agents, recruiters, headhunters, or whatever you want to call them attach executive candidates (talent) to client companies. People are *the* most important component of an organization. They are the difference between success and failure. Unfortunately, the recruiting industry is full of unethical, dishonest people trying to make this month's quota. Often they are not honest with the candidates or their clients. The best thing to do is to work exclusively with an executive talent agent you know and trust. The second best option is to ask your friends for a referral to an honest, ethical agent.

REPRESENTATION FROM AN EXECUTIVE PLACEMENT FIRM

For most of you, this section will be the most important one. Executives at $100,000+ compensation have two alternatives for finding jobs: their personal/professional network and executive recruiters. About 95 percent of your opportunities will come from these two sources.

It is important that you *read this section* and understand how executive placement works. Doing so will give you a clear advantage over other candidates, who routinely get the boot because they do not understand the process. You will understand the model and what talent agents find attractive *and* unattractive. Here are some tips:

- **It is *not* an honor and privilege to represent you.** Number-one tip: Recruiters have an almost limitless choice of candidates. There is nothing that says a recruiter is required to represent you. They are looking for humble, honest, hardworking people. Most recruiters represent candidates only by referral, and actually they represent only about 10 percent of the many who approach them. If you come across as arrogant and elitist, no one will represent you and no one will hire you. Be humble; be genuine. Lose the attitude.
- **Understand priorities.** A recruiter's top priority is matching great talent with great companies. Recruiters make money only if they place candidates. For that reason, they are laser-focused on finding candidates for an existing open position. They do not "market" candidates unless the client relationship is longstanding and intimate. So although they have compassion for your situation, they are not in a position to drop everything to get you a job. All executive recruiters follow this same model.
- **Do not give a line-by-line description of your compensation package.** Getting a job is like selling a house in a bad economy. If you price it right, you can still sell your house reasonably quickly. If you want to recoup your investment or refuse to take a loss, it may take a year or two to sell the house or it may never sell at all. The same principle applies to your job search. If you set your compensation expectations in line with the market, you will get a job. If you set your expectations too high, you will price yourself right into the unemployment line. Be realistic about compensation.

- **Display honesty and integrity.** Ethical executive recruiters use honesty and integrity to place their candidates. They submit only qualified candidates, and they strongly guard their reputation. As a candidate, you need to have the same mantra: 100 percent honesty. Dishonesty from the candidate or a lack of integrity is the primary reason recruiters drop candidates.
- **Maintain confidentiality.** Recruiting work is extremely sensitive in nature. In some cases, the incumbent has not been terminated yet. All discussions, including any positions you are submitted for, are 100 percent confidential. Betray that confidentiality and your recruiter will drop you immediately.
- **Use your representation.** Once you are submitted to a client company, the recruiter is your agent of record for the next 12 months at that company. If you get hired, the recruiter gets paid. The most important point to remember is that you have an agent representing you. You should not contact the client directly unless asked or given permission to do so by your agent. Any time you interview or have contact with the hiring company, you need to update your agent. If you circumvent the process for any reason, you will be withdrawn from consideration and dropped as a candidate. It is essential that you understand the executive placement process and stay within the boundaries.
- **Your job search must be your priority.** You need a job, not the recruiter. If finding a new career opportunity is not a priority for you, do not waste the recruiter's time or, more important, the client's time. Recruiters dread candidates who are "tire kickers," "just testing the waters," "not really looking," or "just gauging the market." They get paid to place people. Engage a recruiter only if you are 100 percent committed to making a move.
- **You need to make yourself accessible.** Recruiters will not play phone tag with you because you are too busy to schedule an interview or take a call. You will find out quickly that they will not chase people around. They typically have a dozen qualified candidates for every position that becomes available. If you make them chase you, soon you will find them not returning *your* phone calls.
- **Value long-term relationships.** Business is based on long-term relationships. There is a recruiter on every corner, and most will be happy to spread your resume around town. But you need to be very careful regarding who represents you. Successful recruiters represent executives who stay in touch with them, maintain their relationship, and express their gratitude when they are placed in a new job. If your plan is to call a recruiter only when you need a job and disappear until you need the next one, you will not be an attractive candidate.
- **It's all about the money (part 1).** Everyone wants to be compensated fairly. A recruiter's job is to examine your resume and skills and align your compensation to market conditions. This determines your "fair market value"—what a company will pay for you at a given time.
- **It's all about the money (part 2).** Focus on the opportunity, and if it is a match, then you can discuss the compensation. If you start the conversation talking about your stock options and car allowance, you will be challenged to find a recruiter to represent you. Always be about the opportunity and the value you can provide, and the compensation will line up.

- **Patience is a virtue.** A typical recruiter receives 300 e-mails, 100 resumes, and 50 phone calls every single day. Remember, recruiters get paid only if they find you a job. If you are submitted for a position, they will get back to you when it is time to move forward. If you are in the interview process, they will update you as information becomes available. *Do not e-mail and call your recruiter for daily/weekly updates. It will not make the process go faster and will paint you in an unfavorable light.* It makes you look desperate even if you are not. And desperation is completely and totally unattractive. If you want to get on a recruiter's bad side, be sure to bug him or her repeatedly for an update. When you do this, you are stealing time from other clients who have patiently waited their turn.
- **You must be able to pass a background check or drug test.** If you cannot pass a background check and drug screen, you typically cannot get a job. A background check looks for a criminal record, driving under the influence (DUI), bankruptcy, foreclosure, or tax lien (depending on the industry). The only thing worse than failing a background check is lying about it up front. If you disclose an old DUI or personal bankruptcy, your recruiter can probably work through it. If it shows up unexpectedly during the background check, you will be disqualified from the job and dropped as a future candidate. If you are already on the payroll, you will soon be terminated.
- **No bigger names on the other line.** The executive recruiter's job is to get you in front of clients and insert you into the interview process. Your job is to interview well and sell yourself. Once you are in the process, you need to be completely honest with your recruiter regarding other opportunities you are pursuing. It is very disconcerting to recruiters to spend hours on a candidate's behalf and then have the rug pulled out from under them at the last second. You may get the other job, but you are burning a valuable bridge. If you are contemplating an offer or close to accepting an alternate position, just let your recruiter know.
- **One job per customer.** If you get a job and quit within a year of your start date, most recruiters will add you to their do-not-use list. Job hopping is very unattractive. Recruiters devote significant effort to matching talent to clients. There is an expectation that it will be a long-term engagement and that you will be a committed team member even through rocky times.

THE RESUME—IT'S JUST A BOOKMARK

At the CIO level, resumes are just a point of reference for the conversation. Having the most pristine resume adds little value. The resume is just something to glance at during the interview. There is no need to spend hours and hours editing and re-editing. The three biggest mistakes you can make are: listing college coursework when you do not have a degree, trying to hide holes in employment, and flowery speeches about how wonderful you are. Here are a few important qualities of an effective resume:

- **Honesty and integrity.** First and foremost, do not lie, embellish, or stretch the truth on your resume. No company wants to hire a dishonest candidate. If you get caught lying on your resume, even after you start the new job, you will be terminated. The most common issues involve embellishing compensation, tenure, job title, or education. *Make sure the content of your resume is 100 percent truthful.*

- **Your unique value proposition.** This is far and away the most important takeaway on resumes. You must have a unique value proposition. The more unique, the better. If a CEO cannot read your resume in 60 seconds and know exactly what value you can add and exactly what problems you can solve, your chances of landing the job are zero. CEOs are busy and do not have time to figure it out or read between the lines to find your value proposition. You need to stand out from the noise. *Make sure your resume quickly and concisely spells out your unique value proposition.*
- **One-line objective.** If you insist on having an executive summary at the top of your resume, make it a simple one- or two-line statement. The best summary is an explanation of your unique value proposition and how it can solve the client's problem. *Keep your objective to one or two lines.*
- **Just the facts.** Most CEOs want to get all the information they need out of a resume in 60 seconds or less. Place your full contact information at the top: name, address, mobile number, and e-mail address. The address lets prospective employers know if you are local or in need of relocation. Always use your mobile number, not your home or work number. List company, title, tenure, and three to five bullet accomplishments for each position. Be careful about disclosing any personal information. It is bad enough that employers can infer things incorrectly, such as "he went to BYU so he is a devout Mormon." You do not want to be excluded due to race, ethnicity, age, gender, or religious belief. The more personal information you disclose, the more opportunity to be excluded.
- **Education.** Do not list your graduation dates. You will be too young or too old. Big red flags for my clients include listing a college you "attended." Never list a college unless you received a degree, and never state that you "went to the school of hard knocks" or anything else that gives the appearance that you have a degree when you do not. If you do not have a four-year degree, your chances of securing a good CIO job are pretty slim. At the C level, graduate degrees are preferred. *List your degree if you have it; otherwise, leave college coursework off the resume.*
- **Microsoft Word defaults (no pictures, emblems, or logos).** Anything other than text detracts from the resume. This includes bizarre fonts, color, and strange borders. And no head shots! CEOs want to spend exactly 60 seconds on a resume.
- **Your specialty.** In the 1960s, being a generalist was a wonderful career path. Today, the jack of all trades and master of none is unemployed. The twenty-first-century career path is that of a specialist. Recruiters need a specific angle or expertise that helps them understand where you would be a good fit. Give your recruiter specific industry experience that lifts you above the white noise.
- **No functional resumes.** Functional resumes are old school. For one thing, they make people think you are a "twilighter" in the last few years of your career. But the primary reason for not using them is that they are too hard to read and the business community knows you are trying to hide something.

THE INTERVIEW—NO SECOND CHANCE FOR FIRST IMPRESSIONS

This is a competition. Usually several candidates are being interviewed for a specific job, and all of them are highly qualified or they would not be interviewing. In this economy with very few active CIO searches, you might be up against 100 candidates. And that number may have been winnowed down from 400 who were submitted. Your job is to position yourself as the most qualified candidate for the job. Here are some tips for an effective interview:

- **Prepare.** Do your homework. Check out the company web site and scan the Internet for information on the company and its executives. Formulate three intelligent questions to ask during the interview process. Executives love their companies and will be impressed that you took the time to research them. Pull out your best suit—dress to impress. Bring a copy of your resume and a full-size notepad in case you need to write something down.
- **Be prompt.** Show up 10 minutes early. The number-one fear of American executives is having someone waste their time. Arrive early and send a message that their time is valuable to you. Showing up late for an interview almost guarantees that you will not move forward in the hiring process.
- **Behave professionally.** You get exactly one shot at the interview. It is essential that you represent yourself in a professional manner. This includes professional attire, a can-do attitude, and the ability to articulate your unique value proposition. Remember, this is your one and only chance to sell yourself to the client.
- **Answer the question.** The objective of an interview is to answer each question fully without rambling on. There is such a thing as too much information. Typically, a 60-second answer is appropriate. The conversation should be balanced—you talk for 50 percent of the time and the interviewer talks 50 percent of the time.
- **Send a thank-you note.** Be sure to get a business card from the interviewer and send a hand-written thank-you card or note. This places you in the top 5 percent of candidates. Most candidates do not work very hard at finding a job. They expect recruiters to do all the heavy lifting. Do the little things that make you a unique and special candidate.
- **Never speak negatively about anyone or any company.** Many candidates are eliminated for this reason alone. Do not make negative statements of any kind, especially about former employers, bosses, or coworkers. If you bad-mouth previous employers or colleagues, it is a strong indication that you will bad-mouth this company when you leave as well. Companies would rather avoid the risk.
- **Bitter is not attractive.** Leave the personal baggage at home. If your last job was horrific, get over it. Your last boss is certainly not obsessing over you. Bad things happen to good people. Move on.

CLOSING THE DEAL—NEVER FIGHT OVER NICKELS

You interviewed well, and now it is time to close the deal. Recruiters should always discuss compensation up front with candidates to ensure there is no disconnect at offer time. Although compensation is an important component, opportunity is the number-one decision-making criterion. If you stated that $200,000 was acceptable and you want $300,000 at offer time, you will probably be withdrawn from the running. If you accept the offer verbally, then sign the offer letter, you need to keep that commitment. If you use the offer to leverage your current employer into a raise, it will come back to haunt you—every single time. Your employer now knows of your discontent; leveraging your employer also discloses your lack of integrity. Make no mistake; you will be gone in 90 days. Finally, keep in mind that if you say anything other than yes to an offer, you have declined it and it is no longer valid.

 ## CAREER TIPS FOR CIOs

The following are some career tips for CIOs:

- **Dig the well before you need a drink.** If you take away only one piece of advice, this is it. The wrong time to build a well is when you need a drink. The best time to plant an oak tree is 25 years ago, but the second best time is . . . today. No one is going to return your call when you are unemployed. You are no longer in a position of power, and since you cannot help people with what they need right here, right now, they will not call you back. They have their own drama to deal with, and your employment crisis is not on their list of priorities. Going forward, focus on relationships. Go to the occasional networking event. Call your friends and business associates with no agenda, just to catch up and say hi.
- **Never embellish your resume.** Even after you pass the drug screen, fly through the background check, and start work, you can and will be fired if you were anything less than 100 percent straightforward on your resume. Be absolutely honest about job titles, compensation, job tenure, and education. Do not list a college unless you received a degree.
- **Dress for success.** This is your one and only shot. If you have an Armani suit, this is the time to wear it. Look like a CEO, not a programmer. *Dress one level above the position to which you aspire.*
- **Do not burn your bridges.** There is no upside to burning bridges. The downside is that anyone you alienate will tell all their friends. As one executive put it, "Always back away gracefully giving the golf wave." Successful executive recruiter will make several phone calls and validate every candidate as part of their due diligence. If no one has anything good to say about you, settle in for a long and painful job search.
- **Do not job hop.** Five jobs in five years is job hopping, and no amount of persuasion will get a company to interview you. Employers view job hoppers as people who do not play well with others. Take time *to think about your next*

career move. Do not take bridge jobs for "until I find something better." Find a company you can stay at for a minimum of three years. *Start building a stable resume today.*

- **Make sure you can pass compliance.** If you cannot pass the drug screen and background check (compliance), not many clients will hire you. Arrests, bankruptcies, foreclosures, tax liens, and DUIs are not attractive. Companies consider these incidents to be a direct reflection of your character. *Be responsible.*

- **Know your noncompete.** If you have a noncompete agreement, a recruiter cannot represent you, and his or her clients will not hire you. It may not be enforceable, but your former employer may send a thundering herd of attorneys to the client, and recruiters do not need that aggravation. *Invest $250 with an employment attorney and understand your alternatives.*

- **Do not spray your resume.** Distributing your resume to a dozen recruiters and every online job posting in the city is very unattractive. In the business, this is called "spraying," and it smells like desperation. Use your personal and professional network to find opportunities. Remember, 80 percent of all jobs are landed through your network. Less than 1 percent are landed through online job postings.

- **Be a specialist.** Clients want executives who fill a specific business requirement. That means a specific skill set and specific industry experience. This is the age of the specialist. You may be able to change industries or transfer skills, but that will not get you a first-class CIO job.

- **The grass is not always greener.** This is the worst economy of our lifetimes. If you have a great job with a huge compensation package, stay put.

 ## CONCLUSION

The average executive career is four years. That means you can expect to change jobs 5 to 10 times over the course of your career. There are always jobs for talented people, but finding the next opportunity takes hard work. The most common stumbling block to the next job is unrealistic expectations. Be aware of the economic realities and set your expectations accordingly. Understanding how the recruiting process works will give you a clear advantage over other candidates. Resumes are a reference point for the conversation with the hiring manager. The most important thing your resume should do is quickly and concisely state your unique value proposition. The interview is your one chance to sell yourself. Prepare yourself to do so. Finally, remember that the most important thing about your next job is the opportunity. Focus on it, and the compensation will follow.

PART TWO

Process

CHAPTER EIGHT

Strategic Alignment

Tim Campos

I N TODAY'S BUSINESS, CIOs have tremendous opportunity to have a major strategic influence on their businesses. This opportunity arises from the rapid adoption of information technology over the past three decades across nearly every aspect of business. When a company wants to merge with another organization, the IT organization is one of the first corporate departments to be involved. When a new plant or facility is opened, the IT organization must be involved to help connect it to the rest of the company's systems. Even when a company reaches into a new line of business, the IT organization is involved to help set up the information systems to support the new business.

This opportunity, however, can also be the CIO's greatest liability if the organization's focus is diluted. IT has been adopted in nearly every business process, even those that are not very strategic. Nearly all employees at companies have e-mail accounts, and every corporation has a web site, regardless of whether it delivers products or services through that web site. Because all of these technology operations must function in order for the business to operate, CIOs must divide their focus and resources across the entire company.

This breadth of demand creates tremendous challenges for IT organizations. It is not good enough simply to focus on those portions of the business that are strategic, to the detriment of everything else. Although this might work in the short run, over time the neglected business functions become a drain on the success of the business. (This is one of the reasons so many firms reimplement enterprise systems.) Moreover, what is "strategic" depends on whom one asks. A customer portal may not be that important to manufacturing, but it is critical to the strategy of the service organization. The resources allocated to the IT department are finite, yet the demands on the IT organization can at times appear infinite. It is this challenge that separates the mediocre from the exceptional IT organization. The secret to addressing this challenge is to strategically align your organization to the business.

FRAMEWORK

Strategic alignment results from structuring the IT organization around the needs of the business. To explain how this is done, let me break the operations of the IT organization down into four basic functions. Two are delivery functions: support delivery and project delivery. The other two are management activities: value attainment and strategic alignment. All activities of the IT organization can be categorized into one of these four functions, although, as we will see later, these functions are typically spread out across multiple teams, which is the source of much of the misalignment IT organizations face (see Figure 8.1).

These functions layer on top of each other such that failure at one level affects everything above it. Strategic alignment is achieved when all functions operate in harmony to achieve business results. However, how these functions are managed directly impacts how strategic an organization is. A tall skinny pyramid will generate far more value for a firm than a short fat one. For the rest of this chapter, we explore each function in more detail and highlight the management issues the CIO and the IT management staff must address to achieve strategic alignment.

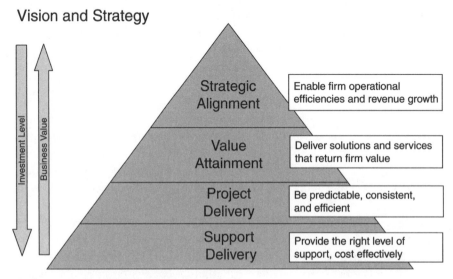

FIGURE 8.1 IT Strategic Alignment Framework

Support Delivery

Support makes up all of the break-fix activity of the IT operations. It is the most fundamental and, in many respects, the most important activity the IT organization engages in. Support includes the help desk and monitoring organizations but also aspects of technical operations, such as system administration, database administration, development, and business process analysts. All aspects of the IT organization provide some level of support back to the business.

Support delivery is critical not because it is strategic but because it is the foundation from which everything else is built. Put in simpler terms, if you are in the CEO's office and her personal computer is broken, what do you expect you will be discussing with her when you meet: supply chain strategy, or why her PC has been down for the past four hours? Support is the function that all IT organizations are engaged in regardless of size. In some IT organizations, support is *all* they are engaged in.

Support delivery involves several management decisions including scope, service levels, and overall investment. A widely circulated metric asserts that most IT organizations spend 70 to 80 percent of their budget sustaining existing systems. Whether this is the right level is the subject of some debate, but the metric highlights the fact that support delivery is not only the foundation of all other aspects of the IT organization, but it is also the dominant expense.

The key support delivery management challenge is to provide the right level of support cost effectively. This balance is subtle but important. Although a corporation might enjoy IT support levels so high that any time a PC failed, an IT representative was there in person instantaneously, the cost of providing such support far outweighs the benefit. Therefore, the CIO must find ways to provide the maximum amount of support for minimal cost. Benchmarking is an effective technique to determine where an IT organization falls on its support investments as support costs are fairly easy to compare across companies. Formal and informal customer surveys are an effective way to determine whether the right level of support has been achieved in the eyes of the IT organization's customers.

In my experience, when support delivery is spread across multiple teams in an organization, it dilutes the effectiveness of those teams. Support activity is urgent and requires immediate attention, while most other IT activities require planning and coordination. Centralizing support activity enables an IT organization to separate out proactive from reactive activities, allowing it to specialize in both. In addition, most support delivery activity is commoditized, which has enabled outsourcing as one of the most common ways of achieving balance between capability and investment. The right outsourcing partner brings economy of scale, geo-economic process, or some other efficiency that cannot be achieved within the IT organization. Centralizing also facilitates outsourcing by concentrating all functions likely to be outsourced under one structure.

Project Delivery

Once a company has its support issues under control, the next function the IT operation is engaged in is project delivery. Although IT organizations typically have a broad-ranging definition of what constitutes a project, for the purposes of this framework, a project is defined as any structured IT deliverable that is not part of support delivery. (Note: I exclude from this definition management deliverables such as metrics or quarterly executive reviews.) Projects are the basis of how value is delivered from an IT organization. For example, if a company is looking to streamline its sales operations, it will employ a customer relationship management and/or enterprise resource planning solution to accomplish this. However, the decision is not simply a purchase decision, much as the company may wish this were the case. Implementing any enterprise software or even technologies based on software as a service requires an implementation project complete with a scope, timeline, and a set of resources (including financial resources). System implementation, merger activity, cost savings initiatives, and infrastructure upgrades are all examples of projects an IT organization might take on. The entire set of projects an IT organization is engaged in defines its project portfolio, while the set of projects the company plans to implement in the future represents the IT organization's road map. The sum of all resources for its portfolio represents the IT investment decision for the company.

With project delivery, the operational challenge for the CIO is to get the greatest bang for the buck in the most predictable fashion. Whether the investment is spread across one project or 100, a company will want the most output possible from its IT organization relative to how much it invests in IT. As one of my staff members used to say, "It needs to cure cancer, taste like chocolate, and cost less than a buck."

In addition to efficiency, to build trust with the business, it is also important that IT organizations be predictable in their project delivery. An IT organization's credibility rests on doing what it said it would do. When an IT project delays or goes over budget, it not only takes resources away from the rest of the company, it also pollutes the decision-making process as executives will discount the forecasts of an IT manager who has been unreliable in the past. I have seen many CIOs fail not because they chose the wrong investments, or failed to deliver them, but because they consistently overcommitted and underdelivered.

The most important challenge with project delivery is determining what is in the portfolio itself. The portfolio of the strategically aligned IT organization directly links to the company's strategic plan. Accomplishing this requires an effective demand management process. Over the years, I have experienced many different approaches to demand management. Some IT organizations employ IT steering committees, others make the decisions at the executive staff, and some leave the decision up to the CEO. Each approach has its own relative strengths and weaknesses that are highly dependent on the company's culture and overall decision-making process. The CIO simply must ensure that sufficient input from the business on what IT should work on is gathered and that a process exists for determining what the IT organization will work on. Whatever the decision approach is, I have found that the most successful demand management process requires that the business bring its own money to the table for new IT investments. Business functions are well positioned to determine the trade-offs of an IT investment when they are financially committed to them. When a business function provides input on a portfolio that it does not fund, trade-offs are not internalized, and it leads to overallocation of IT resources.

Key to addressing all of these challenges is to have the right management team and processes in place. A project management office (PMO) is a key function in strategically aligned IT organizations for governing the project delivery process. A well-functioning PMO will identify projects that are at risk of missing commitments so the IT management team can address the right issues. A PMO can also lead the portfolio planning process to help identify project dependencies and resource conflicts that must be addressed before an IT governing body can decide on the portfolio.

Another key issue for project delivery is where IT resources are sourced from. IT projects are technical, and the technologies evolve very quickly. Therefore, a sourcing strategy is important to ensuring that an IT department has the right skills available to it when it needs them so as to minimize resource conflicts and maximize utilization. The strategically aligned CIO will specifically define which skill sets to develop and retain on staff and which skill sets to outsource or hire on a staff augmentation basis. The business itself is also a great source of talent for IT for both process analyst and management roles. Demand management in particular is a role where I have been very successful in bringing business resources into the IT organization to manage the process, as this puts resources with the right business context and relationships in control of the process.

Project delivery and support delivery are functions that nearly every IT organization has. The next two functions are less common and differentiate the strategically aligned IT organizations from the rest of the pack.

Value Attainment

Companies invest in IT to achieve a business result. Although many organizations implicitly include this activity as part of project implementation, I call it out separately here because it is a different activity. In fact, many IT organizations do not even attempt to ascertain whether the desired business result has been achieved. In these organizations, determining whether or not a system initiative achieves the expected results is either relegated to the business, or it is not done at all. Failing to assert the value of past IT investments almost certainly dooms a company to fail to achieve these results. Just as purchasing a system is insufficient to implementing it, completing a project does not guarantee that the business value expected is achieved. Only if a company monitors the value from its IT investments will it know if that value has been attained. More important, monitoring will help a firm determine what adjustments are necessary to achieve the expected value from an investment.

Failing to monitor value attainment also sets the stage for companies to improperly set the investment level for IT. If the perception is that IT investments have not yielded results, the company will underinvest in IT in the future. If the perception is that IT investments have achieved results when in fact they have not, the firm will continue wasteful spending. Neither is desirable for a CIO.

One of the best examples in my career of why value attainment is so important was an international travel and expense solution I implemented at a major Fortune 500 company. The desired business result of this solution was the reduction in overhead from processing paper expense reports. The solution was implemented exactly to the business requirements on time and on budget. At the end of the project, the project team and the business were ready to pat themselves on the back and move on. However, I required that the team assess whether the value proposition for the project had been achieved. They were shocked to learn that not only had no operational savings from the project been realized, but the additional overhead from using the new system had actually created additional cost! While the finance organization was spending less time processing paperwork, there had been no staffing reductions as a result of the system. Moreover, the employees using the system spent twice as much time filling out the online forms as they did the paper forms. What had seemed like success was in fact a total failure, which had resulted from an overemphasis on the requirements to the exclusion of the business results for which the project had been funded. However, by assessing whether the business results had been attained before ending the project, we were able to make adjustments to the system to reduce the overhead on employees and provide better reporting to the finance organization that enabled it to achieve its staffing targets. In short, by monitoring value attainment, we ensured that the value from the project was attained.

A successful process for value attainment is a subject worthy of its own book. However, in its most basic form, it requires three things:

1. An intimate understanding of the business
2. Proper oversight of projects
3. A commitment by both IT and the business to manage to results, not just requirements

As such, it is a crucial element in aligning the IT organization with the business. The IT organization that leads the value attainment process will find itself asking the question: "What can be accomplished with an additional 10 percent?" rather than "How can you cut an additional 10 percent?"

Strategic Alignment

IT organizations that have successfully led value attainment within their firms will almost automatically find themselves strategically aligned. Nevertheless, what got you here is not what keeps you here. With value attainment, the objective is achieving a specific desired result with a specific investment. Strategic alignment involves defining what those results and investments should be. In other words, everything discussed to this point will get you a seat at the table. However, once at that table, your responsibility is to define business strategy from the perspective of IT.

There are many exceptional examples of the accomplishments of CIOs and IT managers operating at the strategic alignment level. In each, the managers define the desired result and necessary investment rather than waiting for the business to define it for them. An example from my experience was a strategic change to the services organization of a major supplier to the semiconductor industry. I had been tasked with developing an upgrade strategy for the organization's case management system. The service organization had been running on the same version of Clarify for over seven years, and the business knew it was time to upgrade the system. I was tasked with developing a plan for accomplishing this.

I chose to approach this problem purely from a business perspective. I began by asking several questions: Why did the business want the system upgraded? What result were they trying to achieve? Why couldn't they be achieved with the existing system? What were the limitations of the existing system? How were these limitations tied to operational issues in the service organization? How might an investment in systems enable the long-term growth strategy of the services business? Working with the staff of the general manager (GM) of service, I developed answers to each of these questions in both business and technical terms. I developed a business case not only for a systems upgrade but for a complete overhaul of the organization's business processes worldwide that would lead to improved efficiency, higher customer satisfaction, and ultimately greater profitability. I aligned the proposal with the strategic plan the rest of the GM's staff had developed, and together the GM of service and I pitched the initiative to the chief financial officer. The resulting initiative, once implemented, transformed the capability of the service organization, helping it to exceed $500 million in sales, at record levels of profit. What started as a maintenance investment became a transformative initiative for one of the largest business units in the company. Operating at the strategic alignment level, I defined what needed to be done not just for IT but for the business as well.

 ## BUILDING THE STRATEGICALLY ALIGNED ORGANIZATION

This framework can be applied to any IT organization in any company in any business. The key to success is applying it properly. To do so, I have found the following approaches to be quite useful:

- **Understand the business firsthand.** It is very difficult to align to something you do not understand. When I joined a company in the semiconductor industry, I found myself in a mature company largely run by insiders, where few outsiders have succeeded in learning the nuances of the business. To overcome this, I chose to embed myself in the business. I participated in training sessions for business functions I supported. I traveled with other business leaders to build relationships. I built a day-in-the-life presentation for my organization to teach others in IT how the business worked. All of these activities were investments necessary to understand how IT worked in the business and, more important, where specifically it did not work.
- **Hire from the business.** The implementation of IT continues to simplify as more of the technology stack is commoditized. Implementing Salesforce.com, for example, does not require programming experience, system administration, or many of the skills associated with IT. At the same time, the use of IT by the business continues to increase in both importance and complexity. I have found recently that it is easier to teach a nontechnical business resource how to use, manage, and implement IT than it is to teach an IT resource how the business operates.

Hiring from the business brings other benefits as well. Managing business expectations requires effective relationship management skills, and resources from the business already have many of these relationships. This approach also enables you to create a rotation scheme with the business that elevates IT's visibility within the company and provides the CIO with access to some of its up-and-coming talent.

■ **Develop relationships with key stakeholders.** As stated earlier, IT supports nearly all functions within the company. Therefore, regardless of whom the CIO reports to, there will be key stakeholders outside of his management chain. By developing close relationships with these stakeholders, the CIO can gain important allies, which are particularly important when making trade-off decisions on the IT portfolio.

■ **Have measures for everything.** The framework works as well as it is managed and you manage what you measure. Successfully implementing formal processes for each of these described functions necessitates having key performance measures for each. Some examples that I have used in the past are included in Table 8.1.

TABLE 8.1 Key Performance Measures

Function	Key Performance Indicator	Description
Support delivery	Service-level attainment	How effective is IT in delivering to its defined service commitments?
	Customer satisfaction	How satisfied are customers with the level of service from IT? Note: This is a subjective measure.
	Cost per supported user	How cost efficient is IT support delivery? This is a benchmarkable metric and should be evaluated as a trend.
Project delivery	Value delivered	Aggregate sum of business value enabled through the completion of IT programs over a period.
	Schedule performance	Is IT delivering its programs to its commitments?
	Budget performance	Are IT programs aligning to their estimated financial costs?
	Stakeholder satisfaction	Are initiative stakeholders satisfied with what was produced by IT?
	Delivery efficiency	How efficient is the IT delivery engine? Again, the trend here is as important as the absolute value.
Value attainment	Value attained	Measure of business value that has been achieved from past initiatives. Typical maximum horizon for measurement is two years postcompletion or less.
	Agility	How quickly can IT deliver solutions from initial business demand?

CONCLUSION

The role of IT and that of the CIO is changing rapidly. The days of the CIO as a "propeller head" are gone. Today both the CIO and the IT manager need to be effective business leaders who know how to apply technology. Understanding the framework of the strategically aligned organization and applying its concepts will help you to realize your full potential as a leader within your business.

Take control over your organization's support delivery and ensure that you are providing the right level of support cost effectively. Utilize organization, process, automation, and outsourcing to adjust your investment in support to free up resources and dollars that can applied on more strategic activities.

Develop effective project delivery capabilities to ensure that you focus on the right initiatives for your company and do what you said you would do. Leverage a PMO to develop project oversight and portfolio management processes for your organization to help you achieve the most output from your company's investment in IT.

Develop a capability in value attainment to ensure that the business results desired from your investments in IT are achieved. Leverage your value attainment process to help your firm make the right level of investment in IT so as to avoid lost opportunity and wasted spend.

Finally, once you have achieved your seat at the table as a strategic business leader, earn the right to stay there by leading business initiatives that leverage the opportunities of new information technologies to create sustained value for your firm.

I will leave you with one parting thought from an anonymous source: "It's not where you're from; it's where you're going. It's not what you drive; it's what drives you. It's not what's on you; it's what's in you. It's not what you think; it's what you know."

CHAPTER NINE

Developing an IT Strategy

Mark Egan

F RED "FIREFIGHTER" FORSYTH HAS been leading the IT organization for his online commerce company for the past five years. Fred's company provides e-commerce sites for organizations that cannot afford to build their own sites and depends heavily on IT to support its customers. His team works very long hours and has gotten into a pattern of saving the day when users experience issues with the company's systems.

Fred does not have time to develop a long-term IT strategy, and since the company does not have a well-articulated business strategy, he has never spent much time in this area. His boss has raised systems reliability issues and customer complaints several times, and Fred has countered that more money is needed for IT and these problems will go away. Fred does consider his team very good at responding to issues and earned his nickname, "Firefighter," based on the countless times his staff members have had to respond to emergencies. He rewards his team for their rapid responses to these issues and feels his company has developed a greater appreciation for his team's abilities after the countless times they have responded to systems outages.

Fred rolled into the office on Friday around 10 AM after spending most of the night dealing with a recurring network issue that prevented customers from accessing their systems. His boss called him into his office. Fred expected a hero's welcome for resolving the network issue and wondered if he was finally going to get that senior vice president promotion to add to his CIO title. He was surprised when he was introduced to the new

IT leader who had just been hired and would be focused on developing a long-term IT strategy for the company.

This chapter shows how to develop a strategy for your IT organization and avoid getting overwhelmed with day-to-day issues. Many CIOs get caught up in tactical issues and never take the time to establish a future strategy for the organization. The process is not new or difficult, but many CIOs fail to devote the time to this area and end up like Fred.

 ## OVERVIEW

Developing an IT strategy is critical for IT leaders. Unless your organization has developed an understanding of your future goals and objectives, you will not be successful in leading it forward. In the same manner that you must first decide where you want to live and build your dream house before engaging the architect and building contractors, you need to develop a future strategy in order to successfully build your IT organization.

This chapter is written for someone who has never developed an IT strategy in the past or needs to revise an existing strategy to align with the company's future direction. We first review the methodology you can use to develop your strategy and then go through the actual steps necessary to complete the strategy. It is important to note that this is a collaborative process between the IT organization and its business partners. You must actively engage them during the process and solicit their input during the development of the strategy. The IT strategy should be considered a component of an effective business strategy. Finally, we recommend that your strategy is a living document that is updated on a regular basis to support the evolving nature of your business. If you decide to enter a new market, offer new products or services, or change your business model, the IT strategy must be revised to support the business.

 ## IT STRATEGY METHODOLOGY

The methodology for creating your IT strategy consists of three steps, and development of your improvement road map encompasses three critical elements, as shown in Figure 9.1.

The first step is to understand the current state of the IT organization. Key questions for determining current state include:

- Has the organization been successful in meeting the needs of the business?
- Are the relations between the IT organization and its business partners collaborative?
- Does the business feel that investments in the IT organization are providing the desired benefits?

It is important to take an objective view of how the organization is operating today and not assume that things are going great.

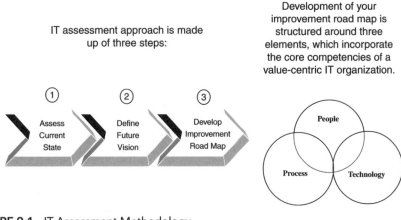

IT assessment approach is made up of three steps:

Development of your improvement road map is structured around three elements, which incorporate the core competencies of a value-centric IT organization.

① Assess Current State   ② Define Future Vision   ③ Develop Improvement Road Map

People

Process   Technology

FIGURE 9.1 IT Assessment Methodology

Defining the future vision for the IT organization is the next step. During this step, it is important to understand the future business strategy and how the IT organization can enable the business to achieve its goals. Interviews with key business partners, such as product development and sales, are required to understand their future direction and areas that technology can assist. You should also conduct external research on how leading companies in your industry are providing technology solutions to support their business.

The final step is developing a road map to get you from where you are today to your future vision. This includes taking into account how much your company is willing to invest in the IT organization, along with realistic estimates for the time required to achieve your future state. We recommend that you develop a six-quarter (18-month) IT road map. Six quarters are long enough to make significant changes within the IT organization and in your ability to deliver meaningful benefits to the business. Note that your six-quarter road map will not be stagnant and should be updated on a quarterly basis.

The critical elements of your strategy include *people, process,* and *technology.* By far the most important is people:

- *People* means having the right team aligned with your business partners. This is essential for your success and we recommend that you devote considerable attention to this area. It is very often the case that you do not have an effective team and need to make some organizational changes. You need to take a hard look at the organization and decide if the team needs any upgrades to achieve your future vision. These upgrades may include hiring more senior-level staff, addressing skill-set gaps, or conducting additional training.
- *Process* can be thought of as glue that holds together the people and technology elements of your strategy. Frameworks such as the Information Technology Infrastructure Library (ITIL) and Control Objectives for Information and Related Technology (COBiT) exist with best practices for managing an IT organization. You need to evaluate the process maturity of your organization and determine whether

you need to make improvements in this area. Staff members often resist processes and view them as bureaucracy; however, as you grow your organization, you can no longer operate effectively without basic processes like incident, problem, and change controls in place.

■ *Technology* is the remaining element of your strategy. Often CIOs spend an inordinate amount of their time in this area and do not give adequate attention to people and process. Technology is certainly important, considering the fact that the IT organization is expected to provide automation capabilities for the company; however too many CIOs get enamored with technology and focus primarily on this area to the detriment of the others. Key elements of your strategy include solutions that are flexible, cost effective, and can scale to meet future demands of the business.

We now walk through this methodology in greater detail and describe how it can be used to develop your IT strategy.

Step 1: Assess the Current State of Your IT Organization

When assessing the current state of your IT organization, we encourage you to take a very objective view and expect to identify many areas of improvement. If you are an incumbent CIO, it is very easy to think that things are going well in your organization based on how hard you and the staff are working. You may well need to bring in a senior consultant to assist in the assessment. Newly hired CIOs have an easier time of taking an outsider's view of how well things are operating and identifying areas of improvement. Regardless of the situation, most IT organizations have areas that can be improved, and this is the time for a careful review.

Examples of key questions that should be answered during this assessment include:

■ Are current business needs being met?
■ Is the expected return on investments in technology being achieved?
■ Is the project portfolio aligned with business objectives?
■ Where does the technology directly touch your customers?
■ Does the current organizational structure create barriers or inefficiencies?
■ Are the skill mix and staffing levels in place sufficient?
■ Are third-party resources being applied effectively?
■ Are outsourcing opportunities identified and leveraged?
■ Is your spending in line with that of your peers? What are your cost drivers?
■ Is there an effective process for approving, managing, and overseeing projects?
■ What is the vendor/partner selection and management process?
■ How do you assess business risk and put risk mitigation programs in place?
■ Are standard development processes defined and adhered to?
■ What gaps exist in the architecture?
■ How are new technologies evaluated and deployed?
■ Will systems scale with corporate growth plans?
■ How are new technologies evaluated and deployed?

We encourage you to spend a lot of time with your business partners to understand their future strategies and discuss how technology can assist in achieving their goals. We recommend that you interview your key business partners and ask these open-ended questions:

- Tell me about your business and plans over the next one to two years.
- Do you have any strategy documents that I can review?
- How well is the IT organization serving your business today?
- Do you have any suggestions on how we can improve our services?

The goal is to spend the majority of time in these meetings listening and learning more about your partners' current challenges and potential areas that technology can assist. A word of caution: If you ask for feedback, be prepared to hear about things that are not working well within IT today, and use this information to identify areas of improvement. Communication is very important during this process. We recommend that you summarize the results of your discussions in an e-mail to your business partners to validate what you heard and explain what you intend to do to improve things. The end result of this phase is to summarize your current state. Table 9.1 provides an example that you can use.

Red, yellow, and green ratings can be used to highlight areas of improvement in simple terms that your business partners can understand. Do not use a lot of technical

TABLE 9.1 IT Assessment Summary Example

IT Element	Current State	Rating	Corrective Actions
People	Very complex IT organizational model	Red	Simplify IT organization model and align to business partners.
	Inexperienced staff responsible for applications functions		Hire experienced IT leader who can build a management team.
	Business partners unsure whom to contact for IT services		Clarify IT roles and business partner engagement process.
Process	No formal process to review and prioritize IT requests	Yellow	Establish executive-level governance board.
	Limited management metrics on effectiveness of IT group		Develop small number of IT performance metrics.
	Basic IT processes, such as change control, not in place		Adopt process framework, such as ITIL, as overall methodology.
Technology	Systems instability and staff focused on day-to-day activities	Yellow	Develop overall IT architecture to guide future investments.
	Limited business intelligence capabilities exist today		Invest in business intelligence for competitive advantage.
	Recent security issues and no formal risk management program in place		Hire experienced security leader and develop security program.

jargon, as this will confuse everyone and limit the effectiveness of this assessment. Based on the results of your current-state assessment, we are ready to proceed to the next step of defining your future state.

Step 2: Define Your Future Vision

When defining your future vision, you need to strike a balance between a bold, forward-looking strategy for your organization and something that you can reasonably deliver in the next two to three years. The overall vision for your organization should not really change over time, and your strategies should be focused on major deliverables that you plan to accomplish over the next couple of years. This is the time to reach out externally to understand industry best practices for similar companies that you can implement for your business. Too often CIOs are internally focused. Now is the time to reach out to your peers, industry analysts, consultants, and vendors to understand the possibilities that exist for your company.

Major components of your future vision should include:

- IT vision statement
- Key business strategies that the IT organization will assist the company in achieving
- Major IT strategies that you plan to employ over the next couple of years to assist business partners in achieving their business strategies

An example of an IT vision statement might be: "Company X business partners are delighted with the services provided by the IT organization." This vision will not change over time, and staff members within the organization will strive to provide excellent services to their business partners.

It is important to understand your company's future business strategies in order to identify areas in which the IT organization can provide the most value. If these strategies are published, you can validate your understanding during interviews with members of the management team. Otherwise, you will need to draft your under-standing based on these conversations. Key business strategies for your organization might include:

- Grow the business 30 percent over the coming year by introducing two new product lines.
- Improve customer satisfaction and achieve highest industry rating as measured by independent survey.
- Reduce costs by 25 percent through selective outsourcing and supply chain management.

From an IT perspective, it is important to have IT align with these business strategies and demonstrate how the organization is adding value and contributing to the business goals. Note that it is possible that the company may not have well-articulated goals; this may make it harder to demonstrate how the IT organization is enabling the business. In either case, your IT strategies should contribute to one or more of these areas: increase revenue, improve customer satisfaction, reduce costs, and meet compliance requirements.

Major IT strategies fall into two categories: internal IT and business enabling. Internal IT strategies might include IT organizational structure, technology refresh, governance, or process improvements. Examples of business-enabling strategies would be specific initiatives that would assist the sales organization to grow the business, help the product development organization develop products quicker, or cost-savings initiatives through automation of tasks that are performed manually today.

Provide management with alternative proposals, usually based on level of investment and desired time frame, to achieve the future vision. IT is competing with many other investment priorities. You need to be realistic regarding the level of resources the company can devote to this area. Table 9.2 shows a high-level framework that you can provide to management to determine your investment strategy.

TABLE 9.2 IT Investment Alternatives Framework

Alternative	Major Programs	Time Frame	Estimated Incremental Costs	Business Benefits
Aggressive implementation	Hire third-party integrator to accelerate IT strategy implementation. Reorganize IT under experienced leader. Establish IT governance board to oversee program.	12 months	$10–20 M	Improve IT performance in shortest time frame possible. Will require considerable shift in business priorities and IT funding.
Accelerated implementation	Hire third party to assist in IT program implementation. Continue with existing IT leadership and reevaluate management team. Provide business executives regular updates on IT program.	18–24 months	$5–10 M	Improve IT performance with minor shift in business priorities and funding.
Incremental improvements	Leverage third parties in selected areas. Maintain status quo with existing IT leader and management. Formalize program and provide regular updates on progress at lower levels in organization.	24–36 months	$1–2 M	Least costly alternative. No shift in existing business priorities or funding.

When generating alternatives, start with your existing organization and budget, and provide management with an estimate of how long it will take to achieve your future vision. Your second and third alternatives can add additional resources and/or shorten the expected time frame. This is an iterative process and a great opportunity to spend more time with your business partners to ensure that you understand their business requirements and how the IT organization can enable the organization to be successful. Once you have locked down the investment envelope and desired time frame to achieve your future vision, you are in a position to develop a more detailed implementation road map.

Step 3: Develop Improvement Road Map

The improvement road map is how you take your future vision for the IT organization and convert it into reality. Based on your investment envelope, you need to flesh out the individual elements of your strategy. These strategies fall into the three elements that we discussed previously: people, process, and technology. Each of these elements will have three to five individual strategies that will comprise your overall IT strategy. Next we review each of these elements in more detail.

People

As discussed previously, people are the most difficult area and the one that we recommend you devote considerable time and attention to. Having a great IT team that is well organized and aligned with the business is essential for success. For this reason, consider structuring your organization like the business. For example, if you are functionally organized with global leaders of sales, product development, and so on, we recommend that your IT organization have teams that support these functions. However, if you have a line-of-business structure with general managers, we recommend that you have IT groups aligned with these businesses. Your goal is to make it very easy for your business partners to do business with the IT organization, including knowing whom to contact for assistance.

IT governance is another critical area that needs to be established in order for an IT organization to be successful. Demands for IT requests always exceed the company's ability to fund this area, and a fair and consistent process needs to be established. It is critical to establish an IT governance board, IT steering committee, or other mechanism for business leaders to evaluate major IT initiatives and determine which ones are the most important for the company. These groups should be cross-functional and include senior-level staff members who can make investment decisions for the company. Critical objectives for these groups include oversight of the major IT programs and approval of future IT investments, and meetings should be held on a monthly or quarterly basis. Of equal importance is the governance that is put in place beneath this executive level to execute to the direction provided by the business leaders. Typically, this working-level group is supported by the establishment of a program management office and accompanying methodologies and processes.

Staff development and training is another area that should be included in your overall strategy. Because the IT field changes rapidly, programs need to be put in place to ensure that your staff members are trained on the latest developments. If this area is overlooked, IT organizations either have to use consultants or continuously hire new staff with current skills. Included in this area is the need for individual development plans for staff members and documented succession planning for key executive and management roles. Finally, one word of caution: Beware of a strategy that overemphasizes staffing your key positions with internal resources only. Although such a strategy may have worked well for prior IT generations, today's IT world is moving far too quickly to be able to rely only on resources who have been brought up through company ranks. An appropriate mix is suggested to ensure that new thinking is introduced into your organization when and where needed.

IT sourcing is another area that you need to include in your overall strategy. No organization can be good at everything, and you need to analyze what you view as your core competencies, areas in which you will spend the time to hire and develop skilled staff. Examples of skills that we recommend you always keep in house would be architecture, business analysis, vendor management, and program management. Context skills are those that you should consider for outsourcing to third parties. Applications maintenance, quality assurance, and help desk functions are examples of functions that you may want to outsource. Keep in mind that each company will have unique requirements. You need to go through core/context analysis to determine your company's sourcing strategy.

These are a few examples of people strategies that you should consider for your IT strategy. Each organization is different and will have unique areas that need to be developed. As mentioned, the people area is the hardest one to perfect. Hire the best staff possible, and keep them closely aligned with your business partners. Do not compromise in this area or be pressured to accept less effective staff since your success relies heavily on having the right team in place.

Process

Process is the glue that binds the people with the technology to ensure that the overall IT organization works effectively. Many IT organizations do not spend enough time in this area, seeing it as slowing things down or downright boring. Process should be viewed like brakes on a car, which are provided to allow the car to go faster, not slower. When approaching overall IT processes, consider following a framework such as ITIL. This framework has a catalog of standard processes, such as change management and problem management, that should be adopted by your organization. The infrastructure organization, in particular, needs to pay close attention to processes, and following this framework can speed up the adoption cycle. If your team or clients are not ready for ITIL terminology, many ITIL concepts can be adopted in advance of a full-blown ITIL implementation. Start by setting up ITIL training for IT leadership and some of your most forward-thinking business partners.

Focus on a couple of processes at a time since it takes a while for the organization to adopt them in their day-to-day operations. Typically, an internal IT program should be established that prioritizes the processes needed and launches focused projects in a staggered fashion to ensure optimal adoption and minimize disruption.

IT investments are often one of the largest capital expenses in the company, along with facilities, and processes need to be put in place to ensure that these investments are carefully evaluated. The IT leader should partner closely with the finance organization to ensure that business cases are developed for proposed IT projects and return on investment (ROI) analysis has been performed. IT projects are competing for scarce resources with other investments within the company, such as the decision to open a new office. The business has many competing priorities and IT projects should follow the same ROI analysis as IT investments. Too often departments that are very vocal about their needs, without adequate business justification, get all the attention (projects); checks and balances need to be in place for these investments.

Development of critical metrics to measure the overall effectiveness of the IT organization is essential to demonstrate that the organization is improving over time. Service organizations, such as IT, can be viewed as merely cost centers. Metrics can be used to identify areas of investment along with key drivers for these expenses. For example, the help desk may be spending an inordinate amount of time supporting a given department with e-mail issues and may determine that some training is required. The majority of applications development staff members may be spending time on an end-of-life finance application while ignoring requests for a sales application that can generate additional revenue. At the very least, you should establish a typical best practices operations review process. Each of your direct reports should identify the top three performance metrics that are critical to their success and present these metrics over time with clear goals identified for each one. These metrics should be compiled into a single report and reviewed monthly. Each missed goal should result in a remediation plan.

Communication is another area to which many IT organizations do not devote the necessary time and resources. Technical staff members are not always the best communicators and can easily confuse business partners with technical jargon. This can lead to bad relations between the organizations, and a decline in the level of cooperation. Hiring a communications staff within IT or soliciting help from the corporate communications organization can assist in this area. Implementing new technology will require changes to how the business is operating, and human nature does not always embrace change. Clear, crisp communications inside and outside of the IT organization can help in this area and facilitate change within the organization. A top-notch communications manager will implement a variety of mechanisms, such as business partner and department-wide meetings and newsletters, to ensure that expectations are clear and well managed with your business partner and internal IT staff.

These are a few examples of processes that you should consider for your organization. Implementation of a continuous improvement program can help to drive the overall process maturity within the organization. Your continuous improvement program should identify those processes that are critical to running an effective IT organization for your company and track progress toward achieving your ultimate goals. Keep in mind that these programs will require time, and management focus and discipline are necessary for them to be successful.

Technology

Technology is the final element of your strategy and an area that some IT organizations overemphasize. Do not underestimate the ability of technology to assist in the transformation of the business; however, first you must ensure that you have the right people and processes in place. One of the first areas to address is an overall technical architecture for the company. Just as an architect develops blueprints of a house for a builder, an IT architecture serves as the broad basis for deployment of technology. Your architecture should encompass these areas: business architecture, data architecture, applications architecture, and technical/infrastructure architecture.

Business architecture covers business goals, business functions or capabilities, and business processes and roles. This architecture is direction-setting for the business and should drive all other architecture development. Business functions and business processes are often mapped to the applications and data they need in order to operate. Keep in mind that this information may not exist for your organization, and you may need to draft your understanding of the company's business architecture based on interviews with business leaders. From a pragmatic perspective, it may be easier to focus on a few key areas of the business, such as order to cash, and identify how process simplification and automation can assist the business achieve future goals.

Data architecture is very important. Be prepared for multiple sources of key information, such as customers, products, and employees, and poor data quality that must be addressed before new systems can be implemented. Identifying business owners for data is important to ensure that you can clean up data and keep it clean on an ongoing basis. These data owners are often referred to as data stewards, and they play a key role in systems projects. If they do not already exist, partner with the appropriate business leaders to develop key integrated data sources, such as customer and vendor master files.

Applications architecture includes all the major business applications that are used to run your business. These systems are often separated into back-office enterprise resource planning and front-office portals and customer relationship management (CRM) systems. Portals and CRM systems support the revenue-generating activities of the company. This is an area to which you should try to devote more IT resources. Investments in these systems can provide the highest ROI, and IT organizations should attempt to place a great focus on this area.

Technical/infrastructure can be viewed as the "plumbing" that everything runs on and includes the hardware, network, and voice technology. These systems need to be scaled to support future business growth and resilient to ensure they are available

24 hours a day. Recent trends are headed toward renting infrastructure resources via cloud technology and paying for resources only when required. Infrastructure investments can be costly. IT organizations are encouraged to develop a balanced strategy of investing in critical infrastructure that cannot be easily purchased as a service and relying on third parties for the remainder.

The technology section of your IT strategy will be very company specific. Your focus should be on identifying areas in which technology can have the highest impact on the business and quickly delivering solutions. Technology evolves very quickly. IT organizations need to constantly evaluate new offerings to determine if they can be of use. Further, keep an eye on end-of-life systems and technology, and ensure that you develop upgrade plans that will allow you to provide continuous support of these systems.

Improvement Road Map Summary

Your IT road map should consist of a series of individual strategies that you intend to deliver over time. Strategies that you might include for your company are:

- **People:** IT organization, IT governance, sourcing, staff development and training
- **Process:** ITIL implementation, metrics and reporting, investment analysis, and communications
- **Technology:** Business, data, applications, and infrastructure architecture; company-specific technology initiatives such as sales force automation; technology refresh initiatives

The template in Figure 9.2 can be used to summarize each of these individual strategies in a consistent and easy-to-read format.

Each of your strategies will have a long-term objective, along with specific milestones that you plan to accomplish in the area. For example, your IT organization strategy may include an overall objective to be customer focused and include several milestones, such as a reorganization and training required to meet that objective. It is important to strike a balance between identifying all the key strategies for your organization and focusing on a limited number of areas that you can expect to improve over the next one to two years.

The summary of your strategy is your overall IT road map and includes the expected time frame to deliver your strategy. Recommendations in this area include organizing your road map by key business partners, such as sales and marketing, and using a six-quarter time frame. Six quarters provides adequate time to deliver programs that may take more than one year to complete and provides visibility into the organization's longer-term strategy. Figure 9.3 provides an IT road map example.

Note the legend that identifies projects that are approved/proposed, along with project that have been delayed from their original delivery date. Most IT organizations should be able to summarize their strategy in two pages. This road map can be an

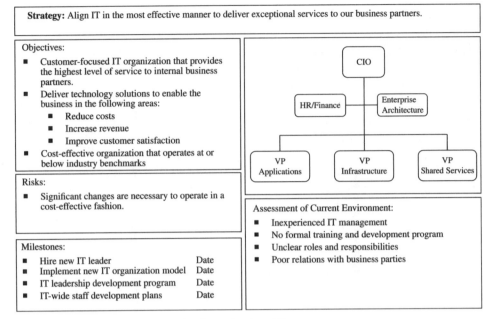

Strategy: Align IT in the most effective manner to deliver exceptional services to our business partners.

Objectives:
- Customer-focused IT organization that provides the highest level of service to internal business partners.
- Deliver technology solutions to enable the business in the following areas:
  - Reduce costs
  - Increase revenue
  - Improve customer satisfaction
- Cost-effective organization that operates at or below industry benchmarks

Risks:
- Significant changes are necessary to operate in a cost-effective fashion.

Milestones:
- Hire new IT leader   Date
- Implement new IT organization model   Date
- IT leadership development program   Date
- IT-wide staff development plans   Date

Assessment of Current Environment:
- Inexperienced IT management
- No formal training and development program
- Unclear roles and responsibilities
- Poor relations with business parties

FIGURE 9.2 IT Strategy Example: Organizational Structure

effective vehicle for management discussions on IT programs. The IT road map should be viewed as a living document and updated on a regular basis.

Final IT Strategy Document

The final IT strategy must be easily understood by management and must address critical business objectives. Guidelines for developing the document include:

- Highly graphical
- Management summary of one page
- Overall document is 25 pages or less
- Include bold recommendations on sweeping changes you plan to make in order to transform the organization over the next two to three years

Your IT strategy should establish aggressive but achievable plans that you are committing to deliver. The costs associated with your recommendations are going to be significant and normally will require board approval, so you must deliver on these commitments. You need to keep a high level of communications during this time frame and test your recommendations during the development process to improve management acceptance. Finally, you must ensure that the key objectives are understood by the entire IT team and that your management's objectives are tied to successful delivery. Whenever you have the opportunity to address large groups of staff members, reinforce the strategy and key priorities.

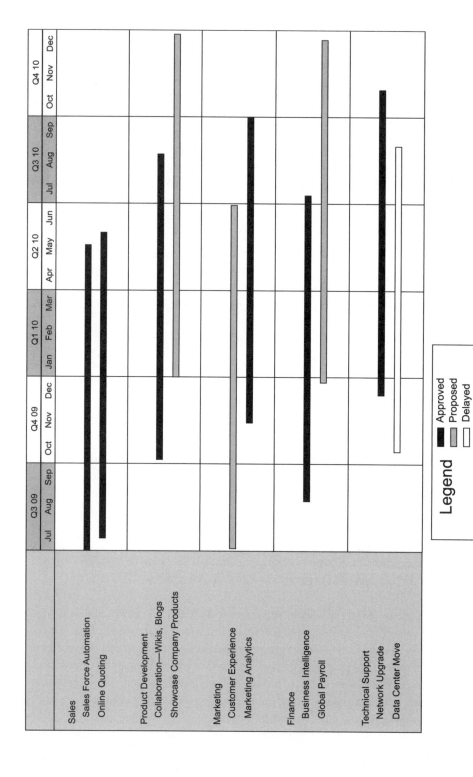

FIGURE 9.3 Six-Quarter Road Map Example

SUMMARY

Developing an IT strategy is the most effective way of communicating with your business partners about how you intend to support their business strategies. The day-to-day pressures of running an IT organization can easily divert team attention to tactical activities, and people can lose focus on delivering business value. This chapter provides a three-step process of assessing where the IT organization is today, defining your future vision, and developing an improvement road map. IT leaders need to allocate time each year for their teams to go through this process and ensure that the organization has a clear path going forward. Resist the urge to go into firefighting mode and solve today's problems. In partnership with key business leaders, today's CIO needs to be bold and establish a vision for his or her organization and lead teams going forward in order to be successful and add maximum value to the organization.

10

Competitive Applications of Technology

Michael Skaff

CHIEVE A COMPETITIVE ADVANTAGE. Understand your audience. Innovate or die. Everyone has heard this advice, but what does it actually mean? Everyone knows that innovation contributes to success, but what sort of innovation is the most important? There is a sense that consumers and audiences have changed and will continue to do so at an increasingly rapid rate. How do you simultaneously meet your customers' needs and stay ahead your competition, even as the fundamental nature of the marketplace shifts? How do we maintain our relevance in this new world? Today's innovation ever more rapidly becomes yesterday's news.

These questions strike at the heart of a growing problem in business. More than ever before, businesses require novel means of achieving a competitive advantage as margins become increasingly slim, product release cycles diminish, and what was previously highly specialized knowledge becomes ubiquitous in a few clicks from a search engine. As one of the primary catalysts in the acceleration of business evolution, technology remains one of the most effective means of achieving a competitive advantage. In this chapter, I discuss some of the ways that technology can be used to achieve a competitive advantage and some of the external factors that influence its success and examine the example of technology applied by the San Francisco Symphony to extend its competitive positioning in the marketplace.

Businesses of all types are evolving at an increasingly rapid rate, as are customer demands and purchasing habits, creating an unprecedented need for sources of strategic differentiation. The methods by which a business once might have distinguished itself from its competition are now considered standard business practice, or have been supplanted by new tools, process, and strategy that have left these old standards defunct, relegated to the status of commodity, shelved, or evolved out of the market entirely.

The increased significance of technology as a source of competitive advantage can be attributed to several factors, fundamentally the accelerating rate of change. Just to survive—let alone capture greater market share—companies have acknowledged the need to become more agile and adapt more quickly to changing market demands. What was historically a more localized set of interconnected economies based on physical products and services is quickly being supplanted by a growing global economy that is based on information which, as a result of technology's influence, moves at an increasingly rapid rate.

Subject to accelerating change and sometimes equally rapid obsolescence if they do not adapt, companies are using technology to reshape themselves by optimizing their presence in existing markets and prospect in new markets. In some cases, businesses that were once competitive in a specific vertical industry have been able to shatter barriers previously crossed only via mergers or acquisitions and reposition themselves to meet equally fast evolution of demand. Examples are plentiful and range from the traditional power companies that leverage technology to break into solar or wind generation, to the new generation of businesses that have grown from the wellspring that is the Internet. This type of expansion is achieved successfully only after careful planning and significant research of the target market; what amounts to relevant technological and competitive advantages in one industry may not be as meaningful a differentiator or even applicable in other industries. The utility company offering cloud-based services to its customers may be a key means of distinguishing itself from its competition, but in many parts of the software industry, offering cloud-based services has become the norm.

Other advances in business process have obviated many competitive advantages originally achieved through more traditional means, which is largely due to technology. Even the more traditional industries, such as manufacturing, have accepted founda-tional elements of technology such as e-mail and file sharing, which highlights the impact that accelerating flows of information now have on highly localized, physically oriented businesses. No longer is technology viewed by those who value their competi-tive position as merely a basic operational element or means to achieve efficiency. It is fully infused into the lifeblood of the business.

Consumer behavior has also shifted because technology has expanded to become fully integrated into a broadening scope and geographic breadth of consumer culture. Accelerating changes in consumer purchasing behavior reflects this new cultural norm and has had far-reaching effects on business. The concept of e-commerce, once an outlying case and only a few years ago considered simply a novelty concept rarely related to the core of most businesses, has become a powerful and growing influence on the global economy. Evidence of this shift is everywhere. Just recently, online advertis-ing surpassed print advertising for the first time. This historic shift marks not only a telltale reallocation of resources but one of the many visible examples of technology being used to reshape business and competition as we know it.

The process of achieving a competitive advantage is not without a few caveats. Despite the clear impact technology has had both on business and modern popular culture, the maximum benefit of technology as a tool for competition cannot be derived without a few key factors present that have little to do with technology and far more with what amounts to fundamental business knowledge.

To achieve a competitive advantage in any sphere, whether in sports or business, there must first and foremost be an understanding of the rules of the game or, in this case, an in-depth understanding of the nature of the business. Although often starting with the best of intentions, the halls of institutional history are strewn with savvy technologists who failed by not taking the time to ask the right questions first and fully understand the relevance and context of the endeavor. Information technology projects have one of the worst reputations for failure because, despite what may be a command of the technology, these projects often become disconnected from the business core they were designed to enhance. When they are not seamlessly aligned with the business need, adoption rates plummet and these projects become more casualties, written off without ever achieving their promised value.

One of the keys to success is industry-specific experience. Without understanding the key factors that define a business, such as the nature of the particular industry, the current state of the markets it operates in, and any other pertinent influences, even the best designed tool will fail. It is far better to lead the charge with business analysts to first illuminate and clarify the problem (or opportunity) than to lead with a technology solution that may not be the right fit. Every opportunity must be fully understood before it can be realized, and the greatest strength of technology is its ability to deliver the right knowledge to the right people at the most opportune moment. The difficulty lies in identifying the confluence of these factors and acting at the right moment, collaborating with the appropriate people, and applying the best technology for the need.

The core of the most effective, and therefore most competitively positioned, applications of technology can be found by identifying key points in the business that can be improved and determining where technology can be leveraged to achieve that improvement. This improvement can take many forms, from collaboration between the pursuit of artistic excellence and technology to utilizing technology to enhance product delivery. These applications of technology are particularly visible within the technology industry itself for several reasons. The business objectives and culture of technology companies are already so closely aligned with the potential of technology as a tool—plus the industry changes so rapidly—that these companies leverage any opportunity possible to achieve a competitive advantage and tend to lead other industries in its application. Technology companies also occasionally fail in their application of technology because they overapply it in instances where it does not belong. They also are prone to overinvesting, sometimes infamously.

The technology industry is somewhat unusual because the process of differentiating technologies sometimes becomes a product in its own right. Whether by design or by evolution, and instead of serving as enhancements or catalysts for maximizing the impact of other products or services, the tool sometimes becomes the business. These cases often produce exceptionally fine-tuned, effective technologies, because they emerge directly from the need. The greatest efficacy in competition is achieved by those technologies that are developed to meet a defined business need or to help a company anticipate an evolving demand. Business intelligence technologies are a clear example of this type of evolutionary product. Businesses have long known that a real dollar value can often be assigned to the timely, effective presentation and analysis of data, but a whole software market has emerged around this once-peripheral business function. These timely, demand-driven scenarios are what separate the most successful applications of technology from the norm of their vertical market. Rather than incremental, they are, at their most effective, revolutionary in some way, either reshaping the organization itself or helping it better understand and therefore serve its customers.

Another important factor to consider in determining the competitive value of any given technology is timing. Like most other aspects of competition, a competitive advantage remains relevant only as long as it distinguishes, extends, or otherwise enhances an organization's operations in a way that has a meaningful impact. Given the increasingly short shelf life of many technologies and the speed at which the technology industry innovates and then obviates these advances, execution and timing have a particularly profound impact on the overall effectiveness of a technology in generating a competitive advantage.

Consider the Web, for example. A few years back, it could be argued that maintaining a presence on the Web could be considered a competitive advantage for some companies, as it provided increased visibility and perhaps implied that the company was forward-looking and savvy as to invest in a web site. These days, having a presence on the Web is viewed by most companies as important and de rigueur as having business cards or a physical office—a web site frequently provides a potential customer with the first and potentially lasting impression of a company and is by no means considered unusual or different. This expectation therefore reduces the competitive advantage of simply having a basic presence on the Web. Interestingly, given the rapid evolution of Web-based technologies, it is still possible (at least currently) to leverage a web site as a competitive advantage, but the elements of that equation continue to change rapidly.

 ## AN EARLY PIONEER

Consider the example of the San Francisco Symphony. A globally recognized cultural institution with a rich artistic history, it is also a multimillion-dollar business. But can technology advance live classical music? Live classical music is, by definition, steeped in the tradition of individual artists, ensembles, and instruments that come together to play for a group of listeners who are completely unplugged and dedicated to the experience of hearing the music (although even this has begun to change). Does technology threaten the communion between artists and audience, or enhance it? For almost 100 years, the San Francisco Symphony has embraced the use of technology in order to amplify the connection of live classical music and make it part of more people's lives, although the nature of the use of technology has evolved considerably during that time.

Is technology a strategic differentiator in the arts? If you had attended the San Francisco Symphony's concert on January 31, 1919, when the orchestra was merely a teenager, you would have heard some groundbreaking early experiments between orchestra musicians and technology. Author Larry Rothe captured one of these early competitive applications of technology in a selection titled "Poltergeist at the Keyboard" from his forthcoming book, *Music for a City, Music for the World; A History of the San Francisco Symphony.*

Ray C. B. Brown wrote an article entitled "Player Piano's Art Is Eerie."[1] The article highlighted the fact that even in a traditional artistic environment, advanced technology has been used to expand the reach of the artist, enhance the "distribution" of the "product," and enable the symphony to perform a concert that would otherwise have been impossible without the physical presence of the artist.

The evolution of music making continues today, with artists like Mason Bates seamlessly blending classical theory and music making with modern technology tools to sample and remix instrumental music in real time. In more traditional business terms, this use of technology helps bring to market a whole new set of products. In fact, technology has become an increasingly frequent presence in music making, from tools used in the editing and production of music to creating entirely new instruments from technology (the Smule Magic Piano, e.g., an iPhone and iPad application). Even a discipline so steeped in tradition and history as music has found ways to creatively leverage technology to evolve and expand the borders of what is possible. In doing so, it appeals to broader audiences, redefines the best practices in production, and even develops entirely new genres of music. What could be more of a competitive advantage than the creation of an entirely new market segment?

Beyond music making, there are a variety of other ways that technology enhances the mission of the San Francisco Symphony. At its core, the Symphony is simultaneously an educational nonprofit, a performing arts organization, a multi-site retail operation, and a multimillion-dollar-per-year global business. Each of these components is enhanced by technology. Like any other business, the San Francisco Symphony relies on a portfolio of business systems investments to maintain normal operations, but there are myriad other ways that technology supports the mission of the Symphony and help it maintain a position of leadership in an increasingly competitive marketplace. The nature of competition in the arts world is in some ways similar to the private sector, but in other ways starkly different, most notably the competition for donor funds—a transaction that is similar to normal commerce but requires an arguably greater understanding of customer behavior and sentiment than does a traditional sale. Thus, business-focused technologies such as customer relationship management become critical to the prosperity and in some cases the very existence of the organization.

Even in this unusual vertical industry, the notion of competition still exists by necessity—at the heart of the business core, performing arts organizations compete, either implicitly or explicitly, across two marketplaces: primarily in the sale of tickets to concerts and shows, but also for the finite pool of donation dollars. The San Francisco Symphony also maintains both a physical and an online retail presence, like many performing arts organizations. The concept of competition in retail is familiar and highly developed, but in the more collaborative world of the arts, it takes on a different form. It is at once a portion of the core business but also serves an important supporting role in strengthening and extending the customer relationship. From optimizing the delivery of the music and enhancing the overall event experience to strengthening the connections with its patrons and broadening the educational footprint in the local and global communities, the San Francisco Symphony uses technology extensively to maintain its position of leadership in its marketplace.

 ## DIFFERENTIATION IN EDUCATION

In 2002, the San Francisco Symphony launched what has become one of the world's top web sites for children's music education, SFSKids.org. In its original conception, the goal of this site was to enhance children's appreciation of music by providing an educational resource that was engaging, fun, and easy to understand. It seeks to educate children (and adults) about the basics of notation and helps them visualize the use of rhythm as a fundamental element of music. Visitors explore pitch, harmony, and tempo and even have the chance to both compose and play music on the site. It familiarizes visitors with the different instruments of the orchestra, both visually and aurally, and acquaints the nascent music student with the layout of a standard symphony orchestra. Through a broad range of fun, fanciful illustrations and sounds, it seeks to make symphonic music more approachable and entertaining for those who are unfamiliar with its breadth and depth.

In these goals, the SFSKids site has been a resounding success. In the years that have followed the launch, millions of visitors have flocked to the site to explore and learn the wonders of music. Teachers from all over the world use the site to enhance their curricula, and the site continues to see traffic in the range of 1,500 to 2,000 visits per day. As one component of a portfolio of educational offerings, this site has had an enormous impact on raising the global profile of the San Francisco Symphony. Combining some of the best minds in education with an unusual delivery mechanism on the Web, the Symphony has advanced its "competitive position" in the educational community as well as its global stature in the symphonic world.

Timing counted here too. By executing this project early on in the evolution of the Web, the San Francisco Symphony extended its visibility, credibility, and even its operational capabilities by automating and extending the delivery of a best-of-breed educational practice on the site. Each of these achievements could be considered competitive advantages for the Symphony, as they elevated the awareness of the symphony's "product," positioned the Symphony as a more attractive candidate for donations, and increased interest in concert attendance and therefore ticket sales.

There are two important points to consider: Technology can clearly be seen as both the catalyst and the mechanism for delivering an industry-leading web site, but critical to the successful launch of this site was the expert, industry-leading knowledge of the two core business components: music and education. The development of industry-leading educational programs based on technology platforms has continued with the launch of the Keeping Score web site (www.keepingscore.org), and its success can be measured both by the number of unique and repeat visitors and the site's recent nomination for a Webby Award.

The importance of timing in the application of technology is clear in the case of the San Francisco Symphony. Through the launch of its social network (http://community .sfsymphony.org), the Symphony was the first orchestra worldwide to both recognize the importance of evolving its relationship with its patrons and take immediate steps to address the opportunity. There was little precedent for it. Historically, orchestras have closely controlled the distribution of any information and have had little appetite for open, unmoderated forums. There was a prescribed way of interacting with the public, and more specifically the formal critics, but as the media landscape changed, the San Francisco Symphony recognized the need to adopt this new paradigm, where patrons have the ability to interact with the Symphony more directly and with each other in a public forum.

The Symphony recognized that while this new venue exposed a potential risk of negative comments from patrons, it also presented a significant opportunity. The formation of a community of like-minded people who have an interest in the Symphony has been a powerful catalyst for increasing community involvement, supporting event attendance, and deepening the connection the patrons felt to the Symphony, an important factor for any organization that relies on the generosity of its patrons' donations for a percentage of its revenue. While still in its early stages of evolution, the opportunity was recognized, and has resulted in the formation of an active, vibrant, and highly engaged community of over 2,700 people from around San Francisco and around the world.

 ## MUSIC MAKING

The concert experience, which is really the center of an orchestra's life, is limited to the number of concerts and size of the audience that can attend over the course of a season. From a business perspective, this structure results in a finite, well-defined inventory and means that it must maximize the impact of that inventory on its bottom line. But technology also allows the orchestra and musicians to move beyond the walls of the concert hall and connect with a larger audience that can access its music through recordings, broadcasts, and the Internet. Technology is used to open entirely new markets that would not have been accessible previously.

Technology not only allows the Symphony to differentiate itself competitively by highlighting the world-class, Grammy-winning artistic qualities of its musicians and music, but it facilitates the delivery of the services of the organization to each of its representative markets, from education to the ticket-buying patrons. In this space, the San Francisco Symphony has used technology both to maintain a competitive advantage and to extend its mission as an educational ambassador for the growth and development of classical music, locally and globally.

Whether it is executed in a concert hall or a corporate headquarters, backed by the right combination of industry and organization-specific knowledge, the right timing, and a fully invested team, technology can be leveraged as a powerful agent for change. Every organization has the potential to recognize and unlock a competitive advantage and evolve the business, but the concept of achieving a competitive advantage is bifurcated and not necessarily linear. It is achieved either by understanding the business and the competition and identifying a means of surging ahead or by breaking new ground and redefining the rules of the game. As one of the fastest-moving, most rapidly evolving forces for change in business, technology is often the best-suited catalyst to be that game changer and help an organization compete. If the factors of industry knowledge, company culture, and appropriate timing align, technology can reshape the market entirely. Simply look to the monumental impact Facebook, Twitter, and Google have had in just the past few years for evidence of this fact.

Overall, the competitive applications of technology can take many forms. A technology that may be used effectively to establish dominance of a market at one time may at another barely be sufficient to stay relevant. Today's competitive landscape is evolving faster than ever and, with it, the nature of differentiation in business. Only by thoroughly understanding the unique character of each industry, organization, and team and by carefully aligning with the right emerging trends can technology achieve its full potential as an effective means of strategic differentiation.

 ## SUMMARY

First and foremost, get to know your industry and understand your organization's value proposition within it. Begin with an honest assessment of your business relative to its peers, and educate yourself about the current norms in your industry so you learn where it may be possible to exceed them and differentiate your business. This knowledge will help you distinguish ideas that have no potential for success from those that will take you into the lead.

Partner with your business counterparts—they will be your subject matter experts, valuable inspiration, and best ambassadors to their discipline, whether it is sales, marketing, or engineering. Learn their language and test ideas with them to gain invaluable perspective. Your success depends on theirs.

Achieving a competitive advantage is more often the result of an ecosystem of contributing factors than due to an individual component. Test these factors to gauge their relevance and relative impact, and prioritize your project planning accordingly.

Timing is, truly, everything. A competitive advantage this month may become the new lowest common denominator or irrelevant by next month.

Recognize opportunity when you come across it, and do not hesitate. The best opportunities often masquerade as something uncomfortable, unusual, or strikingly different, and as a result, they are often brushed off, ignored, or dismissed. There is no crystal ball, so learn to recognize the common elements of opportunity, pause when you come to something novel, and evaluate its potential.

Do not fear failure, but studiously capture and learn from the lessons buried in your mistakes. Identify precisely which aspects of the initiative did not succeed, and apply that knowledge in the next project.

Recognize the spectrum of competitive opportunities—from incremental to tactical to game-changing, there is a time and place for each. Do not lose sight of short-term, more incremental opportunities while you seek out the game-changer. The cumulative progress achieved by many small steps can outpace the big jump, and they may help you recognize the extraordinary when you come across it.

Be methodical in your approach to identifying opportunity, as the greatest opportunities are sometimes in pieces around you. Many may recognize parts of the solution, but they either give up or they cannot synthesize the components. Until you can see or understand the whole, keep looking. The most effective technologies often sit at the center of disparate parts or are a catalyst for another reaction. Differentiate your business through the integration or synthesis of those components.

Remember that technology is only one of many ways to achieve a competitive advantage. Be agnostic in your application of technology and judicious in its use.

 NOTE

1. Ray C. B. Brown, "Player Piano's Art Is Eerie," *San Francisco Examiner*, February 1, 1919, p. 9.

11

A New Paradigm for Managing a Suite of Business Processes Inexpensively

Charles Follett and Jeff Goldberg

LARGE ORGANIZATIONS TODAY MUST manage many business processes—often numbering in the hundreds. Often these processes have evolved organically over the course of years, creating a working—but inefficient—collection. Rarely does an organization have the luxury of organizing its business processes in a coherent fashion.

However, as things become more complicated in a business, this lack of coherence can cause all kinds of problems: employee and customer dissatisfaction, missed opportunities, lost profit, loss of business, and even legal issues.

Managers in such organizations are typically acting in the dark—blind to the big picture of what is really happening in their organization because their tools do not provide enough feedback. Some of their processes will produce exquisite measurements and others no measurement at all. But worse is the fact that the measurements are not comparable and not visible together.

Many software vendors have developed tools to help automate business processes, with the promise that these tools will solve their clients' problems. However, this promise cannot be fulfilled by tools alone if the underlying processes are chaotic in and of themselves. It makes no sense to automate and streamline the wrong process; it is better to fix a process first before introducing automation.

Lack of clear process definition, in turn, leads to another issue: Which process needs fixing first, or most? Even for small financial service support organizations, the number

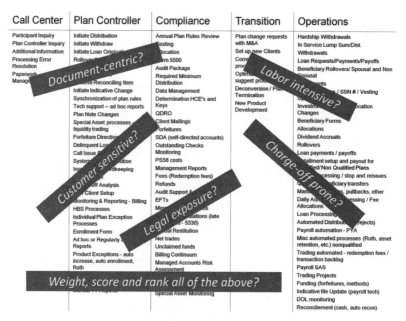

FIGURE 11.1 Where to Start with Business Process Management?

of processes runs into the dozens. Competing concerns, as depicted in Figure 11.1, make for a long, encumbered prioritization exercise that no one is happy with.

Furthermore, fixing a process is expensive; typically doing so involves developing new software, integrating with back-end systems, and/or deploying a new application on people's computers. If you want to fix 100 processes and each one will take two months' time, you're in for eight years of upheaval. Meanwhile, your organization is still exposed to risks that include undetected catastrophic errors, mounting charge-offs, penalties for service level agreement noncompliance, and customer retention issues due to lack of differentiation in services provided.

Finally, fixing each process one at a time will not show how the essential processes are performing to maintain a vital business. Without a coherent system to see how all the processes are performing, it is impossible to determine what to do, and the answer almost always comes down to politics

We can do better—much faster and more cheaply.

 WHAT WE SHOULD BE DOING

If focusing on individual processes is the wrong answer, what is the right answer?

We believe that four fundamental design principles must guide improvement efforts:

1. Start with top-down design.
2. Design for coordination among participants, not individual steps.
3. Measure performance and make it visible.
4. Provide automation that supports coordination and performance improvement.

Top-Down Design

Top-down design starts with discovering the processes that constitute what a business or organization does that provides value. By "constitutive" we mean integral, "business is not viable without." For example, a financial services support organization will have a host of processes for dealing with money coming in. Once the constitutive processes are identified (such as "money in"), the next order of business is to discover the distinctively pragmatic instances of a constitutive process; that is, processes that address the same general concern but are distinct from one another. More about that later.

Many organizations cannot describe the constitutive processes for their business. They can always list their business processes (as in Figure 11.1), and sometimes, after a bit of research, they can enumerate the steps in each process, but often they cannot create a hierarchy of processes that describes how the list would be organized into larger groupings.

This counterintuitive fact follows from the ad hoc way their processes have arisen over time—and because they simply do not think of their daily work in an abstract way. This is often true even of top-level management, who are not necessarily paid for thinking abstractly. However, without such abstraction, it is impossible for anyone in the organization to understand what is really going on—especially for new hires or people who are not part of top-level management.

For instance, the handful of constitutive processes, such as "Provide Service" shown in Table 11.1, are typical for a financial service support organization. Interestingly, all of the myriad of processes listed in Figure 11.1 fit neatly into one of the constitutive processes shown in the table. This immediately provides everyone in the organization the same view of what exactly the organization does, in a way that otherwise will never develop. Starting at the top is the secret to managing what seems like an insurmountable number of processes.

Once you have the constitutive and pragmatic levels worked out, you often can find parallels among processes that you did not think to look for. For example, one financial services company had not recognized that its processes for "incoming checks," "incoming stock certificates," and "incoming transfers from another financial institution" were each examples of a "money in" process—obvious as it was in retrospect—and that the processes could be made more similar than they were, increasing efficiency all around.

TABLE 11.1 Top-Level Processes for a Financial Service Support Organization

Constitutive Processes	Pragmatic Expression
Win business	Develop product or service, sell product or service
Enroll clients	Client setup
Provide service	Money in, money management, money out
Renew service	Plan review, client deconversion
Supervise and support	Plan changes, change request, issue resolution, compliance monitoring, periodic reports

Each of the pragmatic processes typically has between one and five *concrete instances*—for example, "money in" includes such pragmatic processes as "check in," "certificate in," and "transfer in." Each of these instances is distinctive enough to maintain as a separate process, but all share a basic pattern, often requiring only a simple additional step or document or special routing because of a business condition.

These pragmatic processes provide leverage; they are the ones that supervisors and staff engage in on a daily basis to take care of external and internal customers. Almost all of the "hundreds of processes" in an organization will turn out to be variations of a pragmatic process.

To organize all of this in a simpler fashion, we recommend adopting this three-level classification:

Level 1	Constitutive processes—these define the essence of the business
Level 2	Distinct pragmatic instances within constitutive processes that define daily or periodic interactions for taking care of customers and industry-related obligations
Level 3	Variations found within pragmatic process

We show a partial view of the variations found at Level 3 for financial service support organizations in Figure 11.2.

In this way, rather than having to model hundreds of processes, it is possible to control the entire organization by modeling only the two dozen or so pragmatic processes defined in Level 3.

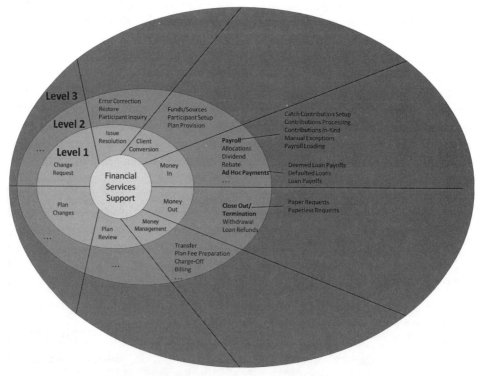

FIGURE 11.2 Hierarchy of Processes

As we see next, this simplification follows from the fact that we are not trying to model the details of what happens in each step of each of the hundreds of procedures at the bottom level.

Design for Coordination among Participants, not Individual Steps

We have discovered that when people redesign processes, too often they focus immediately on the "steps, tasks, and activities" of a process—aspects we advocate putting to the side until after the overall conditions for success for a given process, role accountability, and milestones have been worked out. Not surprisingly, our clients are almost always surprised to discover that, in large measure, their "problematic process" is problematic mostly because nobody has overall accountability for making sure the work is completed correctly and the customer is satisfied.

What matters most is defining how participants will coordinate action to satisfy the customer. In Figure 11.3, we briefly introduce the conventions used in the four-phase commitment-based management (CbM) process model. In phase 1, the necessary action is specified. Phase 1 is complete when a clear request is made by a person acting in the role of the customer to another person acting in the role we call the performer. In Phase 2 the customer and performer come to mutual agreement about what the performer will in fact, promise to fulfill. Sometimes this is exactly what was originally requested but often modifications to the initial request surface as the fit between need and solution is explored or constraints on capacity or capability are exposed. Phase 3 is where the actions needed to fulfill the promise are taken by the performer, resulting in a declaration of completion with the work performed. Finally, in phase 4, the customer either accepts and makes a declaration of satisfaction with the promise or asks the performer to take care of what is missing to arrive at satisfaction.

Say, for instance, a customer with a question or dispute calls a customer service representative, who forwards the question to an account manager, who in turn gets legal advice or other support as needed to reach resolution on the initial issue. Once resolved, system updates may need to be performed before communicating the final disposition to the customer. If delays or other problems stall the process, escalation

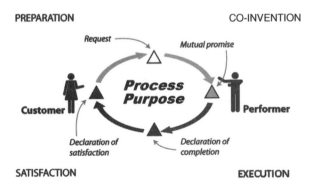

FIGURE 11.3 Four-Phase CbM Model

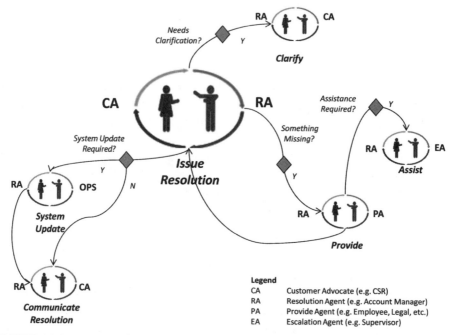

FIGURE 11.4 Issue Resolution Process Modeled with CbM

support may also be requested. In all, there may be as many as five roles involved as the process moves through the four phases, as depicted in Figure 11.4.

What is fundamentally important is establishing with absolute clarity that accountability for satisfactory resolution of the initial question or dispute falls to the role of *resolution agent*. The resolution agent in turn, acts as a customer to anyone assigned the role of *provide agent* as well as the *escalation agent*, or *OPS*, role.

Referring back to Table 11.1, we recognize issue resolution as one of the Level 2 processes previously identified. Designed in the fashion shown in Figure 11.4, this process can handle a whole variety of related customer queries ranging from lost stock certificates to requests for taking loans against accrued assets.

Not only does this adaptation reduce the number of processes that need to be supported with infrastructure; it also sets up a convenient basis for making comparison of performance meaningful, something we discuss in more detail in the next section.

Measure Performance and Make It Visible

Many management executives tend to have trouble measuring the performance of their processes. It is not that they do not measure; it is more that the ad hoc structure of their processes does not allow them to compare different processes, and the results from different processes have different meanings.

Focusing on coordination among participants by following a consistent model, as found in the four-phase CbM approach, allows us to compare any two processes, even those with wildly different characteristics (e.g., time frames, complexity, importance to the organization, or different teams). We can tell that some processes are completed in an orderly manner and in proper time while others are constantly being mishandled. We can tell which individual steps are taking too long—without caring what actually happens within that step.

Because our solution focuses entirely on the coordination among people, and coordination is an innate part of every process, our strategy allows us to show coherent measurements across all processes without getting mired in the details of specific processes.

The corollary is that we are measuring the entire suite of processes from top to bottom of abstraction. We can pinpoint which processes are problematic and, within those processes, which steps are problematic (meaning, usually, "This step often is completed beyond the time we allotted it").

Then, once we know which processes (and which steps within those processes) need fixing, we can meaningfully dive into the details of the troublesome processes and fix them. We are no longer guessing which processes need fixing because now we know exactly how much not fixing them is costing.

Measurement is also vital in day-to-day work. We like everyone in the organization to have a simple dashboard of where their work stands at every moment. The dashboards, like everything else in the system, show only coordination details and not "step" details ("This step is past due," "You haven't received an answer to your question yet," but not "Now calculate the amount the customer is owed"). A sample dashboard is shown in Figure 11.5.

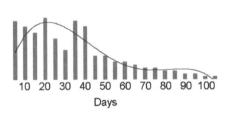

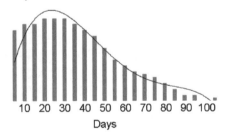

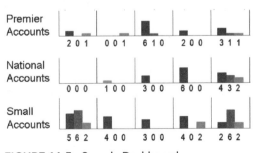

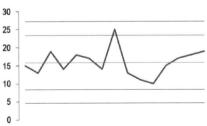

FIGURE 11.5 Sample Dashboard

Design Automation that Supports Coordination

It stands to reason that we should be using software to manage processes. Once again, because of the ad hoc history of process design within a large organization, often there is no such software. That makes perfect sense since without coherent processes, there can be no coherent automation.

Let us suppose that we accept the principles outlined earlier. We have defined our Level 1 and Level 2 processes. Now we are going to write the software to go with them. What will we build?

 CASE MANAGEMENT

The main part of this kind of application is a "case management" tool, as shown in Figure 11.6. Each process that the organization performs is "instantiated" as a case when a user clicks on a "create case" button in a browser, specifies which kind of process to create (at Level 3, which implies a corresponding Level 1 and 2) and a very small number of details pertaining to the case.

Once a case exists, it is automatically routed from one participant to the next, based on defined process logic and role assignments. Each person can see what they have to do on a "work list" page as exemplified in Figure 11.7. When they complete their step, the case is automatically routed to the person responsible for the next step. Should a step fail

RPS Case Management

Refund Checklist

☑ Review Call Issue
☑ Verify Participant Info

5330 Required?
☑ Prepare 5330 Packet

☐ Update Checklist and Spreadsheet
☐ Send forms to sponsor
☐ Process refund

more help with Refunds

Refund 0000293191 for ABC Co.

Case Id:	0000293191	Plan Name :	ABC 401K
Originator :	Cathy	Amount:	$4,000
Sponsor Name:	ABC Co.	Date:	12/20/08
Sponsor Id:	21312313		

Case Description [Change]

Level 1 Process:	Money Out
Level 2 Process:	Refund
Level 3 Process:	Annual Refund Processing

Associated Documents [Add More]

Refund Checklist
Refund Spreadsheet
Email 12/01/07 from Steven Sponsor: Wait! Looks Wrong!

Previous Actions

12/01/07	Cathy	Compliance Specialist	Created
12/01/07	Cathy	Compliance Specialist	Send data to Sponsor
12/01/07	Patrick	Plan Controller	Forward to Prepare Package
12/03/07	(automatic)		Automatic Escalation
12/03/07	Cathy	Compliance Specialist	Returned to Prepare Package
			Hey! Get to work Cuthbert!

Next Action

Action: * [Review and Approve Refund List ▼]
Comment:

[SAVE & EXIT] [CONTINUE] [CANCEL]

FIGURE 11.6 Sample Case Management View

Work List

Past Due

12/20	●	Refund	Houston Univ	Avis Lofthouse	21311231	$4,000	complete view
12/23	●	Rollover	LA General	Hugh Gagliardi	12351565	$6,000	complete view
12/24	●	Rollover	SF State	Darcy Lembke	80847190	$14,000	complete view

Due Today

1/19	●	Refund	UC San Mateo	Amie Schwebach	19275103	$4,500	complete view
1/19	●	QDRO	Glidden College	Noreen Hilliker	87531278	$2,000	complete view
1/19	●	Rollover	Kubrick Hospital	Selena Rimer	86103476	$80,000	complete view
1/19	●	Refund	Larchmont High	Clinton Goodrow	14761416	$9,000	complete view

Due This Week

1/20	●	Rollover	St. Stegen's	Malinda Blanca	65786548	$3,000	complete view
1/21	●	Refund	Nebraska State	Mathew Trepanier	43784537	$5,000	complete view
1/21	●	Rollover	MT Teachers	Rosalinda Easterly	87125352	$4,000	complete view
1/22	●	Refund	Shoestring CO	Max Cambareri	87157126	$8,000	complete view
1/22	●	Rollover	Land College	Roslyn Eddie	12341616	$5,500	complete view

All Other

1/29	●	Refund	Baccarat	Odessa Meli	34610167	$3,200	complete view
1/29	●	Refund	Hollywood Teachers	Kurt Copher	23526109	$4,400	complete view
2/3	●	Refund	State Pension	Milagros Boysen	09712310	$5,800	complete view
2/3	●	Refund	The Mountain School	Christian Remus	98734613	$6,000	complete view
2/5	●	Rollover	Sandy Unified	Marylou Boulanger	23468238	$9,000	complete view
2/7	●	Refund	ABC Co	Sharron Scaife	12461601	$3,000	complete view

● Due to me
◐ Due by me

FIGURE 11.7 Sample Work List

to be executed in a timely manner, the case is routed to someone "committed" to making sure it is completed, who then takes whatever action is necessary. When the case is complete, it no longer appears on anyone's work list.

Dashboards/Reports

Since each step is timed, the system knows which ones are coming due or overdue and, by aggregating information over many cases, which processes and steps are chronically overdue. The resulting reports lead directly to continuous improvement.

It also makes it easy to show any participant how they are doing as an individual or as a team.

Process Descriptions

Because we have modeled all the organization's processes into about two dozen processes, describing those processes for everyone to see is a straightforward task. That makes it easier to train people and show them how their piece fits into the larger picture. It also makes it easier to show people where the step they are required to complete fits in the overall case they are working on.

E-mail Integration

Finally, good integration with the organization's e-mail system makes it easier to work without having to go to the case management tool at all. Since the cases do not manage details, it is easy to complete steps via e-mail. In fact, with e-mail integration, the need to go to the case management tool can often be avoided entirely.

CONCLUSION

Obviously, in a brief description like this, we have glossed over a myriad of details.

However, it should be clear by now that our fundamental premise—the *reason* we believe that managing an entire suite of processes could be done both more effectively and quite inexpensively—is that the way we pretend to manage them today is just too complicated.

By reorienting the way we think about managing processes, we can remove the extraneous complexity and manage what is left with very straightforward tools. By understanding the overall model of the entire process suite and identifying the relatively few *key* processes, we can extract the coordination and collaboration issues and manage them directly. And by providing a single platform for managing coordination in the entire suite of processes, we can effectively manage the entire business.

CHAPTER TWELVE

Information Technology Portfolio Management

Pamela Vaughan

NFORMATION TECHNOLOGY IS AT a critical juncture in today's business climate. The proliferation of business applications, increased scrutiny to cost-justify expenditures, and regulatory changes like the Sarbanes-Oxley Act of 2002 have contributed to an increased need for greater discipline and control within IT organizations. With seemingly exponentially increasing information requirements coupled with reduced budgets and staff, most CIOs face demand for projects that far outstrips their ability to deliver. With IT investments typically ranging from 1.5 to 7 percent of revenues, it is clear that an approach is needed to ensure that these investments meet or exceed expectations. This chapter prescribes Information Technology Portfolio Management (ITPM) as the commonsense approach to aligning, prioritizing, selecting, managing, and monitoring IT investments to ensure optimum alignment with and contribution to the organization's goals.

WHAT IS INFORMATION TECHNOLOGY PORTFOLIO MANAGEMENT?

ITPM is increasingly recognized as a management discipline to improve returns on IT investments and overall align IT with the business. ITPM has become a critical component in the IT business lexicon. It provides structure and consistency to the processes associated with the planning, prioritization, management, and control of IT investments. ITPM is a blend of management disciplines that combines:

- A business management focus to ensure that all IT projects align with and support the corporate strategy
- A project management focus for reviewing, assessing, and managing IT projects to ensure that they are meeting or exceeding their planned contribution to the portfolio
- A general management focus for managing an organization's resources and risks

Combining project management disciplines with business and general management practices at the portfolio level gives an organization the ability to:

- Select the right projects that are aligned with the organization's strategy
- Provide resource optimization, ensuring that resources are working on the highest-priority projects
- Regularly assess how projects are contributing to portfolio health
- Take management action to keep the portfolio in compliance with business objectives

ITPM is the best means of addressing the issues of aligning projects with strategies and attempting to select the best projects for the health of the organization. ITPM enables us not only to do projects right but to select and do the right projects in the first place. Flawless project execution is meaningless if the right projects are not being tackled.

ITPM is the nucleus to assure that IT is aligned with the business, avoiding the costly problem of overspending or unnecessary spending, and bucketing investments according to categories that help run, grow, and transform the business. ITPM provides the discipline of balancing risk against expected returns, evaluating the performance and utilization of existing systems, analyzing and assessing alternatives and trade-offs, and removing waste, resulting in significant efficiencies and cost savings.

ITPM is a set of business practices that brings the world of projects into tight integration with other business operations. It brings projects into harmony with the strategies, resources, and executive oversight of the enterprise. ITPM focuses on all IT projects across an organization and consolidates one view of the overall value and risks, providing a unified view of IT spending in its entirety.

ITPM provides a sound and proven business approach to optimizing investments in IT. Much the way an investment manager dynamically manages a portfolio of financial investments, business leaders must make a series of buy, sell, or hold decisions around their IT investments, balancing the organization's needs, resources, and risk tolerance to optimize revenue and growth opportunities, improve customer experience, and streamline operations. When ITPM is done properly, the productivity improvements and cost savings that result will positively impact the bottom line and allow organizations to fulfill their primary obligation of increasing shareholder value.

UNDERSTANDING WHAT ITPM IS NOT

Some may view ITPM as just another technique of project management, but it is not that. ITPM is above and beyond project management because it spans all the way from the vision of those in the executive suite, through project management, to the realization of benefits to the enterprise and its successful competitive positioning. Key to this new project portfolio life span is selection of the right projects in the first place.

The core mistake is to think that ITPM is fundamentally the management of multiple projects. This definitely is not so. ITPM is the management of the project portfolio so as to maximize the contribution of projects to the overall success of the organization. Project management is focused on completing individual projects successfully. In contrast, ITPM is aimed at simultaneously managing whole collections of projects. Project management ensures that projects are done right, while ITPM ensures that the right projects are done.

 ITPM PROCESS

Most IT organizations are currently structured around projects. Investment decisions are evaluated individually. Projects are defined, initiated, and funded by individual functional departments and managed discretely. Success and failure are evaluated individually rather than as a whole. Trying to prioritize projects in a holistic sense has been impossible because of the lack of comparability and different data sources used. ITPM changes the way IT investment decisions are made for the better.

The processes of ITPM, in order, are discussed in the next sections.

Inventory of All IT Projects

An inventory of all significant IT investments, both current and planned, is created. Each potential IT investment is captured in a standardized business case, allowing for a more apples-to-apples evaluation of proposals and vastly streamlining the administrative effort involved in determining which projects should be undertaken. The right type of data and level of detail will vary according to the specific needs and processes of each organization, but some common information to require includes:

- Project description
- What strategic goal or high-level objective the project aligns with
- Business unit/department involved
- Business benefits
- Expected resource requirements
- Project costs, milestones, and timeline
- Return on investment (ROI) analysis

The organization gets a comprehensive view of its entire portfolio of IT projects. This visibility allows the business and the IT organization to manage the portfolio as a single unit. They can finally see needless duplication of IT projects across business units.

They can see systems in one business unit that would be useful to other business units, and they can see opportunities for collaboration on systems across the enterprise.

Ranking and Selection of Projects

Strategic project selection is crucial to ensuring that teams are focused on those initiatives that align with the business strategy and deliver the highest value. Priority should be based on both individual project benefits and overall impact to the project portfolio. Organizations need to develop a consistent and standardized set of criteria with threshold levels. Portfolio priority criteria should be limited in number, understandable, measurable, and consistently applied. The decision criteria should be linked to the organization's business strategy and objectives. The process for prioritizing and selecting projects should go beyond financial objectives, such as profitability, ROI, budgeted costs, and revenue growth. It should encompass other considerations, including risk tolerance, customer demand, entering into new markets or expanding existing ones, and operational or mandatory initiatives. Various criteria can have different weightings, based on their importance to meeting business strategy and objectives.

Establishing well-defined, consistent criteria against which proposals will be scored allows projects to be evaluated more objectively. The end result should be a single, easy-to-grasp scorecard, with the highest-scoring projects representing the most valuable IT investments. I recall at one company the vice president of marketing was amazed by the ranking and selection process in action and after the meeting praised me for how effective it was. No longer is IT deciding which projects to work on; it is a collaboration of the business focused on ensuring that the right projects are selected to add the most value to the organization as a whole. The CIO's role is to facilitate this process.

Once the business case, ranking, and categorization are deemed complete, IT investments are presented to the governing board, comprised of a cross-functional leadership team. The collaborative and shared commitment from the leadership team ensures accountability and authority to make enterprise-wide decisions. This group evaluates the numerical value assigned to each investment and assesses the ratio of investments within each category to make go, hold, and cancel decisions regarding IT investments. IT governance is the structured executive oversight of IT investments to ensure alignment with strategic priorities.

Managing the Project Portfolio

By frequently monitoring performance of active projects against both the project goals and the selection criteria, the portfolio can be adjusted to maximize return. Receiving accurate and timely feedback is required to manage the current work within the portfolio effectively. Normally, the mechanism for gathering this feedback is the status reporting process. One effective technique is to have one or two lines of information for each project within the portfolio. Each project is marked with a color that indicates whether it is okay (green), at risk (yellow), or in trouble (red). When projects are complete, information should also be collected on how successful they were. The results are then summarized at the portfolio level.

The ITPM discipline ensures consistent, timely, and disciplined reviews of the entire portfolio. It is a continuous gating mechanism to ensure that projects remain aligned with the organization. A successful portfolio depends on how you plan, prioritize, and manage work, but another key aspect is managing change, a constant of business. The changes could be the result of business priorities, new management, new ideas that become important, or regulatory requirements. Changes also could be forced on the portfolio because previously agreed-on commitments for delivering on time and within budget were not met. Portfolio changes must be managed similarly to the ranking and selection process. This means being willing to restructure, delay, or even terminate projects with performance deficiencies or because of changing business requirements.

ITPM BEST PRACTICES

Although the specifics of ITPM differ from organization to organization, the fundamentals of best practice are nearly universal. Successful ITPM initiatives take a top-down approach, starting at the top with senior management buy-in. It is an ongoing activity, not just an annual event. The discipline is based on creating a comprehensive view of the IT portfolio. Further, its primary goal is to align the IT portfolio with business requirements in order to create the greatest possible value for the organization—not the other way around.

Several other beneficial best practices to help increase success rates and the benefits of ITPM include:

- **Start small and add capabilities as you go: Do not overwhelm the organization with a big-bang approach.** ITPM is not a quick fix; bringing it to full maturity within an organization takes time. Significant savings via incremental optimization can be achieved, such as identifying and eliminating redundant projects.
- **Involve stakeholders.** An important means by which to ensure support of ITPM disciplines is to engage stakeholders throughout the organization in the process and have them provide input into the portfolio metrics, criteria, and prioritization.
- **Assess the portfolio regularly.** The status and performance of each project should be evaluated regularly to ensure that projects are collectively meeting the portfolio strategy as well as reviewing any changes in the business. By monitoring performance of active projects against both the project goals and the selection criteria, the portfolio can be adjusted to maximize return. This means being willing to restructure, delay, or even terminate projects with performance deficiencies.
- **Communicate on a regular basis.** Since ITPM can bring significant changes to the way an organization validates, manages, and maintains its portfolios, the need to communicate decisions effectively is critical.

ITPM BENEFITS

ITPM provides significant business benefits, including:

- **Reduced costs.** ITPM provides a unified view of IT spending in its entirety. Redundant or overlapping projects become visible and can be eliminated. The rigorous review process also ensures that the right projects are selected and that decisions are based on well-defined business criteria, which helps to avoid the tendency to select projects by political means, power plays, and emotion, and eliminates projects that have become ineffective.
- **Better resource allocation.** Maintaining a single repository for projects allows the organization to better allocate and schedule resources, avoiding the need to bring in external, and more expensive, resources to deliver on committed schedules and goals.
- **Greater agility.** As ITPM provides a complete view of the portfolio, it helps bring agility, enhancing an organization's ability to respond to change with a better understanding of the effect on the entire portfolio.
- **Increased communication and collaboration into IT investments.** ITPM helps organizations overcome the communication disconnect between the business and IT by putting a value on IT and better aligning it with the business. By helping to create standardized and highly visible decision processes, ITPM engages business stakeholders and makes them partners in the process. Giving stakeholders more collaborative input into decisions earlier in the process means greater buy-in and more effective decisions on an ongoing basis.
- **Elevation of IT's role within the organization.** When IT can report that we spent x and delivered y for an overall return of z, the discussion changes. IT moves from being considered a cost center to a contributor to business goals.

 CONCLUSION

ITPM provides the decision-making framework to proactively and visibly manage IT investments, optimizing the ROI by identifying which investments will produce significant value-enhancing capabilities and which investments are low-value-added and redundant. Investments made in low-value-added projects are eliminated or minimized, freeing up important resources to focus on core issues and opportunities.

ITPM is the nucleus that aligns IT with the business. It is a continuous process to ensure that IT projects remain aligned with the corporate strategy. It provides the framework to translate IT into a common taxonomy that both business and IT executives understand. It is conveyed in business terms, and business management is responsible for making IT investment decisions. The critical importance of alignment to corporate strategy and planning, and the sequencing of priorities to migrate from the current as-is state to the future to-be state, is driven primarily by business needs and supported by IT. ITPM is the change agent that is making this happen with the most efficiency and optimal results.

CHAPTER THIRTEEN

A Beginner's Guide to the Software Development Life Cycle*

Stuart Robbins

L ET'S IMAGINE TWO SCENARIOS. In the first, you are asked to host Thanksgiving dinner for your entire family less than one week before the event, and you have never cooked for more than five people in your entire life. In the second, you are invited to attend your neighbor's Thanksgiving meal, a tradition the family has happily participated in for more than a decade.

Of course, you try to do the best you can in the first scenario, given your other time commitments and your limited budget, with much of the work tackled at the last minute with numerous urgent trips to the store for missing ingredients, utensils, napkins. The results are somewhat entertaining but far too chaotic, with too much anxiety and not enough turkey, overcooked stuffing, and relatives who plan to find a restaurant after they leave your house. In the second scenario, you sit down at the precise time on the invitation to a well-organized menu (even an alternate dish for the vegetarian cousins) including two different salads, coordinated wines for each stage of the meal, and a perfectly timed baked Alaska for dessert. The hosts are relaxed and charming, without

---

*Author's Note: There are many sources of information on the "best practice" known as the software development life cycle, from college texts written for software programmers that explain the "waterfall" development methodology to papers extending those principles into contemporary development techniques such as Agile, Scrum, and so on. While I will summarize the basic tenets of SDLC theory whenever appropriate, this chapter is not a substitute for established research in the field. Instead, this chapter concentrates upon strategies for introducing SDLC-style processes where none exist, and on tactics for addressing two of the major risks to SDLC initiatives in such early-stage implementations.

a single stain on their clothing, and the biggest crisis of the evening involves their cat and some spilled soup. (They had soup!)

It should not be difficult to identify the reasons why one meal was successful and the other was a nightmare that in-laws will find amusing for years to come: planning, execution, and delivery. In scenario 1, with no previous experience and too many distractions, the ad hoc event suffered from poor timing, inadequate supplies, and a main course that triggered a health panic among those who are concerned about undercooked poultry. In scenario 2, based on experience and supported by tried-and-true recipes along with advance knowledge of certain guests' special needs, the meal itself was the denouement when many different actions came together in a coordinated manner with sound results.

Simple anecdote, obvious conclusion: If presented with a choice, most of us would prefer to attend the well-executed meal.

And yet, in large and small companies around the world, we suffer from software products of poor quality delivered late and failing to meet even the basic expectations. We may know how to organize a dinner for 25 people but fail to apply that same wisdom to software development, which (for many) remains an ad hoc process that suffers from poor requirements (how many people are coming and what they want to eat), poor planning (frozen turkeys purchased on the previous day require more cooking time), and low marks for customer satisfaction (at least we didn't get sick, but we're never coming back).

For the purposes of this chapter, the software development life cycle (SDLC) can be summarized (not unlike a complicated meal for many guests) as composed of five primary stages:

Plan → Design → Build → Test → Launch

As noted, there are many detailed expositions on these primary stages with various naming conventions and alternate definitions. However, the objective (in the next sections) is not to declare one superior to another but rather to provide a basic primer for those organizations that want/need to move from scenario 1 to scenario 2 (Getting Started) and offer antidotes for two of the major risks to long-term adoption, once the new process is under way.

 ## CASE STUDY: PROJECT X

The trigger for SDLC initiatives may originate from many sources such as quality complaints, customer requirements, and compliance mandates. In the case study outlined in this section, these organizational characteristics, present before and during the launch of Project X, should be considered environmental factors or boundaries within which the SDLC methodology emerged:

- Limited project management resources with hundreds of open projects to lead
- A small quality assurance (QA) group

- A Web development team burdened by support for existing products while new development was launched without testing
- An enterprise resource planning (ERP) team with rigid protocols and fully documented processes
- An infrastructure team that rarely learned about a request for new servers until the day they were needed to be operational
- Ten different ways to submit a request to IT
- No agreed-on governance for budgeting or prioritization

These factors created an environment where everyone worked as hard as possible on as many projects as possible, often in the evening and on weekends. Management understood the need for a more orderly environment, but the inevitable fire drills of unexpected requests from the business kept its teams, and the entire organization, in spinning-plate mode—attending to the most urgent issues, juggling multiple projects with inadequate resources, often resolving conflicts in the hallway between meetings with dissatisfied constituencies.

It was in this challenging environment that the company's IT audit staff of 10 to 12 senior developers and analysts, preparing for the pending arrival of SAS auditors, attended an exploratory meeting to discuss the compliance requirement for SDLC process documentation. Previous audits focused solely on methodologies within the ERP team; however, the director of compliance was now requesting policy and procedure documentation that established IT policy for the entire organization.

 ## THE FIRST MEETING

Participants were identified by the IT management team based on a broad set of guidelines: All groups needed representation; seniority (based on experience with a variety of projects in this environment) was balanced by those who are predisposed to cross-functional communication and collaboration. We decided to drive adoption of basic SDLC practices from the ground up by creating a task force of individual contributors, on the theory that successful adoption is proportionally related to the degree that employees felt involved in the decision-making process.

Our objective was to draft a proposed policy/procedure document that would be presented to the management team for approval. Our deadline was the next scheduled visit from the auditors, less than three months away.

We opened the meeting with a clear outline of the task force objectives. Following that was a venting session that lasted for two hours, with each attendee identifying barriers and roadblocks that projects suffered from: too many ways, most informal, for a new project to begin; no standards for gathering requirements or clarifying scope, which changed constantly; inadequate time to complete the project, with schedules often preventing the limited QA staff from having any substantial impact; hallway decisions that often shifted the direction of projects midstream with no escalation path to clarify the inevitable confusions; teams frequently working at cross purposes; underlying platform (ERP) development that was not synchronized with either the application developers or the server; and storage teams who rarely learned about the project until the eleventh hour.

An SDLC policy, even the most rigorous and well-documented one, would not resolve these challenges.

However, it was clear—from the group's enthusiasm and the mandate from the IT audit department—that there was an opportunity to shine a light on each of the challenges. Using the SDLC process as a vehicle for identifying other IT processes in need of improvement, the task force eagerly committed not only to the initial objectives but to the broader ambition of improving the overall operational capability of the IT organization.

Each of the representatives recognized the benefits to their particular function: The Web developers aimed for tighter coordination with the ERP team, and the ERP representatives recognized the chance to expand their rigorous procedures in ways that would influence all major initiatives; the QA staff anticipated stronger sanctions for test cycles; and the infrastructure representatives also wanted inclusion in project planning and advance notification of procurement or configuration requirements. The latter change would, by itself, contribute to better budgeting alignment. Everyone agreed to take the issue back to their teams and return, in two weeks, with three specific steps their functional teams wanted in the policy document's first draft.

One of the attendees, within minutes of the first meeting, declared that this was the first time he felt hopeful that things could get better. Everyone's energy and commitment was palpable.

The result, in three months and without impact on any of the individuals' existing responsibilities, was a policy document of enough substance to address audit requirements and drive agreement at the management level that the SDLC proposal should be implemented for all new projects.

The high-level work flow documented by the task force emulated SDLC best practices yet was quickly embraced because it was organically constructed through collaboration by teams and individuals who found immediate value in the model (see Figure 13.1).

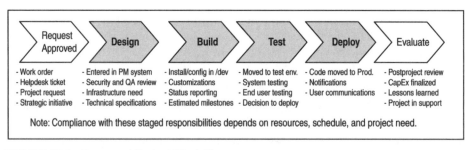

FIGURE 13.1 Proposed Project Work Flow

Source: Selection from *Systems Development Lifecycle: Proposal for Management Consideration,* TriNet, Inc., August 2008, based on "best practice" models in the public domain.

THE EXPERIMENT

It looked good on paper, sounded good to management, and was applauded by various business groups that hoped to model their new processes (i.e., product management) on IT's direction. The explicit objectives of the task force were complete and the initial audit requirements (demonstrable progress) had been fulfilled, but the task force members were not ready to disband. Moreover, they insisted on continuing their weekly meetings with a new and more focused goal: implementation. Among the many barriers facing the SDLC team as they sought to be compliant, not only in principle but in practice, was the immense and complicated list of multiyear projects and initiatives that plagued IT, each attendee involved in too many in-flight projects to consider adding yet another to their workload.

The task force needed a pilot project with sufficient urgency to capture management's attention and sufficient breadth to demonstrate the value of an SDLC-style process yet a project that required no one's *time*.

Project X was formally documented as an urgent tactical request from executives, entered in the company's portfolio management system, and milestones were tracked with status reports delivered at the SDLC team's weekly meetings. The company's CIO, in support of the pilot project, agreed to serve in the role of the project's executive sponsor and immediately sent a priority e-mail to the team with an all-too-familiar demand: Project X, estimated in the initial project plan as a four- to six-month effort, must be delivered "to the market" in four weeks.

For years, dramatic changes in scope and hurry-up schedules were the norm. The CIO was confronting the SDLC task force to face 10 years of habit, and they wilted in the face of executive pressure. Their next meeting began with a flurry of rapid and emotional proposals to meet the new deadline by eliminating all documentation and testing requirements and redefining any Project X objective as unimportant if it could not be delivered by the end of the month.

Organizational habit, and the absence of any conceivable alternatives, had transformed their passionate drive for change into yet another unmanaged and under-resourced race to an irrational deadline over which they had no control. Their deflated morale was almost palpable in the conference room.

 THE FIRST OBSTACLE

In any work environment, and particularly in the technology and service sectors, hierarchical authority is reinforced economically, politically, and socially. In the absence of alternate governing principles offering the check-and-balance function, and in time-constrained situations that favor moving fast, it is human nature to opt for the default momentum of command-and-control decisions. A supervisor says "just do it" and employees "just do it," often spending evenings and weekends in a relentless effort to accomplish the impossible. The results of such environmental dynamics are well known: schedule delays, poor product quality, and overspending.

To compensate, a governance framework (tools, policies, templates, and distinct exception management guidelines) is a foundational component, and the SDLC policy (which had been approved in principle by the management team) simply needed someone to enforce its basic themes.

A template was designed, and an escalation meeting was called for the following morning.[1]

Everyone knew the sponsor's demand was unreasonable, yet there were no clearly defined methods for business case analysis (justification) or project review (document approval), no agreed-on roles and responsibilities (chartered accountability for cross-functional oversight), no shared vocabulary for communicating urgent issues. They knew it could not be done; they simply had no method for explaining that potential failure to the business. Armed with a template and an agenda for discussion with the executive sponsor, the team now had the means for review and feedback, an essential component of life cycle methodologies: At each stage, those with the relevant expertise have checkpoints, gates, and channels for communicating risk whenever and wherever it appears.

Based on the team's one-page escalation document, the executive (CIO) lifted the schedule constraint he had previously imposed. In doing so, his team learned a secondary lesson about the need for professional candor and good process as precursors to good decisions.

Only in its design stage, Project X had already accomplished a key objective by emphasizing that attention to process, however lightweight and timely, increases the likelihood of successful delivery by quickly responding to unexpected changes that otherwise would increase risk.

THE SECOND OBSTACLE

There is an even greater barrier, in the early establishment of SDLC-style governance for IT projects, than the absence of governance principles. This informal case study would be incomplete without identifying the challenge that looms larger than most change management issues yet can be traced to any organization's resistance in the face of dramatic transformation.

On a purely tactical level, it is the challenge of orchestration. Once a new development methodology has been (a) defined, (b) embraced, (c) sanctioned, and (d) successfully prototyped, it can be very difficult (if not impossible) to identify a good time in the company's schedule to implement new rules: It is not advisable to introduce new methodologies in the middle of a project's timeline (i.e., it is futile to redesign an airplane midair), and yet there are always in-flight projects that need to be granted exception status. Doing this, however, reinforces the very habits (urgency, "just do it," etc.) that the new methodology aims to address. Therefore, upon being sanctioned by the company (particularly in regulated industries wherein compliance with published policy is mandatory), the management team must carefully identify the road map for implementing new guidelines. In some cases, a complete moratorium on new development may be required for a period of time (two to three months) to ensure that the SDLC takes root and is given a well-needed foundation.

On a strategic level, there is the broader challenge of organizational architecture. New teams will be needed and new management principles will be required. Behaviors that for many years have been successful and even rewarded (code without embedded comments, testing completed by the source engineer) will become less important to the overall health of the organization than the newer skills of planning, prioritization, and communication. Ensuring that the organization's architecture is redesigned in coordination with its processes can not only complement but also enable the objectives of any SDLC: planned and well-managed execution of projects, consistently, within projected budgets and with reliable levels of quality that are improved incrementally over time.

 ## CONCLUSION

Corporations mature in standard developmental cycles—launched by entrepreneurs like innocent small children at play among skyscrapers, then struggling through the awkward adolescence of stronger competition—and yet, we forget that our "parenting style" should change as the company matures. I would no more recommend the adoption of a software development methodology to venture-backed start-ups than would I encourage algebra in kindergarten. Each stage of a company's growth brings with it the opportunity to shed behaviors no longer relevant.

The introduction of process-oriented governance methods (like the SDLC) should be similarly considered, after a candid self-assessment by executives who themselves may be holding on to behaviors that may have once been, but are no longer, useful.

"We must rearchitect ourselves" to the degree that we yearn to redesign our systems and methods.[2]

I had an opportunity to use this metaphor and will share this anecdote in closing, to explicitly reiterate the importance of thoughtful management (parenting) in the move toward SDLC-style policies and procedures. The conversation occurred during the early weeks of the task force, before the value of review/oversight was widely shared. The compliance team (in the face of an impending audit) was insisting on complete (documented) evidence that each production-ready server had been "hardened" to meet accepted security standards.

The manager of the company's small but resourceful UNIX team challenged the benefit of lengthy checklists, standardized templates, and submission with signatures, on the accurate prediction that it would slow down his team's ability to respond rapidly to requests. He noted that they were highly skilled and capable of moving very quickly, as the company needed in its early years.

I asked if he had children, and he acknowledged a young daughter and younger son with a smile. With this in mind, I offered another perspective for him to consider:

We all know that very young children (two to three years of age) become enamored with Mommy and Daddy's car keys, and these often become a favorite toy. Perhaps it is the jingle, or the cool touch of metal on their skin, and perhaps it is because the keys are objects that serve as a connection with the parents. Whatever the reason, the manager of our UNIX team agreed that a good set of car keys is a great way to keep a baby happy at a restaurant. I observed that using the keys in this fashion was not only convenient but appropriate in those circumstances.

However, as time passes and the baby becomes a young woman, nearly 16 and stridently independent, what parent would calmly hand over the car keys for fun? Same girl, same parent, same tool, yet as the family matured, different challenges present themselves, requiring different boundaries, different rules. What was once appropriate and convenient can become thoughtless and even dangerous over the course of time. The health and welfare of a company may require a much stricter code of conduct as it strives to be compliant, meet contractual commitments, and reach for even more growth.

Good governance, like good parenting, is as much a matter of timing as it is wisdom. If the company needs discipline and rigor that process-oriented methods provide, as executives, we should not neglect those needs.

 ## SUMMARY

Rare is the organization in which best practices actually exist—they are goals that serve as milestones for organizational growth. Most of us work in less optimal environments, yet the desire to improve (as individuals, as teams, as institutions) remains strong in healthy companies. I prefer the term "better practices" for it more accurately describes our efforts to constantly improve.

One such "better practice" is an SDLC that is supported by management and nurtured by good engineering principles. In this chapter, I have shown that even the most underdeveloped software development environments can be improved in ways that allow technical teams to govern themselves by choosing which phases need improvement, then modestly adapting their approach over time. The SDLC, like so many practices, is best appreciated when it is a grassroots effort rather than a regime imposed from above.

 ## NOTES

1. It is beyond the scope of this chapter to identify the key factors that lead to successful executive escalations. However, one or two aspects are appropriate to note in the context of Project X. Escalations, like any other business process, can be done efficiently or awkwardly, and the results are a microcosm of an institution's process health. When efficient, they can be vehicles for clearer and more accurate decisions.
2. Steve Yatko, director of IT R&D, Credit Suisse, New York, 2002.

CHAPTER FOURTEEN

Office of the CIO*

Makarand Utpat

TODAY WE FIND THAT certain trends, such as globalization, mergers and acquisitions, competition for market position and market share, regulatory compliance, and maintaining strategic advantage, have become cornerstones in radically shaping business dynamics.[1] Agility, having a holistic view of the enterprise, doing more with less, and lean methodologies have become more than just buzzwords in the corporate IT world. As a result, CIOs and their leadership teams are demanding that IT investments be spent wisely and that there is a compelling business case that demonstrates why they need to approve and fund new IT projects and justifies the risks and rewards.

Many global corporations have launched dedicated efforts and/or disciplines by forming enterprise architecture departments, program management offices, or strategic planning groups.[2] These disciplines exist at various levels of maturity ranging from intermediate for some to advanced for others. These disciplines typically work in concert with each other. The goals are many, including, but not limited to, rationalization of the IT landscape; building the next generation of the core competencies; leveraging real-

*Acknowledgments: The author is proud to have worked with competent individuals and would like to thank them for their contributions in creation and implementation of the strategy: The vice president of architecture, governance, and strategic IT services for the sponsorship, acting as a project champion, and for the overall leadership related to IT leadership and business leadership committee aspects; cross-functional team members for the successful delivery of the strategy; Scott Seifried (Informatica) for demonstrating the strategic partnership skills; and Drew Wright (Technology Finance Partners) for collaboration and guidance on the data integration business case, and for introducing the author to The Office of the CIO.

world guidelines and applying industry best practices; and identification, prioritization, and management of portfolio investments in order to assess value, increase efficiencies, and realize long-term gains.

The content described in this chapter represents the results of such rationalization efforts for a global corporation, which led to: the key recommendations in the form of the creation of various project proposals and business cases; provision of project oversight by establishing cross-functional organizational structures, processes, and governance mechanisms to maintain alignment over time; adoption of standard software suppliers; and creation of integration competency centers (ICCs).

 ## SITUATION

For the aforementioned global corporation, the information landscape was comprised of the multifaceted portfolio of tools, applications, and projects across data warehouses (DWs), data marts, master data management, extract-transform-load (ETL), and business intelligence (BI) areas.

The peculiarity of the portfolio was characterized by the complexity; geographical diversity; and heavy investments in projects, operations, and maintenance. These investments were primarily driven by functional organizations and affiliate sites dispersed across the corporation's worldwide regions and countries. The portfolio evolved over time in a stepwise manner and was highly disjointed, consisting of an array of fragmented functional implementations with partial integration and no standardization across the enterprise.

Coupled with this, the DWs and data marts were widespread and growing rapidly. The corporation owned multiple supplier software solutions in the BI and data integration (DI) areas, giving rise to the redundancy of functionalities. Enterprise-wide mechanisms to govern the creation and management of DWs, to provide the direction around tools, and to harmonize technology were all lacking. The corporation's cross-functional and/or global needs were being compromised due to lack of production of the integrated views of the data, complex DI issues, and a weak information culture. A few examples of these needs were:

- Exploratory and confirmatory analysis of clinical trial data
- Reporting on cross-study data that required integration across preclinical, clinical, and safety functions
- Reporting physician spend to regulatory authorities
- Generation of a full view of the customers (doctors, patients, key opinion leaders, and key accounts)

The corporation could not transform these needs into a strategic advantage with the implementations that were in place.

Overall, this fact gave rise to critical challenges:

- The current environment was seen as heterogeneous by users. As a result, a holistic (360-degree) view of the underlying information could not be achieved.

- Data redundancies and reporting redundancies gave rise to data quality and metadata issues and users being less confident in the data, which affected business users' decision making.
- Organizational silos limited the reuse of know-how and skill sets.
- Creation of cross-functional views was time consuming. It required a great deal of coordination in the form of copying the data from one environment to another and led to unmanaged data and multiple copy chains.
- High operational overheads resulted, due to the substantial redundant investments in projects, tools, and the infrastructure.
- There was an increased total cost of ownership due to: lack of enterprise-wide maintenance terms; multiple invoices to multiple locations with multiple points of contacts; tactical projects consistently lacking budget, leading to opportunities lost or reverting to manual coding efforts; and absence of cost-effective procurement structure.

Maintaining the status quo had become increasingly problematic. The huge footprint hampered the corporation's ability to respond to changing business needs in a timely fashion and to maintain a competitive advantage. The aforementioned challenges were shared universally by the business and IT. However, since the business was siloed, the corporation faced difficulties in receiving the singular business sponsorship. A fundamental overhaul was necessary via enterprise-wide IT strategy creation, delivery, and implementation that would achieve a sustainable business impact from people, process, and technology perspectives. The IT leadership committee (included the global CIO and direct reports) recognized that further derailing was no longer acceptable and thus decided to sponsor this effort.

IT STRATEGY CREATION PROCESS

The vice president of the architecture, governance, and strategic IT services group acted as the sponsor and appointed the author to lead this effort. The challenges were enormous and the expectations were high with the IT strategy affecting the corporation's five worldwide regions, which included over 30 countries.

The goals were:

- To deliver an overarching strategy that will consolidate and harmonize the complex data warehousing, BI, and DI landscape without compromising the underlying information needs.
- To define future architecture vision and create a long-term road map that will harness the value of information the corporation possesses and leverage the corporation's investment in the operational systems.
- To embrace a federated approach that will promote integration of various DWs in a coherent manner in alignment with the functional area road maps and portfolios. The goal was not to pursue a big-bang approach (e.g., creation of a single, monolithic, enterprise-wide DW) but rather to adopt an evolutionary approach.

- To deliver the guidance for the decision makers and governing bodies on how to respond to new data warehousing, BI, and DI project requests.
- To deliver the key recommendations that, if approved, would lead to concrete actions whereby the aforementioned road map would be executed in the form of creation, execution, and monitoring of specific projects, programs, and/or foundational capabilities.

The formation of a cross-functional task force was proposed to ensure that each of the key constituents had a seat at the table, that their subject matter expertise could be leveraged, and that their needs and pain points could be understood in order to come up with an optimal future direction. The IT leadership committee approved this approach. Some key constituent groups (stakeholders) that had representation on the cross-functional task force were supply chain and finance; human resources; clinical development; sales and marketing; infrastructure; and supplier management.

This cross-functional task force delivered the rationalization in the form of:

- A comprehensive assessment of the current environment (the fact base) in the form of inventory of the number of the DWs, BI tools, DI products, underlying subject areas, data sources, user base, geography, and licensing and maintenance costs for various supplier products and platforms
- Rationale for the change including the pain points, missed opportunities, and suboptimal activities
- Construction of the guiding principles for important areas, such as data warehousing, BI, infrastructure, validated versus nonvalidated environment, governance, and supplier management
- The characteristics of the future state environment with the focus on people, technology, and process aspects
- Articulation of the envisioned future state landscape in the form a long-term road map
- Identification of the standardized tools for back-end DW, front-end BI, and DI to support the future-state landscape
- Concrete recommendations that produced actionable results

 ## CREATING PROJECT PROPOSALS AS A RESULT OF DRIVING AN IT STRATEGY

IT strategy was driven from various fronts that ultimately led to the creation of project proposals, business cases, and organizational structures (e.g., cross-functional programs and integration competency centers). Some of the key elements (not in any particular order of importance) that constituted the successful conclusion of IT strategy were:

- **Active communication between cross-functional team members and stakeholders.** The cross-functional task force was global in nature. The stakeholders were located across multiple geographies that operated in different time zones. Communication took the form of weekly teleconferences, e-mails, and video conferences, with additional meetings coming in the form of face-to-face facilitated workshops. The goals of these meetings were manifold in nature, namely listening and understanding the pain points of the IT stakeholders, leveraging their subject matter expertise, generating a comprehensive understanding of the current environment, and devising recommendations.

- **Regular communication with various leadership teams.** In addition to the lateral communications, upward communication with the governing bodies (such as the IT leadership committee, the leadership and management teams of individual IT leadership committee members, architecture review board members, and the business portfolio planning committees) took place in the form of submitting status reports, discussing roadblocks, escalation of issues, scope verifications, and doing presentations in the formal forums.
- **Subject area–specific DW design.** To design the future data warehousing landscape, the greenfield approach was embraced. The approach here was to go beyond the functional boundaries, adhere to the guiding principles, understand the fundamental information needs, formulate relevant use cases, and then devise the target number of DWs the corporation would need.

  The cross-functional task force came up with about 50 key use cases. These use cases were logically clustered to see which use cases fit into which buckets of the subject areas to construct DWs accordingly. The notion of subject areas revolved around the notion of business processes (which by definition were cross-functional in nature). Subject areas were defined as a logically related set of business processes about which the corporation needed information (e.g., subject areas were defined as sales, customer, clinical, supply chain, human resources, finance, etc.).
- **Strategic road map construction.** The strategic road map was constructed by prioritizing various project activities and by taking into account the functional area road maps. For example, creation of business-driven cross-functional subject area DWs and data marts; reengineering of existing data warehousing landscape (via integration, consolidation, or retirement of legacy environments); design and configuration of the back-end data warehousing landscape; provisioning of ongoing project support by developing a repository of shared reports, queries, data models, guidelines, and naming conventions; and construction of the financial business cases for and set-up of an enterprise-wide BI and ETL platforms.
- **Work stream creation.** A divide-and-conquer approach was followed by creating various work streams for critical areas such as BI, data warehousing landscape, and ETL. The corporation had six software suppliers for BI and five software suppliers for ETL. The primary goal was to conduct rationalization and drive alignment whereby enterprise-wide standards would be chosen.
- **DW and BI software supplier selection process.** The process was geared toward making recommendations around the general-purpose BI tools (e.g., querying, analytics, reporting, and dashboarding). Special-purpose BI tools (e.g., visualization, data mining, and predictive analytics) were omitted due to the

specialized requirements the corporation possessed. Internal users were approached to understand their requirements and experiences with BI tool usage. Finally, supplier days were organized.

■ **ETL software supplier selection process.** ETL supplier selection strategy was handled at a later stage due to high priorities associated with DW and BI supplier strategy aspects. Existing ETL capabilities were assessed in terms of the projects, tools, and the requirements of ETL functionality. Current-state ETL landscape was constructed, and gap analysis was performed.

In both cases described (i.e., DW and BI supplier selection and ETL supplier selection), suppliers were asked to present an overview of their capabilities and to explain the product fit (as they saw it) with the corporation's requirements and culture. Research analysts from Gartner, Inc. and Forrester were consulted to understand the supplier landscape in terms of market leadership, supplier road map, associated risks for the corporation, competitive landscape, industry benchmarks, and best practices. Additionally, would-be suppliers were asked to provide references. The task force members conducted series of interviews with these references to validate supplier capabilities. Finally, product rating matrices were constructed that included various criteria with weighted averages. Task force members completed the matrix denoting BI supplier and ETL supplier of his or her choice. An average was derived from each task force member's evaluation, and a strategic recommendation was formulated.

■ **Development of financial business cases.** Creating a compelling financial business case was vital to obtaining buy-in from the IT leadership committee and other governing bodies. Lists of assumptions, constraints, and rationale were documented, which in turn served as a basis for constructing the business cases for adopting enterprise-wide BI and DI/ETL platforms. Adopting this approach allowed the corporation to set the context for decision making. A number of solution alternatives were articulated that took into account pros and cons in terms of costs, benefits, risks, and complexity. Although the business case benefits were articulated, it was understood that the ability to realize the portrayed benefits hinged on the respective global delivery/implementation teams taking it to fruition.

■ **Business case for adopting an enterprise-wide BI platform.** The notion here was to create optimistic and pessimistic scenarios and to understand which one was most justifiable. Efficiency gains and savings were calculated for each of the key constituent user groups. On the benefits side, several parameters were identified from different angles, such as full-time-equivalent (FTE) productivity gains, generation of standardized reports, reduced manageability costs, in-house expertise, and resource collaboration.

The additional investments needed due to the migration of existing nonstandard platforms, infrastructure scalability to accommodate data growth, injection of external consultancy expertise, additional staffing headcounts (e.g., architecture, programming support, and other FTE aspects) were taken into account. These were then compared and contrasted with the corporation's current BI spend, which came primarily in the form of software licensing and maintenance

costs for multiple BI vendors, projects, and operational costs to keep the environments running.

- **Business case for adopting an enterprise-wide DI/ETL platform.** This step
  was focused on collecting an inventory of current and future DI projects. Various
  parameters were defined to compute the estimated costs—for example, expected
  project start date, months to develop with hand-coding or current ETL tools,
  estimated project completion time, estimated number of FTEs needed in the
  absence of a standardized ETL tool, ETL development costs (e.g., extracting data,
  creating mappings and transformations, applying business rules, and loading
  data into targets), and ETL production costs (e.g., code enhancements, bug fixes,
  change management), plus annual resources costs (which differed from continent to continent).

  These estimated costs were then compared and contrasted against projected
  savings, where another set of parameters was defined—for example, impact of
  standardized ETL tool in terms of reduced code rewriting and testing, projected labor
  savings, ability to share know-how consistently across the corporation, incremental
  ICC impact on projects, and cost avoidance (license and maintenance costs savings)
  realized through retirement of nonstandard ETL tools.

  Numerous scenarios were constructed that looked at computing future licensing and maintenance costs for various alternatives, such as staying with the status
  quo, pay as you go, paying based on the wish list, and achieving cost-effective
  licensing structure via enterprise-wide licensing agreements.

 ## RECOMMENDATIONS AND CURRENT STATUS

A set of key recommendations were made:

- Establishment of a cross-functional program to drive alignment with the architecture and redirect DW-related projects and operational activities where necessary.
  The cross-functional program would drive the creation of subject area DWs and
  relevant efforts.
- Funding a business intelligence competency center (BICC) to establish a global
  platform in order to bring together the various BI projects in a coordinated
  manner.
- Funding a data integration competency center (DICC) to establish a global platform in order to streamline DI activities in terms of the resources, infrastructure,
  skill sets, and training aspects.

The recommendations along with the needed funding were approved by the
respective governance bodies.

Current status to date is as follows:

- An organizational model has been established in the form of a cross-functional
  data warehousing department. Geographically dispersed resources with the

right know-how and subject matter experts have been brought together under the auspices of this department. It is currently providing oversights related to cross-functional projects, platform guidelines, relevant processes, and governance. The cross-functional task force is now in its second generation and continues to bring together cross-functional stakeholders via establishment of sounding boards.

■ Design and implementation activities with regard to the subject area–specific DWs have been launched.

■ The BICC has been launched. The first phase of the project has been concluded with the establishment of an enterprise-wide infrastructure and pilot projects. Subsequent phases have started with onboarding of projects for broader usage in all the functions.

■ The DICC currently is a work-in-progress project. The corporation has completed foundational activities, such as the competency center readiness assessment; completion of the financial business case depicting cost-benefit analysis, risk analysis and return on investment (ROI) calculation; adoption of an enterprise-wide DI supplier; and procurement of a cost-effective global licensing agreement. The business case and ROI justifications have been approved by the IT leadership committee. The DICC establishment commenced operations in early 2010.

LESSONS LEARNED

Ten common themes that we have found in dealing with many corporations are presented next. Some may be familiar, and some may be new.

1. **Executive management sponsorship with the support of business executives.** As the team leader working in a cross-functional, global matrix environment, the author had little authority or influence over the team members. Team members were dispersed across multiple countries and sites. Having a top-down mandate and formal sponsorship of the IT leadership committee turned out to be vital in overcoming the organizational barriers and easing change management aspects. Organizational barriers came in the form of team members committed to other projects who needed to negotiate with their supervisors and prioritize their time and their schedules.

   Key Message: Creating and executing enterprise-wide strategies represents a great change management effort from the perspectives of people, technology, and organizational process. It is imperative that organizational commitment exists. CIOs must support the IT strategic efforts through a formal, top-down sponsorship.

2. **Focusing on information requirements analysis.** A lesson learned in early project phases was to keep the future architecture approach and road map recommendations aligned with the underlying information requirements. In earlier recommendations, major emphasis was placed on rationalizing the DW landscape by reducing its numbers via consolidating and retiring DWs.

We realized that this approach was not intuitive enough and could not have accommodated the changing business requirements.

Soon thereafter, we shifted gears and placed the emphasis on collecting and documenting use cases. A set of 50 use cases were collected that aimed to address the pain points. These use cases were classified into two buckets: (1) needs specific to functional areas and (2) needs specific to cross-functional areas. Segregating the use cases in this manner allowed the team to define and solidify the architectural concepts at the right level of granularity. The advantage of this approach was that it achieved outcomes similar to those that the team wanted, but the approach was much more foundational in nature and met the changing business requirements.

Key Message: Think creatively about the future by incorporating the information requirements analysis. Document use cases and brainstorm to define architectural concepts at the right level of granularity.

3. **Coupling portfolio planning and enterprise architecture skills.** It is a well-understood fact that tight correlation exists between key disciplines: enterprise architecture, strategic planning, and enterprise portfolio management.[3] Successful harmony between and among these disciplines allows IT organizations to align process, technology, and people aspects with business strategy; to manage business requirements; and to make IT a credible partner in delivering value to the business.

   As the team leader, the author had to wear different hats as occasions demanded, especially around strategy planning, project management, and enterprise architecture areas.

   Key Message: CIOs should appoint an individual who is well versed in the aforementioned disciplines to drive IT strategic efforts.

4. **Selecting the cross-functional team members.** Due to the aggressive milestones and high expectations of the sponsors, failure was not an option. It was imperative that an agreed-on approach that balanced stakeholder needs along with long-term organizational priorities must be established. A cross-functional team had to be assembled of people with specific skills: a solid understanding of organizational history and culture and of the decision makers and their risk tolerances; substantial knowledge of data warehousing, BI, and DI areas; and the ability to positively influence decision makers. Each task force member had a vested interest since the strategy outcomes directly impacted his or her respective business needs. Thus, there was wholehearted participation.

   Key Message: Amplify chances of strategy success by selecting a team of people in the trenches who are technologically savvy and organizationally astute.

5. **Achieving Shared Goals.** Often the project experienced tough times, due to accelerated milestones, differences of opinions, presence of strong personalities, or simply because the author did not have answers to the issues or questions. Acting as a conduit and not a barrier went a long way. Team members appreciated dedication and forthrightness. Sharing the issues collectively with the team allowed the members to get involved and solve problems creatively, and gained their buy-in from the get-go.

Key Message: When working toward the shared goal, forge sustainable partnerships by developing trust, walking the walk, and demonstrating a high degree of integrity.

6. **Construction of the financial business case.** It is the author's experience that IT organizations typically are good at computing soft benefits. However, they face a perennial problem of computing quantitative ROI in terms of hard dollars to financially justify the undertaking. They are not savvy enough when it comes to constructing financial business cases that involve complex formulas and concepts such as present value, future value, and net present value.

   The construction of the financial business case for the BICC establishment was delivered internally, and it was certainly a tough act to follow. In order to construct the financial business for the DICC establishment, the corporation leveraged a consulting firm, Technology Finance Partners.

   Key Message: Given that CIOs now routinely demand financial ROIs and cost justifications, the author highly advises the hiring of a competent and knowledgeable consultant. Although this expense will be front-loaded, it should be looked at as an investment. You will impress the CIO as having done your homework and it will pay more dividends at the end, leading to successful project approval.

7. **Gathering best practices and understanding the competitive landscape.** The corporation had a subscription to services of research firms such as Gartner Inc. and Forrester. The cross-functional team took full advantage by leveraging their analyses. The added value came in the form of utilizing 30-minute complementary advisory calls. Additionally, the team was able to tap into the brain trust of would-be strategic suppliers and their references. A wealth of information was shared (e.g., supplier competitive landscape, road map, business climate, benchmarking data, and pros and cons of tool set capabilities) that helped facilitate discussions with the suppliers (e.g., requests for proposals and supplier days).

   Key Message: The 30-minute call passes before you know it, so proper homework (e.g., choosing which questions to ask) is crucial prior to making advisory calls. Would-be strategic suppliers had a vested interest in ensuring that the corporation succeeded in its undertakings.

8. **Executive management buy-in.** Getting organizational commitment through top-level sponsorship opened the door. However, it represented just one side of the coin. Keeping that door open was equally important. It ensured that the business case data and ROI justification figures represented the pain points of respective stakeholders. The IT leadership committee was aware of this fact, and hence the final approval process turned out to be a breeze.

   Key Message: Adopt a bottom-up approach by constructing the business case from the ground up to get CIO-level buy-in.

9. **Official communication of the strategy.** The corporation had a structured way to communicate the strategy (e.g., official announcements, web site news, intranet postings, and regular communication with the governing bodies). However, in this case, even before the official communication took place, other project teams started knocking on our door and were eager to embrace the

proposed architectural approach, future vision, and standards. This was a great demonstration of the power of word of mouth and the remarkable traction that was derived from it.

Key Message: Good work is contagious.

10. **Acknowledging completion and celebrating success.** Although leadership is important, successful delivery of any project is never the result of the work of any one individual. Rather, project success is achieved due to the collective efforts of a project team. After successful approval of the strategy, the author, as team leader, ensured that all the participants were recognized and rewarded by sending hand-written thank-you notes and formal gifts.

Key Message: Recognize and reward team members for outstanding performance.

 CONCLUSION

This chapter has described the key ingredients for creating project proposals by providing a real-world example and describing the considerations CIOs and IT executives need to take into account in terms of the linkage IT has with a corporation's strategic objectives.

 NOTES

1. Tony Murphy, *Achieving Business Value from Technology: A Practical Guide for Today's Executive* (Hoboken, NJ: John Wiley & Sons, 2002).
2. Based on the author's personal experiences with global corporations, such as Johnson & Johnson, Merck, and F. Hoffmann-La Roche AG from 1998 to 2009.
3. Meta Group, "Enterprise Program Management—Keys to Driving an Effective Project Portfolio," EPMO Executive Session, Somerset, NJ, November 13, 2002.

CHAPTER FIFTEEN

Requirements

Allyn McGillicuddy

R EQUIREMENTS ARE CENTRAL TO the IT system or solution because they are directly determined by the solution's goals. While goals are often broadly stated, they are not actionable until they are rationalized into smaller elements that can be enabled by the application of relevant technology. In this sense, requirements are actionable goal components.

The definition of a requirement is something wanted or needed. If it is no longer wanted or needed, it ceases to be a requirement. Requirements are classified as either user requirements or system requirements. User requirements describe what a user needs to perform his or her job. A system requirement states what the system must provide to satisfy or help satisfy the user requirement.

It therefore follows that the requirements definition is incomplete if, when all requirements are realized, their achievement has failed to fully implement a system that provides the services the user needs to perform his or her job, and has therefore failed to achieve the project goals. Based on the centrality of requirements to a project's goals, great care must be taken to ensure that the requirements were accurately delineated and understood from the inception of information systems development. The deliverable for the project requirement specification phase is the solution requirements specification document.

SOLUTION REQUIREMENTS SPECIFICATION

The solution requirements specification document identifies four things: (1) all functional and performance requirements; (2) the required formats for user data entry of inputs and screen/Web page or report outputs; (3) any required standards; and (4) all design constraints, such as security requirements. The primary deliverable of the requirements development process is stakeholder validation of all the requirements specified in the document.

This validation step is intended to ensure that the requirements specified in the document accurately reflect the most important business requirements or needs and that all requirements are included. Often a series of requirements reviews are undertaken to accomplish this milestone. A final sign-off, or formal acknowledgment that all requirements are accounted for, completes the requirements project phase and signals the transition to the next step in the project.

The resulting solution requirements specification (SRS) is a document that completely describes what the proposed system should do without describing how the system will do it. The basic goal of the requirement phase is to produce the SRS, which describes the complete external behavior of the proposed solution.

Requirements traceability is concerned with documenting the life of a requirement. Tracing the origin of each requirement should be possible, and every change made to the requirement should therefore be documented in order to achieve such traceability. Even the use of the requirement after the implemented features have been deployed should be traceable. Traceability makes it possible to answer the question, "Why is this feature or function needed?" at any point.

A complex project may have many stakeholder groups with a wide variety of business goals. If so, the review and sign-off process may be time consuming. Stakeholder representatives cycle on and off the project for various reasons, such as medical leave or promotions, and in many cases they may delegate project involvement to a subordinate. Initial orientation of a new project participant usually will add unplanned additional time to the process.

 REQUIREMENTS MANAGEMENT RISKS

It is not unusual for stakeholder groups to have overlapping or even conflicting goals. The challenge to resolve these conflicts falls on the chief information officer and his or her team to manage. Moreover, in the absence of timely management action to achieve consensus, business users can adopt a litigious approach, requiring many rounds of meetings to fine-tune the wording of the requirements. Such a protracted requirements definition process and the addition of multiple, analysis initiatives typically yield unwelcome results.

One common risk associated with this hazard is that the entire project budget might be depleted by the requirements phase, particularly for projects involving technology that was not well understood. In other cases, dynamic business and technology factors over the course of a long requirements phase can render target solutions elusive. Organizational change among developers and business users alike often thwarts timely completion of the requirements phase for projects with large scope and scale. The longer the time period needed to complete project requirements, the greater the risk that circumstances may affect the goals, scope, and/or budget of the project. Finally, financial dynamics often circumscribe the project opportunity and limit the scope in midstream.

Organizations have responded by limiting project scope boundaries to reduce these risks. By limiting the scope of the planned solution, fewer requirements are needed for its implementation. In addition, the lower cost of smaller-scale projects increases the likelihood of successful implementation and benefits realization.

STAKEHOLDER MANAGEMENT

In addition to managing project scope, the requirements process facilitates both communication among stakeholders and consensus as to how the goals will be achieved. This aspect of solutions development can comprise a perilous journey fraught with conflicting stakeholder needs and overt or covert political agendas.

A good example is the insurance company that successfully developed a claims management system for its subsidiary located in an eastern U.S. state. Although its first release was well received, myriad minor requirements remained unmet, awaiting the next release. However, when the development team launched the effort to implement the same system in its California subsidiary, it encountered a technically sophisticated and politically assertive user community determined to ensure the solution addressed every need in its first release. Over an additional two-year period, myriad requirements were defined, reviewed, and signed off.

As a result, at the conclusion of the requirements phase in 2004, the original $20 million budget had metastasized to $60 million. When this fact came to light, senior management scrapped the development project. Layoffs ensued, and five years later a solution was finally nearing implementation. The potential benefits of the earlier system were significantly delayed. Senior-level careers were also derailed as a result—an undesirable outcome for all.

Many projects do not encounter this level of risk, but the CIO's team must always manage expectations and user acceptance, beginning with solution scope definition and requirements definition. The requirements process influences the successful outcome of solution development more than any other aspect of development. It is the phase in which the two dancers of IT and the internal business departments encounter each other amid the music of opportunity.

Critical capabilities for success include agility (the ability to adapt to dynamic influences); commitment to close, effective communication; trust; confidence in each other's abilities; and commitment to a common goal. A well-managed requirement process can yield a memorable achievement comprising collegial, professional, and personal reward; its flawed counterpart may degrade into a nightmare to be dispatched quickly from memory. These are the stakes involved in effective requirements management.

However, in systems development, the dancers are not likely to hear the music in the same way. The systems developer usually lacks insight or understanding of the business client's problem domain, and the client has little empathy for constraints affecting system design. The nomenclature each party employs to discuss its viewpoint and its needs varies widely, further complicating effective communication. This large gap in perspective must be bridged adequately during requirements analysis.

The CIO's team must manage other stakeholders as well. IT development partners, both offshore and onshore, typically play an essential role in enterprises today. Well-understood requirements are central to effective leverage of development partners. Our development partners endeavor to the best of their ability to fulfill the requirements, but they naturally bill us for their efforts. If the requirements are not effectively communicated, the project will be burdened by a sunk cost as a result.

 ## QUALITY REQUIREMENTS

For any important development initiative, the requirements process must address the required quality of the solution. The question, "Exactly *how* round must the wheel be?" is always more easily posed than answered. Important stakeholders often disagree on this point. For the users, the quality must be very high. For the chief financial officer, it may not be as high, because higher quality comes at a higher cost. The CIO cannot be successful without a clear understanding of the business drivers underlying the requirements and parallel insight as to the appropriate quality and associated cost.

For this reason, the CIO must ensure that requirements designed to manage the appropriate level of quality are incorporated into the overall system requirements, along with defined measurement techniques. This is a high-risk area for many IT organizations. The risk is not the failure to measure quality in the results. Rather, it is that the metrics are not well matched to the nature of the required quality. Metrics are extremely effective in shaping development partner focus and behavior, for if we measure the wrong things, we are certain to achieve unintended results.

Mature IT organizations have learned that effective attention to requirements development influences the total cost of an initiative more than any other aspect of the systems development life cycle. If the defined requirements overshoot the appropriate scope of the project, the result is project cost overruns, delivery delays, and sometimes cancellation. If the requirements fail to address the needed business functionality, the expected benefits may decline as users or, worse, customers abandon it. If the requirements are not effectively shaped to yield the intended business benefits, the return on investment is curtailed.

 ## EMERGENCE OF PROTOTYPING FOR NEW REQUIREMENTS

To reduce many of these risks, prototyping emerged as an effective means of achieving the goals of requirements development. Barry Boehm's 1981 breakthrough book,

Software Engineering Economics, offered quantified evidence that prototyping reduces a typical project's completion time and cost by 40 percent.[1] Using this approach, instead of fully elaborating on the high-level requirements and then freezing the requirements before design or coding can proceed, a prototype is built to more fully understand and communicate the requirements.

Based on currently known requirements, an informal representation of the solution aids business users and developer alike to get an actual feel for the system and its functionality. By interacting with a prototype, stakeholders gain an improved understanding of what is really needed and how the system could or should be used.

Many organizations employ a series of prototypes to complete development of the system, refining the functionality through multiple iterations. Each prototype iteration provides increased functional capability until the full system is implemented. Extensions and design modifications can be made in each delivery step. An advantage of this approach is that it usually results in more effective testing, since the testing of each increment is likely to be less complex than testing the entire system all at once.

A wide range of prototyping is available to project teams. These range from paper-based prototypes to interactive prototypes that offer users the ability to interact directly with the system. Various prototyping alternatives are reviewed in the next section. Prototypes employed early in the development process deliver the most significant advantages because they help stakeholders test their assumptions before investing time and money. The dilemma is that it takes time and money to develop prototypes. The team must strike a balance by employing several approaches to prototyping throughout the project.

Wire-Frames/Paper Prototypes

Wire-frames and paper prototypes are useful in the project's early stages, but their utility is limited because they only crudely represent the target solution. They are not interactive and usually represent very broad user options. In one developer's words, "If our project were to be painting a landscape, you might think of wire-frames and paper prototypes as the early sketches on a notepad, or some under-painting. In other words, suggesting the basic shape but not saying much about the details."[2] While rough in nature, this style of prototype is valuable because it can identify problems very early in the development cycle. As a result, significant and unnecessary costs can be avoided.

Visual Prototypes

Visual prototypes are static images representing planned application Web pages. The links portrayed on the page are not functional, but they depict more accurately what the user will see than a wire-frame can depict. They might be visual mock-ups rather than true prototypes, inasmuch as they represent potential appearances and layouts. A facilitator references these while asking the prototypical user, "What would you expect to do on this page?" They are most useful in validating user interface design, but they can also validate various approaches to navigation and functional design (see Figure 15.1).

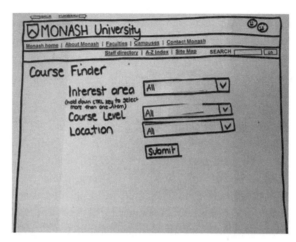

FIGURE 15.1   Paper Prototype of a Web Page

Interactive Prototypes

Interactive prototypes are similar to visual prototypes, but they offer limited interactive functionality. While these are more useful than visual prototypes, they involve increased investment in time to produce. Their goal is to model the system design with greater detail and represent the designed navigation through the system. They typically combine the visual design with limited interactive functionality, such as navigation or the use of real Web controls. These offer the richest, most effective prototype, but they require more time to create, so they become available later in a development project.

Spiral Prototyping Model

The spiral model or cyclone methodology further developed prototyping as a means of defining requirements by adding rigor through risk analysis, measurement, and benchmarking. Proposed by Boehm in 1988, this approach defines iterative prototyping cycles in the spiral.[3] In each cycle, the design team defines potential alternatives to achieve project objectives, and constraints such as time and cost are imposed to discern the appropriate solution approach (see Figure 15.2).

The identified alternatives, using the spiral model, are evaluated against the understood objectives, constraints, uncertainties, and risks. The development team crafts strategies to effectively manage the identified uncertainties and risks: the known unknowns. The selected solution attempts to incorporate risk mitigation by employing strategies that address the uncertainties while satisfying cost, time, technology, deployment, and support constraints. Various alternatives are investigated and prototyped to reduce or mitigate the risk associated with the development decisions.

The spiral approach has enjoyed greater popularity among aerospace, defense, and engineering (ADE) specialists than among business developers. The risks and scope of ADE projects may warrant their use, while the approach may be unnecessarily complex and laborious for less risky business endeavors of smaller scale.

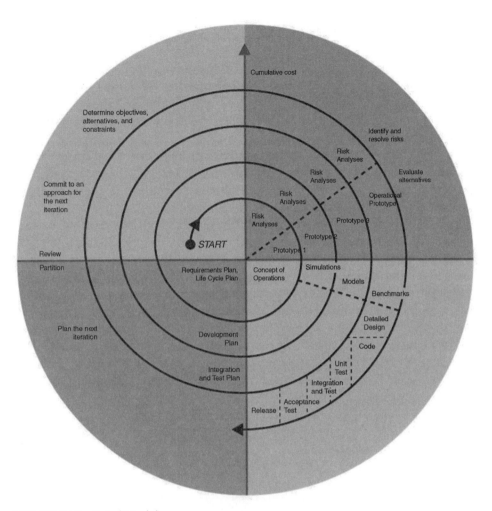

FIGURE 15.2 Spiral Model

Source: Barry Boehm, "A Spiral Model of Software Development and Enhancement," *Computer*, IEEE, 21(5): 61–72, © 1988 IEEE.

When balancing the advantages and disadvantages of prototyping, the CIO's team should consider these factors:[4]

- Breadth of functionality needed in the prototype at first and then later on
- Choice of prototyping tool and its limitations
- Completion criteria for the iteration cycle
- Composition of the team (users, developers, other stakeholders)
- Level of fidelity needed in the prototype at first and then later on
- Maximum length of an iteration cycle
- Purpose of the prototype at first and then later on
- Ways to manage conflict between team members and to build consensus

Some top prototyping risks include:

- Prototyping may encourage many change requests.
- Prototyping may lead stakeholders to believe that the final product is almost ready for delivery.
- The excellent (or disappointing) performance characteristics of prototypes may mislead the stakeholder.
- Stakeholder availability to provide the level or frequency of feedback required for iterative prototyping is often lacking.

DYNAMIC SYSTEMS DEVELOPMENT METHODOLOGY

Dynamic Systems Development Methodology (DSDM) emerged in the late 1990s as a response to the failure of large-scale systems and network infrastructure projects that never reached implementation. A precursor to rapid application development and Agile development methods, a DSDM development project is constrained by an imposed time frame.

For example, a project will be designated as comprising four weeks. In the first week, the requirements will be developed. In the second week, the system will be designed. In the third week, the system will be developed, followed by a week for quality assurance and deployment (see Figure 15.3).

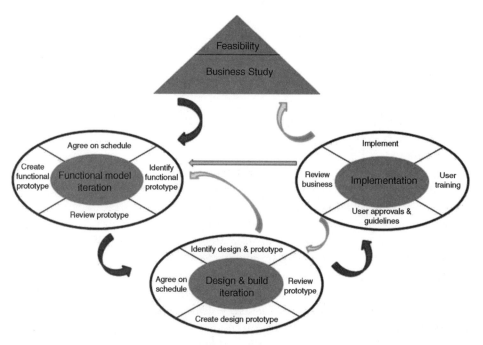

FIGURE 15.3 Process Diagram Depicting the DSDM Model

Full collaboration among business users and developers is assured by sequestering the team for a sequence of iterative development cycles concluding with production deployment. The central stakeholders work side by side on every aspect of the project through implementation, a method that prevents the disadvantages of asynchronous collaboration cycles.

With DSDM, teams avoid a protracted requirements definition and analysis period by quickly defining the baseline, high-level requirements. Rapid prototyping by the converged team of business users and developers serves to develop the requirements further. With fitness for business purpose the primary measurement for acceptance, the team continues incremental prototyping until the functional model emerges. The team collaborates further to develop an analysis model and some rudimentary system components that comprise the major functionality.

 ## MANAGING REQUIREMENTS WITH THE UNIFIED DEVELOPMENT PROCESS

The Unified Development Process, or Unified Software Development Process, is a widely used system development methodology today. The most prevalent version of this approach is the Rational Unified Process, or RUP. The methodology is based on incremental iterative steps or phases. Requirements are developed primarily in the first two phases of the Unified Development Process: the inception and elaboration phases.

Deliverables for the inception phase include:

- Project justification or business case
- Project scope definition
- Expected use cases and key requirements that will drive the solution design
- One or more candidate architecture approaches
- Key project risks
- Preliminary project schedule
- Preliminary cost estimate

Requirements artifacts with greater detail are produced in the Unified Development Process elaboration phase. These artifacts include use cases and scenarios. Use cases define the functional requirements and the scope of each iteration. Ivar Jacobsen, a major contributor to the development of the Unified Development Process, developed a visual modeling technique to create use cases in 1986. During the 1990s, use cases were used increasingly to capture functional requirements, particularly among developers using object-oriented technologies for systems development.

A use case describes how an actor, or user of the system, will interact with the planned solution to achieve a goal or a task. A use case may be related to one or more features, and a feature may be related to one or more use cases. While there is no single standard for documenting use cases, most versions include sections that define goals, actors, stakeholders, preconditions, triggers, postconditions, and business rules.

Use-case templates are widely available, and many development organizations share a standard set of templates to facilitate a common understanding among stakeholders regarding the solution requirements and expected functionality.

There are two types of use cases: business use cases and system use cases. A business use case employs no technical terms. The business use case describes the business process used by actors to achieve the desired business goals. A system use case, however, describes system functionality—a function or service that the system provides. Examples of system use cases are "create voucher" and "schedule future payment."

The Unified Development Process employs "scenarios," along with use cases, to graphically and textually describe the foreseeable interactions of users with the planned system. Scenarios identify the system goals, stakeholder expectations, and user actions and reactions to portray the way in which a system will be used. Scenarios, like use cases, replace or supplement traditional functional requirements. Scenarios often are used in usability testing and in other forms of quality assurance to validate the system functionality.

Many versions of the Unified Development Process have proliferated over the past two decades, including the Oracle Unified Method, the Open Unified Process developed by Eclipse Process Framework software development practitioners, a lightweight version developed by Jacobsen called the Essential Unified Process, and the Agile Unified Process.

AGILE REQUIREMENTS MANAGEMENT

The Agile Manifesto, drafted in February 2001, stated a set of principles that defined Agile system development.[5] Its authors were representatives from various approaches, including DSDM, extreme programming, Scrum, adaptive software development, Crystal, feature-driven development, and pragmatic programming. What they had in common was an interest in finding an alternative to prevailing documentation-driven, heavyweight software development processes. Its original authors met at the Lodge at the Snowbird ski resort in the Wasatch Range of mountains in Utah to discuss various approaches.

The central values of Agile system development that emerged from that historic meeting are:

- Individuals and interactions take precedence over processes and tools.
- Working systems take precedence over comprehensive documentation.
- Customer collaboration takes precedence over contract negotiation.
- Responding to change takes precedence over following a plan.

Agile system development practitioners expect requirements to evolve throughout a project. As a result, they regard any early investment in detailed documentation to be counterproductive. Using this approach, the team believes that initial requirements will sufficiently identify the project scope, enable development of a high-level schedule, and allow estimation of the magnitude of effort and cost.

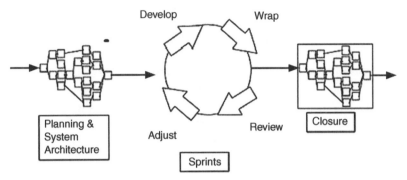

FIGURE 15.4 Process Diagram Depicting an Agile Scrum "Sprint," or One Iteration

Proponents of Agile-oriented requirements management assert that Agile approaches to system development deliver value to organizations and end users faster and with higher quality. The initial goal for Agile requirements management is to implement the highest-priority requirements first. Using a technique called Scrum, requirements are frozen for a defined solution iteration to provide a level of stability for the developers (see Figure 15.4).

Stakeholder collaboration is central for the Agile development process, and there is a need to have on-site access to people—typically users or their representatives—who have the authority and ability to provide information pertaining to the system being built and to make pertinent and timely decisions regarding the requirements and prioritization thereof (see Figure 15.5).

Other requirements for successful Agile development include:

1. **Timely decisions.** Stakeholders must to be prepared to share business knowledge with the team and to make both pertinent and timely decisions regarding project scope and requirement priorities.

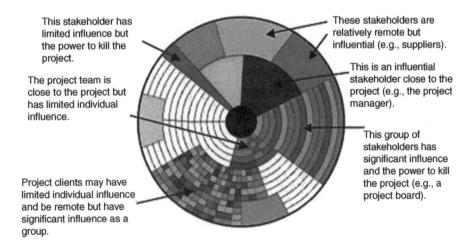

FIGURE 15.5 Project Stakeholder Analysis

2. **Inclusive modeling.** The team employs modeling techniques based on user-centered design and participatory design principles, which stakeholders can easily learn and adopt.

3. **Management requires IT skill and knowledge.** For senior managers to effectively support the project, they must first understand the technologies and techniques that the team is using, why the team is using them, and their implications. This knowledge makes their efforts within your organization's political arena more likely to be effective at the right times in the right ways. Senior managers aren't able to gain this requisite knowledge simply by reading a weekly project status report or by attending a monthly project steering meeting. Instead, they need to invest the necessary time to learn about the things that they manage, and to actively participate in the system development.

4. **Production staff are involved from the start.** Operations and support organizations must invest the resources required to understand both the system and the technologies that it will use. Project support staff must take the time to learn the nuances of the planned system, because they need to work with the system as it is developed. The development team must provide them with training. Furthermore, the system operations staff must become proficient with both the installation and operation of the planned solution. One or two operations engineers should serve on the development team in order to train operations staff on the planned system. Irrespective of development of approach, both operations and support organizations will need to be actively involved with the project development team.

5. **Take an enterprise view.** Designers and developers must work with other project teams when the solution system is integrated with other systems. For example, perhaps the proposed system needs to access a legacy database, interact with an online system, work with a data file produced by an external system, or provide an XML data extract for other systems. Integration often proves difficult if not impossible without the active participation of developers of these systems: Imagine how difficult it would be to access the information contained in a large legacy database if the owners of that database weren't able or available to provide any information about that database. Some initial architecture envisioning will help to drive this integration and interaction.

6. **Don't just hand-off to the maintenance team.** Maintenance developers need to learn the proposed system. When the developers' intentions are to either partially or completely hand off the maintenance of the system to other IT professionals, it is necessary to prepare them to take over the system once it is launched. Even when some original team members are still involved after deployment, an effort must be made to transfer the knowledge to the newer members of the team.[6]

Agile developers are expected to adopt multiple roles during the development process, including responsibility for usability testing and quality assurance testing. Alan Cooper illustrates this point in his seminal book, *The Inmates Are Running the*

Asylum: Why High Tech Products Drive Us Crazy and How to Restore the Sanity, in which he outlines several important techniques for effective requirements definition.[7]

One of Cooper's recommendations is to identify prototypical user groups and their distinguishing characteristics. These can be personalized by naming them, assigning demographic characteristics aligned with their prototype, such as gender, age, education level, role, and so on. The designers then consider product capabilities designed specifically for the prototypical users. Designers will gain insight by developing usability test cases that correspond with identified user prototypes.

 ## AGILE REQUIREMENTS MANAGEMENT: ITERATION 0

Initial requirements analysis, called envisioning, usually occurs in the first week of a project. The objective of envisioning is to identify the solution scope and the likely architecture to address it. Envisioning entails both high-level requirements modeling and high-level architecture modeling. The goal is not to write detailed specifications but rather to examine the requirements and identify an overall project strategy.

For a short project, such as one several weeks in length, envisioning may require only a few hours. For longer ventures, two weeks may be required. More time than this imposes the risk of over-modeling and of modeling something that contains too many problems.

The first stage of an Agile project—iteration 0, or the initiation phase—explicitly includes an initial architectural modeling effort. This initial architecture modeling is viewed as essential for scaling Agile system development techniques to large, complex, or globally distributed development efforts. The goal of the initial architecture modeling effort is to identify an architecture that has a good chance of working. This initial model establishes the technical direction with sufficient information to organize a team around the architecture.

Requirements at this point often entail free-form diagrams depicting the technical infrastructure and initial domain models in order to explore the major business entities and their relationships. Succeeding iterations reflect evolving understanding and refinement of the initial architectural models. The developer considers alternatives to implement each requirement, modeling where appropriate to explore or communicate ideas. This modeling is, in effect, the analysis and design of the requirements being implemented for the immediate iteration.

Developers collaborate with two or three colleagues on an impromptu basis, discussing an issue while sketching on paper or, more commonly, a whiteboard. These "model-storming" sessions typically last for 5 to 10 minutes. (It is rare to model-storm for more than 30 minutes.) The participants gather around a shared modeling tool (e.g., the whiteboard), explore the issue until they are satisfied that they understand it, and then continue implementing the solution.

Model-storming is just-in-time modeling: You identify an issue that you need to resolve, enlist a few teammates who can help explore the issue, and then everyone continues on as before. Extreme programmers call such model-storming sessions "stand-up design sessions" or "customer Q&A sessions."[8]

FEATURE-DRIVEN DEVELOPMENT

Like requirements management in other Agile methodologies, feature-driven development (FDD) is an iterative and incremental system development process. Created by Peter Coad and Jeff de Luca in 2002, FDD combines the Agile methodologies with model-driven techniques that scale to very large-scope projects comprising large teams. The approach employs development of a feature list to manage functional requirements and development tasks. A feature tends to be a "higher-level" objective than a requirement and is usually more focused on business needs rather than implementation.

Solution requirements analysis begins with a high-level examination of the scope of the system and its context. Next, the team assesses the domain in detail for each modeling area. Small groups then compose a model for each domain and present the model for peer review. The team selects one of the proposed models or a combination thereof. The model chosen becomes the model for that particular domain area. Then domain area models are merged into an overall model, which is subject to continuous review and adjustment.

Each domain then is functionally decomposed into subject areas. Subject areas each contain business activities, and the steps within each business activity comprise its feature list. Features in this respect are small pieces of client-valued functions expressed in the form <action> <result> <object>. "Calculate the total of a sale" or "Validate the password of a user" are features, for example. Features typically take less than two weeks to complete.

 REQUIREMENTS MANAGEMENT TOOLS

Requirements management involves organizing an expanding and changing set of details that comprise the final specification. Requirements management tools enable teams to efficiently gather requirements, track them, manage requirements, and measure success. Software solutions are available for storing the requirements for all specifications of a proposed technical system. The requirements are organized into a specification tree, in which each requirement can be traced directly to its "parent" requirement in the higher specification.

Requirements management systems share four goals:

1. Alignment of IT and business requirements
2. Project scope optimization
3. Stakeholder relationship optimization
4. Requirements-driven development

Widely used requirements management software systems include CaliberRM (Borland Software Corporation), Dimensions RM (Serena Software, Inc.), OptimalTrace (Compuware Corporation), RequisitePro (International Business Machines), and IrqA (Visure Solutions).

Another software solution, GatherSpace.com, is a lower-end, on-demand require-ments management product offering tailored to Agile development methods. The solution includes a use case modeling visualization tool. iRise is a popular offering that also allows business users to visualize how the planned system will work. The system and others like it are useful for prototyping widely implemented enterprise resource planning systems such as SAP, mobile device applications, and Web 2.0 features.

 ## REQUIREMENTS MANAGEMENT SYSTEMS

IT organizations that employ requirements management software systems report significant improvement in the solution development processes. While they require time and effort to master, the benefits are significant:

- Requirements management tools enable gathering "structured" requirements. For example, users may define attributes captured for each requirement (e.g., requester, date needed, owner).
- Automated requirements management tasks, such as creating requirements documents, save time.
- Good requirements management software tools have built-in work flow and best practices for tasks commonly related to requirements management.
- A good requirements system enables efficient and effective stakeholder collaboration.

The International Council on Systems Engineering publishes and periodically updates a comparison of features for many requirements management tools. Its web site, found at www.incose.org, also offers a good discussion of the minimum capabilities of requirements management tools. Copies of its survey results can be downloaded.[9]

 ## CONCLUSION

Requirements, and techniques to manage them, are integral to successful solution design, delivery, and deployment. Requirements determine the solution's scope, what is included in the solution, and what is omitted. The resulting scope definition directly impacts both the cost and the fulfillment of stakeholder goals.

Well-defined and well-understood requirements directly determine a project's chance of success. Investment in requirements management definition is a proven contributor to on-time and on-budget project outcomes with acceptable features and functions. Poor requirements management processes (or their absence) have been identified as a leading cause of project failure.

Solution designers and developers have introduced a wide range of methodo-logy and structured processes for requirements definition and gathering. Some approaches are contained in software development systems and tools, while others facilitate collaboration among developers, business users, and other stakeholders. In many cases, the benefits of improved methodologies and tools serve to reduce risk of project failure.

Selection of the best methodology and/or tools may involve assessing the project stakeholders, the risks, and the project constraints and modifying the project scope for the best fit. Prototyping often is used to accelerate a shared understanding of the required solution dimensions and to avoid misdirected approaches as early as possible. An effective methodology facilitates collaboration among stakeholders to identify and manage the risk of conflicting goals.

The trend today is to implement approaches to requirements management that avoid long, protracted requirements phases. Recent successes favor a sequence of rapid, iterative development cycles that incorporate requirements management software and services to optimize project efficiency and foster improved collaboration. Additionally, today's successful CIOs employ rigorous risk management and feature-oriented approaches to improve the chances for project success.

 NOTES

1. Barry W. Boehm, *Software Engineering Economics* (Englewood Cliffs, NJ: Prentice Hall, 1981).
2. Reynard Thomson, "What Is Software Prototyping?" www.reynardthomson.com/what-is-prototyping.html.
3. Barry Boehm, "A Spiral Model of Software Development and Enhancement," *Computer*, IEEE, 21(5):61–72.
4. Walter Maner, "Prototyping," 1997, csweb.cs.bgsu.edu/maner/domains/Proto.htm#1 1997.
5. Jim Highsmith, "History: The Agile Manifesto," http://agilemanifesto.org/history.html, 2001.
6. Scott W. Ambler, "Active Stakeholder Participation: An Agile Best Practice," www.agilemodeling.com/essays/activeStakeholderParticipation.htm.
7. Alan Cooper, *The Inmates Are Running the Asylum: Why High Tech Products Drive Us Crazy and How to Restore the Sanity* (Indianapolis, IN: Macmillan, 1999).
8. Scott W. Ambler, "Agile Model Driven Development (AMDD): The Key to Scaling Agile Software Development," www.agilemodeling.com/essays/amdd.htm.
9. See INCOSE Requirements Management Tools Survey, http://www.incose.org/ProductsPubs/Products/rmsurvey.aspx.

CHAPTER SIXTEEN

Project Risk Management

Sam Chughtai

A NEW AGE OF RISK MANAGEMENT IN A GLOBAL, INTERCONNECTED WORLD

Today, business and projects are different. Today's projects are agile, complex, and characterized by a vast, complicated network of business relationships teeming with technology, process, regulatory compliance, and sensitive information. A single high-risk unmanaged relationship or variable can be a ticking bomb. Today your business or a mission-critical project may be at risk whether you realize it or not, especially if you do not have an independent risk assessment and reporting function in place during the project life cycle.

Today, risk management must be strategically insightful and tactically consistent, and cross-functional across the enterprise—and as fast and reliable as the underlying technology that drives it. Costly solutions for governance, risk assessment, and subjective compliance reporting that offer only compliance comfort are no longer enough. In this new age, you need the independence, transparency, and standardization of an on-demand risk management intelligence as an in-flight check (IFC) to sustain a high degree of confidence in successful project delivery.

WHY PROJECT RISK MANAGEMENT?

Big projects fail at an astonishing rate, causing a multitude of impacts ranging from brand value, market share compromise, reputational impact, and regulatory compliance risk. A lack of transparency and independent project oversight causes a loss of objectivity in project progress reporting. Missed project deadlines and deliverables often are not reported or are misrepresented in reporting until it is too late.

When a promising project does not deliver, chances are that the problem was not the idea but *how it was carried out.* Managers expect they can plan for all the variables in a complex project in advance, but this simply is not possible. *The number and frequency of variables in complex projects create a virtually infinite range of possible outcomes.*

Large projects still fail at an astonishing rate despite a strong project management office, all the Ivy League MBAs, and Big Four audits on board.[1]

KEY EXECUTIVE CHALLENGES

In global enterprise complex projects, what keeps executives up at night?

- "Can I deliver what I committed to my business?"
- "Can I trust the executive reporting provided by my team?"
- "What is my project team not telling me?"

Most executives find out the hard way when it is too late to fix a major failure.

How Big Is the Problem?

It is estimated that of the $255 billion spent per year on information technology projects in the United States, more than a quarter is lost to failures and cost overruns. The Chaos Report by the Standish Group, considered a landmark study, looked at the causes of software development failure.[2] The sample included large, medium, and small companies across major industry segments: banking, securities, manufacturing, retail, wholesale, heath care, insurance, services, and local, state, and federal organizations. The total sample size was 365 respondents representing 8,380 applications.

The report shows that:

- 31.1 percent of IT projects will be canceled before completion.
- 52.7 percent of projects will overrun their original cost estimate by 189 percent.
- U.S. companies will spend $81 billion for canceled IT projects.
- They will pay an additional $59 billion for ongoing IT projects that exceed time limits.
- Only 16.2 percent of IT projects are completed on time and on budget. (In larger companies, this rate drops to 9 percent, and only 42 percent of these retain the original features.)

In a recent study by the Gartner Group, many CIOs reveal that identifying and mitigating project risks are critical steps, especially when cost overruns are no longer tolerated.[3] Cost overruns and outright project failures represent millions of lost investment dollars and opportunity costs that are incurred far too often. Businesses can no longer afford failed projects.

C-level management and the board receive a range of staff responses when they ask, "Why is the project failing?" Responses may include:

- The selected technology did not work as expected and is complicated.
- User requirements and expectations were not managed well or clearly defined.
- Resources were not managed to achieve the desired business value.
- Too many project changes resulted in an overly complex system that was hard to test.
- We have vendor delivery problems or internal management challenges.

Most failed project analysis reveals that even direct staff members fail to admit and were unable to explain why the last project health reports before project failure admission were "all OK" or "all on track." Lack of independent project status reporting has been identified as a fundamental problem in a majority of the failed projects.

Independent third-party objective project data verification and validation is critical to the entire life cycle of a project, and it is essential to minimizing an IT project's exposure to failure. Early project delta identification and course correction results in a high degree of project success.

IFC is a third-party, independent risk management solution for large projects. Research indicates that many complex, high-cost private- and public-sector projects develop significant cost overruns, exceed time estimates, or fail. Failed projects incur tremendous economic and political costs. IFC, which provides objective project tracking and reporting services to senior executives, significantly reduces failure.

IFC is a trust, validate, and delta course correction reporting of project progress. An external project audit framework, IFC ensures that key deliverables meet pre-defined expectations. IFC incorporates technology, media, and subject matter expert resources to direct course correction during the project life cycle to ensure successful delivery or timely cessation. The small budget overhead for IFC is more than offset by mitigation of risk that can easily double estimated project cost or result in project failure.

The cost of a failed project is only the tip of the iceberg. Every project failure incurs both direct costs of the IT investment itself and indirect costs of the lost opportunity.

Project failure impacts include:

- Loss of brand value and market share
- Opportunity costs
- Product release delay resulting in lost revenue
- Regulatory compliance violation
- High cost of supplemental solution
- Loss of internal and external customers
- Loss of competitive edge
- Impact on shareholders' value

In recent interviews, CIOs stated that during cost cutting, they eliminated several high-risk projects and implemented an IFC process to ensure that the remaining projects were managed better and would deliver high-impact value.

A common theme of identifying problems earlier and using an IFC process helped several organizations modify project plans or stop projects due to technical or managerial issues. According to one Fortune 100 CIO, "We previously viewed in-flight check as a luxury, but the cost is such a small percentage of the project budget and it helps ensure the delivery of projected business value with a high degree of trust in all reporting parties. The result is that we're now mandating it on many of our large and high-risk projects."

Multiple CIOs of Fortune 100 companies stated that the enterprise is much better off using an IFC contractor and process because often they identify major technical problems that prime contractors did not recognize. Again, it is the third-party independence and objectivity that is the fundamental building block of IFC reporting.

C-Level Executives' and Boards of Directors' Call to Action

The following best practices will help ensure that both business leaders and the IT organization reap strategic value from IFC engagement:

- Engage a reputable, independent, and experienced third party; internal resources are not independent.
- Determine the scope of responsibilities for the IFC team.
- Ensure that the IFC addresses both managerial and technical approaches, requirements, and the ability to deliver the business value as stated in the project charter.
- Do not treat the IFC as an overhead expense; it is a critical risk management component of the project cost. If the business does not want to pay for an IFC, it must accept the additional risk and conduct more periodic technical and management reviews.
- Ensure that the IFC team reports to the board to maintain its data reporting objectivity and transparency without any inside influence peddling.

Bottom Line: By implementing up-front planning and ongoing due diligence, IFC is an excellent process to ensure third-party objective project oversight and reporting to reduce project risk/cost and schedule overruns. A secondary and often overlooked benefit is reduced postimplementation support, which can save considerable longer-term costs.

Businesses increasingly will have little tolerance for IT project failures and projects that produce suboptimal results. Organizations can no longer afford the additional costs or the potential loss of promised agility or growth when projects do not achieve the business case for which funding was approved.

Project Risk Management Plan

There are four stages to risk management planning:

1. Risk identification
2. Risk quantification

3. Risk response
4. Independent third-party risk monitoring and control

Risk Identification

In this stage, we identify risks. The best approach is a workshop with business and IT people to carry out the identification. Use a combination of brainstorming and reviewing of standard risk lists in addition to IFC.

Business risks are ongoing risks that are best handled by the business. An example is that if the project cannot meet the end-of-financial-year deadline, the business area may need to retain its existing accounting system for another year. The response is likely to be a contingency plan developed by the business to use the existing system for another year.

Generic risks are risks to all projects. Examples include the risk that business users might not be available or that requirements may be incomplete. Each organization will develop standard responses to generic risks.

Risks should be defined in two parts. The first part is the cause of the situation (e.g., vendor not meeting deadline, business users not available). The second part is the impact (e.g., budget will be exceeded, milestones will not be achieved). A risk can be defined as "The vendor not meeting its deadline will cause the budget to be exceeded."

Risk Quantification

Risk quantification has two dimensions: impact and frequency. Both require an independent assessment.

For simplicity, rate each value on a 1 to 4 scale. The larger the number, the larger the impact or probability. By using a matrix, a priority can be established (see Figure 16.1).

Note that if probability is high and impact is low, it is a medium risk. If impact is high and probability is low, it is high priority.

Risk Response

There are four possible risk mitigation options and strategies:

1. **Avoid the risk.** Use another supplier or vendor, for example.
2. **Transfer the risk.** Make someone else responsible. Perhaps a vendor can be made responsible for a particularly risky part of the project.

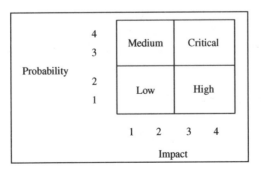

FIGURE 16.1 Risk Quantification

3. **Mitigate the risk.** Take actions to lessen the impact or chance of the risk occurring. If the risk relates to availability of resources, draw up an agreement and get sign-off for the resource to be available.
4. **Accept the risk.** The risk might be small and acceptable to the business.

A risk response plan should include the strategy and action items to address the strategy. The actions should include what needs to be done, who is doing it, and when it should be completed.

Risk Control

The final step is to monitor risks continually to ensure that they remain at acceptable levels. It is best to hold regular risk reviews to ascertain status and keep them within an acceptable appetite for risk.

 ## CONCLUSION

We all know that risk represents something that we would like to minimize. Risk represents the possibility of an outcome that we do not desire. These two statements are related because in order to achieve a desired outcome, we must manage project risks so that they are minimized. Managing risk is always a balancing act. Doing so requires leadership, participation of other team members, the identification and definition of risk, a plan, and steps for implementation of the risk management framework. The alternative is to do nothing, but should you choose that path, you must ask yourself: How risky is that?

 ## NOTES

1. Nadim F. Matta and Ronald N. Ashkenas, "Why Good Projects Fail Anyway," *HBR ARTICLES*, September 1, 2003, http://hbr.org/2003/09/why-good-projects-fail-anyway/ar/1.
2. The Standish Group, "Chaos Report," Standish Group Report, 1995, www.projectsmart.co.uk/docs/chaos-report.pdf.
3. Gartner Research, "Verifying and Validating to Reduce Project Failures," *Gartner Executive Programs EXP Road Notes*, September 9, 2009, http://blogs.gartner.com/road-notes/category/uncategorized/page/5.

CHAPTER SEVENTEEN

Project Cost Estimation

Subbu Murthy

T HE PURPOSE OF ESTIMATING a project varies from assessing feasibility to actually budgeting and managing the project. In the early stages (see Figure 17.1), the purpose of estimating the cost of a project is to assess the feasibility of implementing it or to choose among different alternatives, such as various design options or vendors. Early-stage estimates are typically rough-order-magnitude (ROM) estimates, which can be developed quickly but are not very accurate estimates of the true project costs. Estimates typically are expressed in ranges to account for the inaccuracies.

In the planning stages, the purpose of cost estimation is to establish budgets and allocate them across multiple categories. These allocations may need to conform to both financial and technical structures established within the enterprise. These estimates are more accurate than ROM estimates but often have significant contingency built into them (as much as 25 percent) to account for scope creep, design changes, and other exigencies. During execution, the purpose of cost estimation is to assess planned expenditures with respect to scope changes and getting more granular estimates on project components, and on occasion to assess whether to continue with a project or terminate it. These estimates are more detailed and generally more accurate than those in the early stages.

FIGURE 17.1 Purpose of Cost Estimation

CONCEPTS

Cost estimation of a project is an a priori estimate of the total costs. Total costs of a project may or may not include life cycle cost. Life cycle cost is the sum total of all recurring and one-time (nonrecurring) costs over the full life span or a specified period of a good, service, structure, or system. It includes purchase price, installation cost, operating costs, maintenance and upgrade costs, and residual value at the end of ownership or its useful life. For example, a project that encompasses replacing hardware may include the life cycle costs for assessing a specific vendor selection but may not include the life cycle cost for budgetary purposes. While there are many components to estimating the cost of the project, the most challenging to estimate is the cost of labor associated with developing, testing, training, and deploying the software within the enterprise.

One of the fundamental questions in managing project costs is whether to estimate the cost of the proposed design or constrain the design to a specified cost. Both approaches are commonly used. Most new product development seeks to develop a design to a specific cost, whereas implementation of proven technologies uses the cost-to-design paradigm. A valuable though often ignored component of cost estimation is getting buy-in from all the stakeholders. Stakeholders include not just the sponsor but users and developers as well. The easiest way to get buy-in is to involve the stakeholders at all stages of the cost estimation process.

COST ESTIMATION TOOLS AND TECHNIQUES

The most common methods of cost estimation include parametric estimates, analogical estimates, and work breakdown structure (WBS). A technique often used is getting market pricing. This is not an estimation technique per se but a very pragmatic approach to estimating the costs of very large IT engagements. The process is to ask outsourcers to bid on engagements with the assumption that competition invokes the best pricing. This is a practical technique for all projects that are targets for outsourcing.

Parametric Estimates

Parametric estimation is the process of predicting the amount of effort required to build a software system using mathematical models. The parametric estimating technique involves using project characteristics (parameters) in a mathematical model to predict total project costs. Both the cost and accuracy of parametric models vary widely. Models provide one or more mathematical algorithms that compute cost as a function of a number of variables. They are most likely to be reliable when the historical information used to develop the model is accurate, the parameters used in the model are readily quantifiable, and the model is scalable, such that it works for a large project as well as a small one.

There has been extensive research and development in estimation models for software development projects, resulting in a number of formal methods and tool sets. Older models used lines of code such as COCOMO (COnstructive COst MOdel; visit http://sunset.usc.edu/csse/research/COCOMOII/cocomo_main.html for a full description), and higher-level aggregated models used function points (function points measure functionality by objectively measuring functional requirements; visit www .functionpoints.com for a detailed description of how they can be used to estimate project costs). Parametric models inherently suffer from many disadvantages:

- Lines of code, function points, and feature points have the inherent disadvantage that a great deal of design effort is required to get to a point where the estimate can be made, raising the question of how much it is going to cost to get an estimate of how much it is going to cost.
- Rapidly changing technologies render parametric data obsolete. For example, open-source components and reuse make the estimation process very complex and inaccurate.

Analogical Estimates

Analogical estimates are more common during the early stages of cost estimation, when there is a limited amount of detailed information about the project. They use expert judgment and are less expensive and less accurate than parametric estimates, but are reliable in similar project situations. References of the proposed project are drawn to the existing project and adjusted for differences. When project costs are estimated early in the life cycle, the solution becomes "less known," and therefore the estimation error rises. However, the better the estimators understand the business domain, the more reliable the estimate. Another challenge with analogical estimates is that true costs are rarely available for comparison.

Work Breakdown Structure

The WBS method is essentially bottom up. WBS is a tree structure that shows a subdivision of effort required to achieve a specific project objective. A meaningful and properly organized WBS is essential to developing a granular estimate. A technique for developing the WBS is to start with the end objective and successively subdivide it into manageable components in terms of size, duration, and responsibility (e.g., systems, subsystems, components, tasks, subtasks, and work packages) that include all steps necessary to achieve the objective. Individual schedule activities are estimated to the smallest detail. All costs are then aggregated and used for reporting, tracking, and control purposes. Here, awareness of the individual activity cost is of prime importance.

One very common guideline is to develop a project hierarchy of all activities to the level of detail where a cost can readily be assigned. More granular activities will lead to more accurate cost estimates; however, developing a more detailed WBS is time consuming. Despite the significant effort that is required to develop a good estimate, this method is the most popular technique for estimating the costs of large projects. A significant benefit is that it is also the foundation for managing the project.

WBS-based estimation also suffers from many disadvantages:

- Team productivity can be highly variable. If the estimators know who will do the work, they can produce better estimates. But often estimators are given that job because they are very good developers, and they then estimate how long it would take *them* to do the project, not the resources who actually will be assigned to the project.
- Simple estimator bias exists optimistic estimators make different projections than pessimistic ones.
- Unstated assumptions and misunderstanding can lead to problems.

 ## COST ESTIMATION PROCESS

Irrespective of the technique used in cost estimation, the cost estimation activity is split into three distinct phases (see Figure 17.2). Ideally these phases should be sequential, although often some backtracking occurs. The phases are:

1. Assessment: understanding and sizing
2. Estimation: turning the size into an estimate of effort
3. Adjustment: reviewing and adjusting the estimate and the risks

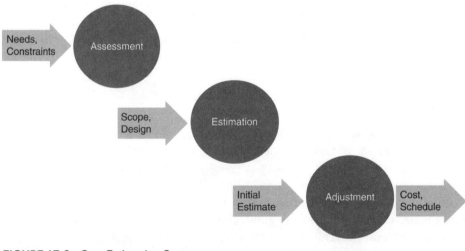

FIGURE 17.2 Cost Estimation Stages

In the assessment phase, estimators analyze the project to be estimated. Time pressure typically constrains their ability to understand the scope of the task, so a focus on ramping up the estimators' knowledge of the business problem is essential. The general approach is to model the solution, identify the components, and then estimate their size and complexity. Finally, tasks that are not strictly mapped to components are added. The essential point is that *effort* is not estimated at this point—just size and complexity. Here we introduce the first bias reduction mechanism: The sizing should be performed independently by more than one person. If the enterprise has never developed a system like this before, cost estimation will be a problem. Looking at similar solutions implemented by competitors can help with understanding the complexity (e.g., there are many details in the shopping cart checkout process: change quantities, cancel item, shipping options, calculating shipping costs, etc.).

The estimation phase consists of turning the output from the assessment phase into effort. Doing so requires analogical estimation—for example, how much time will it take to develop the detailed requirements for, and to design, construct, and unit test, this shopping checkout module? The estimated time is a function of the size and complexity of each task but also of the developers' knowledge and experience. For example, if the project is developed in house, the in-house team may have a better understanding of the business but less experience with the technology.

The adjustment phase focuses on two aspects of the estimate: the difference between the estimates of individual estimators and the assessment of risks. In comparing the estimates of individual estimators, estimates of even experienced estimators for the same task can vary widely for any number of reasons, but chief among them are general optimistic/pessimistic bias and differing assumptions. This part of the adjustment activity is a dialog, which is better if mediated by an independent third party to reduce the risk of one estimator dominating the result. Finally, the riskiest activities should be identified and adjustments made to the estimates. You can think about this as identifying the unknowns. For example, does the solution require the purchase and integration of a software component that we have no experience with? This identification activity often uncovers risks that need to be mitigated as early as possible in the project, perhaps even before the project is committed. This activity could be done earlier in the estimation process, but often these risks get uncovered only when estimation differences are discussed and an unstated assumption is unearthed. Pricing and laying out a timeline are typically the final activities. At this stage, staffing options sometimes have to be evaluated. For example, can this project be outsourced? If it is, what are the assumed offshore rates and the additional project management oversight required?

SUMMARY

Cost estimation is a critical component of project management. It can help in assessing feasibility of a project, choosing among competing designs or vendors, planning the IT expenditures, facilitating budgeting, and managing the project.

Common techniques of cost estimation include parametric models based on project parameters, analogical estimates based on experience with similar projects, and using a detailed WBS. Accuracy of estimates is important, but accuracy has to be balanced with the effort that is expended to get good estimates. The WBS method is the most popular technique as it seamlessly integrates cost estimation with the project management process.

18

Managing Project Quality

William (Liam) Durbin

F OR A CIO TRYING to manage an IT shop, there is nothing more important than project quality.

And yes, really big ticket items come along, such as acquisitions, enterprise resource planning (ERP) implementations, major technology breakthroughs, and other career-making and breaking opportunities. However, in terms of operational processes that the CIO owns, none are more important than project management. Think about it: The vast majority of the bugs that shut down or impair your production applications were born in the implementation process—the project. Even if these business-impacting issues do not show up for years, the seeds were likely planted during the project phase. It could have been a missed requirement, a poorly designed interface, or a data model that is too rigid to adjust to changes in the business. These are the sorts of items that drain millions from an IT organization's expense budget each year to fix what could well have been prevented by better project quality.

So if you have a ballooning operational (expense) budget, before you start turning over rocks in your support shop, look first at your project management process and how you spend your capital. If you do not fix project management first, you might as well be standing in a sinking boat frantically bailing water instead of taking time to understand where the water is coming from and plugging the holes. Projects drive consumption of expense dollars long after the project is complete, but it does not have to be that way.

So project quality is important. Let's discuss how to go get it.

As we begin, let's be clear about another thing: Managing project quality begins way upstream of where your projects actually begin. If you are starting a project and just beginning to think seriously about quality, you are in big trouble. It would be like going into the manufacturing business, your heart set on delivering a high-quality product, but without having spent any time thinking about the construction of the factory, the people who will operate the machinery and their skills and metrics, or the processes that make the factory floor run smoothly. If the factory is constructed properly, you will likely produce quality products again and again with less consideration of the people actually doing the work. It will still be possible to make defective products, but clearly the process is going to steer the workers toward making defect-free products. And bad products will be identified and corrected much sooner in the process, when it is much cheaper to fix. Conversely, if your factory is shoddy, the best you can do is to try to inspect quality on a piece-by-piece basis. We all know this does not work.

INSTITUTING PROJECT QUALITY

Let's say, for the sake of argument, that you are starting to examine project quality either as a manager new to your CIO role or as a sitting CIO who has decided it is time to do something about your project quality issues. The actions are similar if you want to implement a quality process for doing projects or to tune up ones that are already under way.

Here are the six steps for instituting project quality:

1. The bold decree
2. Metrics to make it stick
3. Organize for quality
4. Take the pain out
5. The traceability matrix and test plans
6. The one thing every project must have

Let's explore these steps in more detail.

The Bold Decree: "All Projects Will Follow the XYZ Methodology"

No exceptions. No winking, no turning the other way, no faking it. Do not be sucked into distracting conversations that attempt to compartmentalize what is and what is not a project. Resist the temptation to do "lite" versions of your methodology. This just creates a path for projects to skirt the process by being small. Your bold decree is a no-kidding decree. If it was just a good idea or some guiding principles, it cannot be a decree. Decrees are absolute—even for your closest friends in the business functions. Make sure your team knows it, and make sure your peers know it. Put the decree and a link to your XYZ methodology in your auto-signature. Own it.

For the sake of argument, XYZ methodology could be any methodology. I am a fan of a six-step waterfall method, but the genius is in having a methodology, not in which particular flavor or how many steps you go with. You will find it useful if your methodology lends itself to being measured, and that is why I like waterfall.

If your methodology lends itself to graphical representation (most do), print it poster size and put it on your wall so everyone coming into your office sees it. You will have to repeat it hundreds of times because your resolve will be tested. Make your methodology the project language of the business.

Once you have made your bold decree, have put it in your auto-signature and plastered it all over your walls, and have thoroughly overcommunicated your project management principles, live up to your own decree by attending *every* gate review for your projects. This does not mean every steering committee meeting and project team meeting. But it does mean that at every formal step in your process, where you pause and ask the business, "Is this right so far? Did we hear you correctly? May we proceed to the next stage?" you are in the room, and so is your business champion. In these formal meetings, IT leadership and functional leadership can look each other in the eye and confirm that the project is on the right track.

Once the word gets out that you attend these meetings, you will find your business partners show up too, the attendees are engaged, and the project team is better prepared. This is what quality looks like in practice, and it is much more than what is captured in the old saying "Don't expect what you don't inspect." It is leadership by example. Your attendance demonstrates commitment, not suspicion or mere scrutiny.

These formal graduation meetings become your pulpit for what you expect from your methodology and project teams. In these meetings, you highlight superior results and capture high-quality deliverables to become templates for future projects. You are actively involved in fine-tuning the process. This reinforces the point that your methodology is not static but a process that constantly improves and evolves.

This is particularly important in the beginning, when you are trying to establish a quality process. After a year or so, you may relax a bit and turn specific reviews over to your project management office (PMO) leader. But in the beginning, your decree will not stick if you cannot make it to the meetings.

A word of caution: Making the decree and giving it no more than lip service is worse than no decree at all; to say you have a process only to abandon it when the time comes to actually live up to it will discredit the IT organization. After the decree, listen for process language to become more prevalent and the behaviors to become more natural—language such as "What project phase are we in?" and "I need to make a few changes to my communication plan," "Do we have a template for that?" and similar expressions. If you are not hearing these types of phrases, your decree lacks substance.

Metrics to Make It Stick

Add in a healthy helping of quality metrics that will apply to all projects evenly, objectively, and exhaustively. Not fluffy, how-do-you-feel metrics but meaty, no-place-to-hide metrics. They may embarrass you at first, but in the long run they will keep the factory running without you spending all your time on the factory floor. Here are some metrics that I strongly recommend.

Say-Do

This simple metric is the number of project commitments met on time divided by the number of commitments made. Every step in your methodology is a commitment to the business. Are you hitting them? You can engage in some very interesting philosophical discussions around when to commit to different deliverables or steps in a project, but in the long run it really does not matter.

If you require your project leaders to commit to all deliverable dates at the outset of the project, you will drive some fairly predictable results. What will happen is that project leaders will have a good say-do metric for the early commitments, but the dates at the end of the project will whip around like a loose fire hose. Your team's say-do for the later commitment dates will be horrible at first. Some will say it is too hard to do. Do not let this stop you; measure anyway. As your processes mature, you will slowly work your way down to the end of the fire hose and get it under control.

Alternatively, you can allow your project leaders to commit to project deliverables in chunks (this is what I recommend). In particular, it is difficult to commit to the go-live date before functional requirements are complete. Ask project leaders to commit to the functional requirement date, and once that is delivered, they can commit to the remainder. This gives you some anchor points along the length of the hose and limits the whipping effect.

Your project leaders will tell you that this method of measuring will lead to padding of dates, but it will not—not as long as the business is at the table, perhaps pounding the table, and needs the project. Most projects have critical business benefits that some functional leader needs badly. So keep the business as close as possible, and project leaders will help keep the padding to a minimum.

When a deliverable date is missed, capture it as a miss and also capture the reason it was missed. Limit the reasons for misses to no more than eight and avoid catchall categories. After you have enough data, this collection of fault code data is a very powerful way to understand why your dates are being missed. Share this information with your team and the business. Train out the lumps.

Postlaunch Incidents

For a period of time (a month works well) after any new functionality is put in production, measure all calls (incidents) to the help desk (service desk) for that application. If your tools are sophisticated enough, separate out those calls that are not related to the new functionality. If not, leave them all in. In the long run, it will not matter. It is critical to ensure that *all* calls pertaining to the application are captured. Ideally this is easy, because all calls are already going to the service desk. If not, you have the potential for lots of leakers, but do the best you can to eliminate all of them.

Unmercifully count all calls as incidents, even training and user errors. If you want quality, you cannot take any prisoners. You cannot put up with exceptions. If the users do not know how to use the application properly, you have missed a commitment to the business, and it should be captured. Missing on training and commercialization of an important project is like driving the ball down the field in a grueling game of football, grinding it out yard by yard in a gut-wrenching ground game, prevailing over all obstacles to get within field goal range, lining up to kick the winning goal, and dropping the ball and walking off the field as if getting that far had proven enough. It may sound outrageous, but it happens a lot. If you want your project leaders (business and IT) to focus on these important details, count every call as a defect. Call them defects—doing so will raise eyebrows and blood pressures, but that is what they are.

Year over year you should drive postlaunch incidents down through training on the common causes. Where your business partners are contributing to the defects, make them aware and ask for their partnership in eliminating them. They will thank you for asking as long as you have data to point out how big of an opportunity it is. Present the opportunities diplomatically and ask for their help to drive to higher levels of quality.

Organize for Quality: Split Application Support Out of Project Management

It is not just that having project leaders derailed by critical production issues slows down projects. Although that is true, and it will adversely impact your projects, the bigger concern is the conflict of interest. You might think that if someone has to maintain the code, they will take more care in its development, but things do not work that way in practice. In practice, project leaders under pressure to hit a commitment will cut corners if they know they will be supporting the application when the project is done. Project leaders will skimp on proper documentation or procrastinate on it in order to get other things done. But if they develop the new functionality with full knowledge that they will be handing it off to someone else—and that that person has the right to refuse it (yes, it can be rejected!), project leaders will go to much greater lengths to make sure it is a quality product. Testing and documentation will get a lot more attention when projects and production are separated. (This fits with the Information Technology Infrastructure Library framework too.)

Besides resolving the conflict of interest, such a handoff also allows team members to focus on one set of metrics and skills, depending on which discipline they are assigned to. Being a great project leader is completely different from being a great application lead. If people have metrics in both disciplines, they will be constantly conflicted over which ones to focus on. Split the disciplines apart. Tell your project leaders to become pros at projects and your application support team to be pros at maintenance and enhancement.

This separation of production and project management may be difficult if you do not have enough scale, but it is too important to ignore. In practice, I have found that the split can be made even if one or two people end up straddling disciplines for a period of time. It is better to make the move and ask someone to straddle for a while than to wait for the perfect time to make the split. If you want to focus on quality, the split has to be made. Get creative; use dual-hat roles, contractors, and stretch assignments.

Once the disciplines are separated, establish clear rules for how new functionality will be handed off between the projects team and the applications support team. It is absolutely vital to give veto power to the leader(s) of the support team. If new functionality is not quality tested and documented, the applications support team can say no. This is critical because the support team is where your expense dollars are consumed, and expense dollars get very close scrutiny. This team will have pressure to get more efficient year over year and take costs down. It cannot do that if it is expected to take on junk or depend on poorly documented code. In healthy partnerships, the support team will consult and attend meetings throughout the project so that when it is time to turn it over to support, the support team is ready to go.

Make sure the leaders of both disciplines and your PMO are measured on metrics on both sides of the split, even if the team members are not. This will drive better cooperation between the teams.

Another note of caution: Once you establish the two disciplines (projects, application support), do not diminish the support roles. They may already feel like they're playing second fiddle because projects are considered more glamorous. Make sure you put A players on both sides of the divide. Being good at application support takes people with a head for repeatable processes and attention to detail. They must be self-starting and risk-avoiding professionals. When it comes time to promote and award bonuses, be sure to take care of the applications support pros. If the project leaders are the lead singers, the application support team is the rhythm section.

Organize for Quality: Implement an IT Quality Leader Position

Implementing an IT quality leader position is not always easy because people seem so busy. You may ask how can you possibly spare a strong project leader to drop projects and instead take up quality on *all* projects. But spread across 30 or 40 projects in a year, if a quality leader can find a meager 10 percent improvement in project quality, you will easily cover the difference. In large organizations, it is a very nice model to split the quality assurance leader out from the PMO position, but in smaller organizations, the two roles can be combined.

The quality leader/PMO should be one of the most influential positions on the CIO's staff. The person chosen to fill this role needs to be one of your very best leaders, with enough project management experience to have some credibility with your more junior project leaders and with the functional teams. In our factory analogy, the PMO is the factory operations manager and the IT quality leader is, well, the factory quality leader.

Once the position is filled, make sure you support your quality assurance leader. Even an experienced and credible quality assurance leader cannot be effective without the support of the CIO. So make it continuous and public.

Take the Pain Out

Make project quality implementation easy and make it repeatable, with standardized documentation. This means simple templates, checklists, standard report-outs and project documentation. Extensive use of templates will drive acceptance within IT and with your business partners. Doing the same thing over and over again gives everyone the perception that you are in control. As each project completes, harvest the best and worst practices and tune the templates. If you find a great example of a resource plan, make it the new template. Celebrate and commercialize the success. As usage of the templates becomes second nature, the project team's workload goes down. Team members learn the program and know the steps.

Treat your templates and checklists as living documents rather than static how-to manuals. Every project is another opportunity to cultivate best practices. With good encouragement from yourself and your PMO/quality leader, project leaders will become excited about their role in tuning the project management process. Make sure they know that while the use of the templates is nonnegotiable, template content is highly negotiable. Eventually (two years, notionally) the supporting documents for your project management methodology will become highly tuned, and there will be less change from project to project. But in the beginning, change is constant and expected.

Another word of caution: Use of templates and examples does not mean clobbering your project teams with unnecessary documentation. If you find them creating documents that serve no purpose or are never looked at again, or if a particular document appears to be purely academic, put a stop to it immediately. It waters down your position on why templates are useful. Shoot the non-value-added content publicly. Make sure everyone knows that templates are to improve speed through consistency, simplicity, and exhaustiveness. They are designed to reduce rework by making sure people do not miss important steps and that the company learns from previous projects.

Here are some examples of project deliverables that lend themselves to templating:

- Functional requirements
- Communication plan
- Resource plan
- Test plan
- Tollgate meetings agendas
- Cutover plan
- Project team site (Sharepoint) or other gathering place
- Traceability matrix
- Risk mitigation plan (failure modes and effects analysis [FMEA])
- Use cases
- Infrastructure checklist
- Security checklist

Examples of each of these deliverables are available on the Internet or as handouts from any project management course. Again, the genius is not in having one flavor over another but in having any standard documentation at all, cultivating the documents that drive quality and shooting down the ones that do not.

Can you have a project deliverable that has lots of "Not Applicable" in it? Of course you can! For small projects or package solutions or upgrades, many questions are not applicable. But the template reminds you to ask the questions, reinforces the process, and makes sure nothing gets missed. A standard template with nine questions answered with "NA" and one critical question answered substantively is a lot better than moving past the requirement without answering that one critical question.

The Traceability Matrix and Test Plans

Tying everything together with a traceability matrix sounds scary, maybe even engineer-like, but doing so is actually quite simple. The traceability matrix is a single document that tracks requirements from the voice of the customer, through the functional requirements, technical requirement and testing. After all, once your customers have spoken, shouldn't their wants be represented in the functional requirements, again in the technical requirements, until finally demonstrated in an exhaustive test plan? The traceability matrix will also clearly demonstrate any functionality that fell out at some point in the project, why it was taken out and who approved its removal. It is a critical communication and planning tool.

The final section of the traceability matrix is testing. Give your testing the respect and attention it deserves. Testing should be a part of the PMO or quality assurance role but if it is not, you can either move it there to get it the attention it needs or you can deputize someone on your team to own it. But testing must have an owner. Make sure your team and your clients know that test plans are not done once and then put on the shelf. Encourage (enforce) them to take the time to get the test plans right and then they can be used over and over again each time the system is modified.

Use your position to make sure your business partners pony up qualified testers when the time comes. During the project and whenever the resource plan is first discussed, make sure that sufficient testers are on the resource plan. This will ensure that when the time comes to provide the bodies to conduct testing it is not news to anyone. Resist the temptation to cut back on testing when the project runs long. Set up a war room with all the right resources (PCs, projector, whiteboard, etc.) to get through the testing unabated. Creating a testing facility takes some effort, but it pays back in better focus and shorter, better testing.

The One Thing Every Project Must Have

All the steps just described are important in establishing a culture and a framework of project quality. Yet the success or failure of any single project hangs on *one thing*: the presence of a functional project leader. Do not kid yourself into thinking that a project can be successful without one. The project will be starved of quality if there is not a dedicated functional owner. The impact of this role is quite Boolean: It is success or failure with very little gray area in between. It is well documented but this simple must-do is very hard to do.[1] Your resolve will be tested. Resources are scarce, especially in today's economy. But things worth doing are worth doing well. So bite the bullet and make sure that you do not commit the one cardinal sin of failing to have a functional project leader. If you want quality, you have to have proper ownership.

CONCLUSION

I will end where I began—there is nothing more important in the CIO's world than project quality. If you throw your CIO weight behind project quality, identify yourself as a quality zealot, and adopt these simple recommendations, your PMO, quality leader, project leaders, and business partners will reap significant benefits. Although quite simple, some of these suggestions may seem awkward or difficult, but they are what is required in the pursuit of quality. It takes commitment, particularly in the beginning. But once the flywheel is in motion, the effort drops dramatically and the benefits will come easily. If you made it this far in the chapter, quality is obviously something you want. Go get it.

 ## NOTE

1. Liam Durbin, "Beware These Hazards to Functional Engagement in IT Projects," *CIO Magazine*, August 6, 2007, www4.cio.com/article/128300/Beware_These_Hazards_to_Functional_Engagement_in_IT_Projects?page=1.

CHAPTER NINETEEN

Project Reviews

Subbu Murthy

T HE PURPOSE OF PROJECT reviews depends on the project life cycle (see Figure 19.1). Understanding the purpose of a review is as important as the review itself. In the early stages of the project, reviews are typically held to assess the project impact across the portfolio of other projects, evaluate alternatives, and make decisions to continue the project or abandon them.

In the planning stages, reviews are held to assess the project costs, schedule, and risks. They are also held to establish the high-level scope and interfaces with other projects and to evaluate resource allocations. The reviews in the early stage and the planning phase play a key role in prioritizing and sequencing the project.

In the execution stage, reviews are focused on understanding the project specifications (requirements, design, etc.), assessing the progress of the project, and assessing project quality.

Postimplementation reviews are also crucial as they serve to assess overall performance and review the key lessons learned. They also help understand the true causes of variance. In a majority of IT projects, poor specifications and scope creep are the two strong determinants of cost and schedule variances.

Project reviews share four characteristics: (1) They are measurable, (2) they have specific goals, (3) they deliver direct or indirect benefits to customers or stakeholders, and (4) they are triggered by a specific milestone or a preestablished schedule.

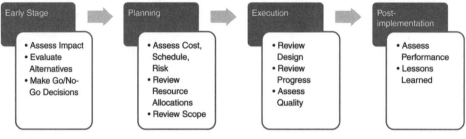

FIGURE 19.1   Project Life Cycle

 CONCEPTS

Every review must have a purpose, and the purpose must be aligned to the specific project needs. In addition to identifying the purpose of the review, some of the fundamental aspects of a project review to consider are the frequency of the review (weekly versus monthly or quarterly), granularity (detailed versus high level), and whether reviews are scheduled (weekly, monthly, quarterly) or event driven (such as completion of a project milestone). The audience for the project review depends on the purpose of the review. Management, technical architects, developers, quality assurance personnel, users, finance, and other functions may have to be involved, depending on the type of review.

While the frequency of review and granularity of reviews depends on the type of project and the maturity of the team working on the project, it is helpful to recognize that projects that are unstructured (not very well defined) and more critical to the enterprise will require more scrutiny. Weekly meetings as opposed to monthly reviews may be required. The flip side of the equation is the cost entailed in organizing and conducting the reviews.

It is a very common myth that project reviews always require face-to-face meetings and are formal. Informal reviews, online project dashboards, and other communication mechanisms are also part of the project review process and very critical to ensuring overall success of the project. Formal project reviews are generally planned as milestone events, but reviews for very complex projects can have mini–life cycles of their own. This is true for reviews where a critical decision, such as deployment readiness, has to be assessed. The phrase "review phase" is quite common when reviews are complex and time consuming.

In addition to compliance with project requirements, the review focus is a combination of assessing the costs, schedule, quality, and risk of a project. Project risk can be defined in terms of criticality, degree of clarity in the specifications, and costs. Projects that are critical, lack clarity of specifications, and are costly to implement are high-risk projects. In contrast, projects that are not mission critical, cost less, and are well specified tend to have the least risk.

In general, smaller, mission-critical projects have a schedule focus (see Figure 19.2); that is, the review focuses on schedule variance since the costs are relatively low and the schedule of when the projects get completed assumes more importance. However, for

FIGURE 19.2 Review Focus

larger, less mission-critical projects, in addition to schedule reviews, cost variance reviews are also important. For smaller but mission-critical projects, reviews tend to focus more on mitigating risk; for mission-critical large projects, the review focus is on all of the four attributes mentioned.

 TYPES OF PROJECT REVIEWS

Some of the common project reviews include:

- **Project go/no-go review.** The purpose of this review is to assess the project need; the desired benefits; the fit within the project portfolio with reference to costs, schedule, and risks; and, most important, how the project aligns to business needs. The desired outcome is a go/no-decision and project prioritization within the portfolio of projects. In reality, decisions are not made in one review meeting, and different levels of granularity of project scope may need to be reviewed, depending on the audience. For example, finance may be more concerned about return on investment (cost and tangible benefits) whereas users may be more concerned about features and prioritization.
- **Plan review.** The purpose of this review is to review the project plan. (Note: For very small projects that are better treated as tasks, the project plan and review process may be less formal.) For most projects, the master plan for a project is usually formally documented in a project plan. The key goals of this review are to ensure that:
  - Project governance provides adequate visibility and is in compliance with IT governance practices.

- The project addresses the critical business, user, and technical requirements.
- The project vision is understood and shared by all team members.
- Project costs, schedules, and resources are realistic.
- Project success criteria are clearly established.
- Interfaces with other projects and external and internal entities are clearly identified.
- Project quality assurance and reviews are well planned.
- Project risks are appropriately identified, and mitigation strategies are proposed.
- Project organization has experience in delivering projects.

  Note examples of what to look out for to determine if you are going in the right or wrong direction.

- **Progress reviews.** The purpose of the progress reviews is to review the status of the project. These reviews address not only the progress to date but the plan for the remainder of the project and any necessary adjustments. The key goals of this review are to ensure that:
  - Project progress (costs, schedules, and resource utilization) is per the plan. Variance in terms of costs and schedule are tracked. If variances exceed established thresholds, replanning may be required. It should be noted that extensive replanning is tantamount to canceling the existing project and initiating a new one.
  - Project success criteria are met. An absolute measure is nearly impossible to achieve. Criteria such as on a scale of 1 to 5 help provide a degree of success of the project.
  - Interfaces with other projects and external and internal entities are assessed.
  - Project technical progress is as per the plan.

  Progress reviews address the technical aspects at a milestone level. Some of the more common progress reviews include preliminary design review, test readiness review, and deployment review.

  The preliminary design review is a key review in the early stages for reviewing implications to the project scope, schedule, and costs, based on design alternatives that meet requirements.

  The test readiness review assesses the completion of the development and the readiness to proceed with the testing. One of the key considerations is the quality of the test plans and the adequacy of both technical resources and users available for testing.

  Deployment reviews help determine whether the developed and tested product (or service) is ready for use.

  The goal of progress reviews is to ensure that mistakes are caught early in the project life cycle. While there is general agreement that mistakes detected earlier in the project life cycle are far less expensive than those detected in the later stages of the project life cycle, there is no uniform data to quantify the costs. Generally it is an order of magnitude more expensive to correct a mistake during testing as opposed to detecting it during early stages of the design and a further order of magnitude more expensive to address postdeployment (see Figure 19.3).

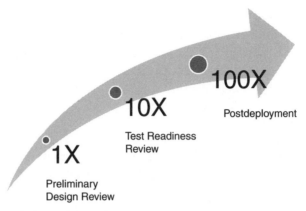

FIGURE 19.3 Cost of Mistakes/Defects

- **Detailed technical reviews.** The purpose of these reviews is to ensure completeness, accuracy, appropriateness, and overall quality of the project. The reviews depend on the type of project and are typically staged to match the project life cycle. Software projects, for example, typically include requirements reviews, design reviews, development (code) reviews, and test reviews. The quality of the delivered project depends heavily on the quality of the technical reviews. While the technical collaterals and checklists depend on the nature of the review (e.g., test reviews should include a mapping to the requirements specification to ensure that all requirements are tested), they all have a few common characteristics:
  - Informal technical reviews should be held frequently to ensure that errors, omissions, and other issues are caught early in the project life cycle.
  - In general, detailed technical reviews should not be combined with project progress reviews. Although cost and schedule considerations are important, the primary purpose of technical reviews is to ensure overall system quality.
  - In addition to development teams, users and members of the quality staff are actively involved in the technical reviews to ensure that the project implementation meets the stakeholder expectations.
- **Project sunset review (aka postmortem review).** The purpose of this review is to capture project successes, difficulties, and resulting lessons learned and communicate these to the project team and relevant management peers. A common myth is that project sunset reviews are needed only for projects that were not deemed successful. These reviews provide very valuable insights and evidential data to improve existing processes, metrics, and often serve as a baseline for future projects. Project sunset reviews for successful projects are valuable in that they reinforce what worked and best practices. Such reviews are arguably more valuable for failed projects in that they show what did not work so as to avoid making similar mistakes in the future. In either case, such reviews provide an excellent opportunity to reflect and learn.

PROJECT REVIEW PROCESS

In the past, reviews were almost always conducted face-to-face. Recent advances in technology have facilitated Web meetings, with tools such as WebEx and GoToMeeting enabling geographically dispersed teams to collaborate as if they were sitting next to one another. A few institutions also use social networks to facilitate project reviews where some of the participants provide "informal" feedback, such as wikis and tweets. While face-to-face meetings are more common, these newer forms of collaborating are gaining momentum. Independent of the review modality, formal project reviews have a mini–life cycle of their own and should be treated in the context of the project.

The three key stages are preparation, meeting/review, and postmeeting follow-up:

1. The preparation stage is crucial to ensure success of the review. Careful preparation results in maximum benefits from the review. The review collaterals, review checklists, audience, review agenda, schedule, and location are critical to a successful review. Typically the review collaterals are sent ahead of time to the reviewers with instructions and road maps for reviewing. This method is particularly useful when reviewing large documents. When preparing for the review, the aim is to ensure that the review goals are met with buy-in from all participants. Review-meeting planning checklists help facilitate the reviewing planning process. While checklists and preestablished templates facilitate reviews, they should always be viewed in the context of the project.

2. Each review should have a review coordinator who conducts the meeting. Also consider designating a note taker and timekeeper. The assigned note taker is responsible for taking meeting notes. The note taker records action items that are then reported in the meeting minutes and any follow-on reviews. The review coordinator is responsible for leading the meeting, setting the agenda, and creating the role rotation. On occasion, the review coordinator may be assisted by a timekeeper to ensure adherence to the meeting agenda. The review agenda may be modified by the review coordinator as warranted. The note taker will ensure that all comments and new and open issues are recorded as part of the meeting minutes.

3. During the review or postreview, the action items are reviewed and assigned to responsible individuals. Any issues/concerns raised during the review are discussed and adjudicated. Accepted issues will have a corrective action plan and rejected issues are documented with the appropriate rationale for rejection. All these items become part of the meeting minutes, which are sent to the reviewers and other stakeholders as appropriate.

 SUMMARY

Project reviews are an essential component of project management. They should be planned taking into account the nature of the project, culture of the enterprise, and project stage. Reviews should be planned to help assess project progress, technology, and other key variables to ensure that the project is proceeding as planned. However, care should be taken to ensure that the review process does not become onerous and dilute the overall purpose of the project. To be successful, all reviews must be planned, conducted according to preestablished agenda, and have a follow-up to ensure that they have achieved the desired outcome.

CHAPTER TWENTY

Compliance

Gary Kelly

W HEN ONE THINKS OF compliance, one usually thinks of having to follow rules—and so it is with information technology compliance.

There are regulatory rules that must be met as well as organizational policy directives from management to be implemented. Additionally, there are also directives from outsiders (such as hackers) or from insiders (such as those with particular departmental or personal priorities that conflict with management's objectives) that must be avoided.

As a result, compliance can be considered to fall into three general categories:

1. **Regulatory:** Mandated actions from outside governmental/regulatory agencies
2. **Procedural/Policy:** Mandated actions from (inside) management
3. **Security:** Prevention of the actions of outsiders and insiders attempting to enhance personal interests that are in conflict with owners' (stockholders' or the public's) best interests

In some cases, categories 2 and 3 may overlap, such as when the actions of management are not in the best interests of the organization. An example of this would be a CEO who treats the company's funds as her own personal piggy bank or a government official who uses public funds for personal gain. For example, consider the actions of former CEO Dennis Kozlowski at Tyco, who threw lavish parties (costing over $200 million) with company funds, and the actions of former Maryland governor Spiro Agnew, who took kickbacks on government contracts.

REGULATORY COMPLIANCE

The IT department—since it is primarily a service department—has very few direct governmental rules that apply to its own operations. However, IT management does have to concern itself with any area that relies on data integrity or information process quality.

Five areas that fall into this category are:

1. The finance department, which is concerned with taxes, internal control over financial statements, and proper recording of costs and revenue recognition
2. The human resources department, which must protect confidential personal information, such as Social Security numbers and health information, and which must safeguard fingerprint or security clearance data
3. The engineering department, which must protect new patents or innovative technology
4. The manufacturing department, which must protect secrets regarding proprietary processes for manufacturing and/or establishing high-level quality products that exceed competitors' capabilities
5. The legal department, which may be involved in high-stakes negotiations or lawsuits

In most cases, IT regulatory compliance involves solely data protection. However, it may, in rare cases, involve establishing the processes that ensure such data protection is afforded to the appropriate other departments. One example of this is the recent IT audit requirements that exist as part of the Sarbanes-Oxley Act of 2002.

Sarbanes-Oxley Act of 2002

The Sarbanes-Oxley Act of 2002 (also known as SOX) was implemented by Congress in response to the fraudulent financial reporting at both Enron and WorldCom at the end of the dot-com boom period of 1999 to 2001. The collapse of these two firms led to a law requiring that large businesses enact very detailed processes to ensure that the financial reporting processes, including the IT processes surrounding financial reporting, were designed such that top management would be directly responsible for any irregularities and could not blame such irregularities on the actions of lower-level management or staff-level positions.

The actions of this law were quite successful and led to a major overhaul and improvement in the integrity of firms' financial statements. Unfortunately, SOX regulations were designed to apply specifically to manufacturing and service firms, but exempted financial firms and brokerages if they were already subject to the restrictive covenants of banking and securities laws. As we now know, these banking and securities laws seemed very conservative, restrictive, and were continually monitored—but in reality, they ignored many of the exact same problems (such as the creation of exotic derivatives and overextension of debt leverage) that had led to the problems at Enron and WorldCom. As a result, in late 2008 and on through 2009, the world suffered a major economic downturn that was largely the result of financial firms (and their clients) being overextended in the credit and debt markets. One estimate put the size of this collapse at the equivalent of $66 trillion. Banks failed at rates not seen since the Great Depression of the 1920s and 1930s, and, as of the time of the writing, the economic depression is still very much affecting worldwide economies negatively.

Many critics state that SOX and any regulatory rules cost companies money and thus negatively affect the companies' economic activity and profit-making capabilities. This complaint brings into question the need of any company to do anything besides make profit. My argument is that even if a company does not have a requirement to contribute to the betterment of its community or be fair to its customers, it still has a commitment to its shareholders to properly report its operating results—and most regulatory rules, such as Securities and Exchange Commission reporting requirements and SOX, are designed primarily with shareholders in mind.

 ## PROCEDURAL/POLICY COMPLIANCE

A second compliance issue for IT is how to help management achieve its objectives. This is the area referred to as procedural/policy compliance.

Whether the organization is a for-profit firm, a nonprofit private entity, or a public governmental entity, the IT department has three primary purposes as part of procedural/ policy compliance. IT must ensure that:

1. The organization's assets are used for improving the organization's value or the value of its owners (which may include the public when the organization is a governmental entity).
2. All assets (including those of human capital) are able to perform at top efficiency.
3. Data are recorded to determine how effective the organization is at achieving purposes 1 and 2.

In the past, organizations often thought that they were performing their activities well, without recognizing the many actions that IT could perform more quickly and the extra data analysis and overview that IT resources could provide to determine the true effectiveness of the organization's activities. Nowadays, most organizations have used at least some of these new processes. The automation of the improved processes has shown the many review and analysis possibilities of IT.

 ## SECURITY

One of today's key concerns is that modern hardware and software configurations be designed such that software assets are maintained intact and not corrupted by inadvertent or deliberate unauthorized changes. This is one of the primary reasons why companies use standard frameworks and comply with suggested regulatory standards such as ISO20000, Control Objectives for Information and Related Technology (COBiT), and the

Basel Accords. It is also the reason that they use Six Sigma methodologies in reviewing system designs and/or system deficiencies.

Most of these technologies are designed not only to detect unauthorized changes but also to streamline existing processes and operational methodologies. By so doing, they establish operational compliance as a by-product, ensuring that the IT organization is meeting corporate and regulatory requirements for the protection of the corporation's valuable information. Vulnerability assessments are a standard part of such regulatory standards, and there are systemic programs available for such assessments as well as standard auditing techniques. Some of the things that should be considered in a compliance audit of a web site audit include:

Backup Controls

1. Ensure that physical security, including environmental and life safety controls, is in place at the hardware site running the Web application.
2. Ensure that network availability and data backup is assured by using component failure architectures that repair themselves, such as RAID, tape or compact disc juke boxes, Bernoulli boxes, or other similar backup media.
3. Review disaster recovery and business interruption plans for the web site, focusing on whether the alternate plan had been tested for validity and readiness.

E-Commerce Controls

1. Ensure that IT is using a set of security mechanisms and procedures, which, taken together, constitute a security architecture—for example, Internet firewalls, public key infrastructure, encryption, certificates, and password management (including nonstatic passwords).
2. Ensure that the firewall mechanisms in place can mediate between the public network (the Internet) and an organization's private network.
3. Ensure that the web site is using a combination of public and private key encryption to guarantee a unique and positive identification of the user.
4. Ensure that digital signatures are being used.
5. Ensure that certificates are being used—including certificate authority, registration authority, certification revocation list, and a certification practice statement.
6. Ensure that logs of the e-commerce portion of the web site are being monitored by responsible personnel on a regular basis. This includes operating system logs, console messages, network management messages, firewall logs and alerts, router management messages, intrusion detection alarms, application and server statistics, and system integrity checks.
7. Ensure that the system has a method, such as SSL (encrypted secure socket layers), to guarantee confidentiality of data.

System and Transaction Controls

1. Check on the ability of the system to counteract vulnerabilities, such as instituting countermeasures to traffic/trend analysis on the part of intruders (e.g., padding messages, sending noise, and providing covert channel analysis).

2. Ensure that hardware controls, such as elimination of unused maintenance accounts, are in place.

3. Test that existing employees have been screened for security and that measures are in place to ensure that they are not using data scavenging techniques to piece together information from bits of data.

4. Check the system logs to ensure that the IT administrators are not taking advantage of initial program load (IPL) vulnerabilities by putting the system into a single-user mode during web site start-up.

5. Review data traffic patterns to ensure that neither existing personnel nor intruders are using network address hijacking to reroute data traffic from a server or network device to a personal machine.

6. Follow sample transactions all the way through the system by use of audit trails to ensure that all the various security events relating to the transaction are taking place; to ensure that the terminal at which the transaction was processed (if internal) is one that is authorized for such a transaction; to look for production job reruns and amendments to production jobs; and to look for computer programmer changes to live production data.

Data Library Procedures

1. Ensure that utility software (used for data correction of inconsistencies on an automated basis) is restricted on a need-to-use basis and that a log is generated whenever this utility is used.

2. Review the check-in and check-out of standard code for the web site to ensure that it was not being reviewed by nonauthorized individuals or those not involved in the web site code process.

System Development Standards

1. Ensure that run-to-run totals of key fields are used and compared to detect alterations between postings per reports from the web site, and posting to the general ledger based on actual sales booked/monies received.

2. Ensure that there is a separation of duties in the upgrade of Web application software and systems software so no individual has the capability to perform more than one of these processes: origination, authorization, verification, or distribution.

3. Review the change management procedure for installing changes to the Web applications.

4. Use mapping to identify specific logic that has not been tested, then analyze these programs during execution to determine whether program statements have been executed, thus identifying potential exposures.

Data Center Security

1. Ensure that reports, such as critical output reports, are produced and maintained in a secure area and distributed in an authorized manner. Access to online output

reports should also be restricted. Online access can be tested through a review of the access rules or by monitoring user output.

2. Run a set of substantive tests on transactions that examine the accuracy, completeness, consistency, and authorization of data currently held in a system in order to see any failures in input or processing controls. Verify the data against the source documentation.

Online Auditing

Consider using at least one (and probably more) of these types of online automated evaluation techniques:

1. System control audit review file and embedded audit modules (SCARF/EAM)
2. Snapshots (of the steps transactions take from input to output)
3. Audit hooks (embedding programs within the web site that act as red flags to indicate when an error or irregularity has occurred that is escalating in size or severity, so as to prevent it from getting out of control)
4. Integrated test facilities (a duplicate site to simulate the entire web site operation and verify its validity by comparing the results at the test site to actual results based on live data flowing through the system)
5. Continuous and intermittent simulation (a system that continuously checks while running transactions, and audits a transaction if certain predetermined criteria are met)

Contingency Items

1. Any other item that has been a serious concern, from business managers or whistleblower calls to the audit committee, or that key executives would like to have checked relative to the operation of the web site
2. Anything unusual relating to the information systems architecture that covers the web site operations (including changes to process synchronization, job scheduling software, data communications software, operating system changeover/upgrade, or new data modeling/reporting software implementation)

 ## HACKERS AND OUTSIDE-THE-NETWORK ATTACKS

As you can tell, many problems can be encountered when trying to protect information in the systems network from outside attack (either from unauthorized access or unauthorized modification).

Hackers, internal and external, are constantly trying to bypass internal controls, both manual and automated, to steal company funds or to obtain data on customers that will allow them to steal or modify customer data.

Hackers perform their work in a variety of ways. Some of the most common methods are shown next.

Looking at Established Automated Diaries

Your company computer faithfully preserves data that most people are unaware of. Sensitive information is contained in bits of deleted files, parts of documents created or opened, cookies from Web pages visited, and chats in instant messenger. Access to these should be restricted by setting your history time frame to one or two days only or by offloading this history to a more secure location.

Computers used on the Internet keep track of all your activities. Every time you give your credit card to a retailer, even a local restaurant, you run the risk of that data failing into the wrong hands. Limiting such access—or monitoring its results—is important to ensure that unauthorized charges are not made. Verify the data against the source documentation to spot inconsistencies. Also, be sure not to access such sites from public locations, such as Internet cafes or local libraries.

Viewing Swap Files

Computer programs require memory to function. While processing is normally handled by the central RAM (random access memory) processing unit, the computer is able to perform its job by creating what is commonly referred to as virtual memory. Virtual memory is a fabulous thing but a privacy nightmare. Files or data encrypted in Windows or Linux often are unencrypted in the virtual memory (usually in the paging or swap files).

Often this problem can be resolved through the creation of a permanently allocated swap file of a fixed size that then can be destroyed periodically by use of a file-wipe utility.

Making Changes to the System Directory

The system registry contains configuration data and tells programs and device drivers when to start and how to run properly. As a result, any changes to this area can stop vital functions or create new programs or tell your computer to go to a web site and post information there. Unlike other parts of your computer, the system register cannot be file-wiped or deleted because its function is vital to the performance of your computer. Hackers love putting new things in system registries, because it makes these things almost impossible to delete.

It is almost impossible for the average person or even system programmer to understand how the system registry functions or what it is telling the computer to do. As a result, average users do not know the processes it initiates or deletes. Some IT people consider this an advantage, because they can then track users' activities when they are using the computer. This is true, but I believe that the loss of local user control relative to the ease of hacker control offsets the advantages gained.

There are many other hacking options, such as stack overrides or placing Trojan programs, but these are generally easily defeated if proper security measures, such as firewalls and the use of proxy servers, are enacted. Other, more advanced methods include denial-of-service attacks or emanation eavesdropping, but these are beyond the scope of discussion of this chapter.

All of the hacker attacks mentioned require the use of network access, whether the hacker is internal (i.e., he or she works for the company) or external (outside of the company). But another possible method to override compliance involves outside-the-network attacks. Better known as social engineering, these activities involve convincing others inside the company (who do have access to the network) to make the changes for them. Hackers sometimes do this by sending spam e-mails that entice computer users to give up confidential information, such as logon IDs and passwords. Other times, "bait" sites are used to encourage people to visit the site and download "rootkits" that contain infected programs. Sometimes all that is needed is to convince people on the other end of a phone to assume that what the hacker tells them is real. For example, if I call and say that I work for a bank at which you have an account, you may well believe that I really do work for that bank.

 ## SUMMARY

IT professionals need to be cognizant of the need for compliance with many different types of rules. There are actual laws that need to be complied with and that may require regulatory reporting to agencies that monitor such compliance. There are company policies that require compliance in order to improve the efficiency and effectiveness of the company's profit-making efforts. And there are security compliance needs to protect the company against attempted theft of company assets or confidential information. The IT department plays a vital role in all of these activities—often, the key role in the company. Recognizing what these rules are, how others are attempting to circumvent them, and what the company needs to do in response are some of the primary roles of the chief information officer in today's company.

CHAPTER TWENTY-ONE

Service Management

Himanshu Shah

NFORMATION TECHNOLOGY SERVICE DESK processes have matured and standardized over the years. Everything about service management can easily be found in the IT Infrastructure Library (ITIL) or in the documents of the International Organization for Standards (ISO). While these and others have become established as standards, the actual delivery of the service, the tools, knowledge management, centralization of service desk, and associated processes have evolved over time. They continue to evolve to ensure cost optimization, automation, and consistency in delivery of service.

In this chapter, we review the service management life cycle, understand the steps and tools required in delivering a service, and explore different models used for delivering the service.

 SERVICE MANAGEMENT LIFE CYCLE

The service management life cycle is an iterative five-step process, as depicted in Figure 21.1.

Service Modeling

The service management life cycle essentially begins by defining a service delivery model (Step 1) that can be a combination of following options, which we discuss in subsequent sections:

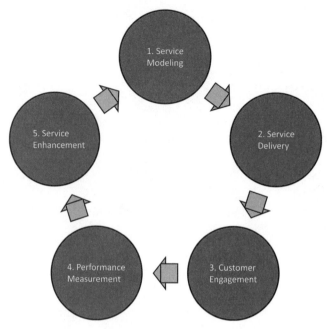

FIGURE 21.1 Service Delivery Life Cycle

- Centralized or decentralized service desk
- Outsourced or in-house desk
- On-site, phone-based, or Web-based support model
- Multilingual options
- Generalist or specialized queue-based support

Service Delivery

Call (ticket) creation, categorization, assignment, and resolution are the activities of the transactional service delivery (Step 2) as managed by the support analysts. In subsequent sections we review the service delivery steps from call assignment until the resolution of the call.

Organizations striving to provide a service delivery differentiation over time need real-time engagement with customers and must consistently measure performance, identify opportunity areas, and enhance the service delivery mechanism through experiential learning.

Customer Engagement

Service delivery managers must have channels for real-time engagement, assessment, and escalation management. Engagement (Step 3) requires real-time understanding of the calls or requests in the queue and the ability to deal with peaks and troughs. Peaks in call volumes are dealt with by pulling support resources from other queues, requesting that resources that are not scheduled be made available on request, deprioritizing noncritical service support, or leveraging resources from other support areas. Doing this also requires an understanding of what drives the high volume. In some cases, interactive voice response (IVR), bulletin board, and plasma updates can be provided to effectively communicate about the issues at hand.

Engagement also requires periodically taking the pulse of service delivery by monitoring calls and interactions. Monitoring provides a greater understanding of the challenges in providing a great customer experience and insight into other opportunities for enhancing the service. Often customers request real-time escalations when their service delivery expectations are not met immediately. The ability to handle escalations, including the number of escalations and the associated resolutions, is a critical element of service delivery process.

Customer engagement through account managers, especially if the service delivery organization is off-site, helps customers understand the process, culture, geography, and knowledge barriers to providing effective service. In addition, receiving feedback based on resolved or unresolved calls using surveys provides a greater understanding of the delivery landscape. We discuss the feedback process in detail as part of the performance measurement process.

Larger service desk operations have specialist roles for managing customer communications. They provide updates on outages, performance measures, and larger process changes in the service delivery model.

Performance Measurement

Performance measurement (Step 4) of service delivery is closely connected with the culture of the organization. Process-driven organizations strive to pay more attention to hard measures of service desk performance. These include the number of tickets managed in a given period of time, ticket handling time, percentage of first-contact resolution (FCR), and the overall resolution percentage.

Higher handling time leads to increased FCR percentage as it gives the customer a greater opportunity to understand and resolve the problem at hand. However, it also increases the cost of service delivery and will increase the hold time of other customers in the queue who are waiting to be serviced. Increased FCR will certainly lead to a greater customer satisfaction.

Organizations driving purely for superior customer experience measure feedback on relatively softer measures. Softer measures include customer feedback surveys, internal assessments from real-time monitoring, and feedback from internal quality audits.

Customer experience feedback typically is gained through a formal survey process. In order to ensure that a fair survey is conducted, larger organizations outsource the feedback process to a third party. Others have an independent audit function that reaches out to customers independently. In either scenario, customers are asked to provide feedback on how their problem/query was resolved. They are also surveyed to understand how the call/service was handled behaviorally.

If the sample of customers surveyed is too large, the cost of feedback will increase and if the sample is too small, the analysis can lead to skewed interpretations. Selecting the right distribution of counts and variants of customers to be surveyed is a critical success factor of the measurement process.

Surveys can be conducted using form-based (electronic or paper) input. In some cases, interactive feedback can be provided at the end of the voice conversation. Answering questions with numerical scores provides only the statistical facts of the overall service provided. Personalized and commentary-based interactions for feedback can yield a greater understanding of the service delivery model and also increase customer confidence in the support delivery model. Interactive feedback sessions can be accomplished through on-site account managers or service delivery managers having a real-time interaction with customers. In addition, attention and response from executive management to critical feedback on service will further strengthen customer confidence in the service delivery process.

Most service delivery organizations have a quality and audit function that measures solutions and behavioral elements from a review of sample calls. Quality processes, on a real-time or off-line basis, can track process adherence as well as etiquette followed by the service delivery organization in its interactions with customers. With this approach, many service improvement opportunities can be identified internally, well before customers get to experience them. Quality checks and input also enable coaching of the IT analysts with the appropriate process knowledge and specific conversational improvements.

Service Enhancement

Service enhancement (Step 5) opportunities identified through soft and hard performance measurement processes provide the input into iteratively evolving the service delivery model, thus representing a complete and continuous cycle. Here are some examples of how the performance process can loop into identifying improvement areas:

- Recognition of those interactions where customers have had a better experience can be used to role model conversations.
- Resolutions on new call types should be fed back into the knowledge base. These will increase the internal knowledge and improve the FCR rate.
- Service delivery training programs built to provide initial and incremental training should directly correlate to the findings from the audit and quality processes.
- Automation and self-service opportunities should be pursued for those call types that are predictable and high in occurrence. Whether it is an IT system or access to Web systems, password resets should be driven through a self-service process rather than being manually reset by the service delivery organization.

Additional system-based enhancements can be provided, from tight integration of back-office systems leading to increased accuracy of customer profile information. The following examples illustrate integration possibilities in the back-office systems:

- Structured information management using a Lightweight Directory Access Protocol (LDAP)-like setup provides a strong integration with business systems and account management.
- Single sign-on access to multiple systems using a single password reduces end-user frustration from managing multiple accounts.

Standardization of software versions, hardware options, image management, and other controlling procedures also reduces the variants in technological environments, further leading to predictable service management and delivery.

Additional enhancements certainly can be driven following ITIL or a similar framework that includes:

- Configuration management to identify, control, and validate all physical assets, service-level agreements, and knowledge. This is also referred to as a configuration management database.
- Effective management of disruptions in the standard service offerings and restoration of the offerings to standard working expectations within the service-level agreements. This is referred to as incident management.
- Proactive management to prevent incidents from happening. This is referred to as problem management. It requires deeper understanding of known issues—expected failures, disruptions, and degradations—with the aim to have a plan to attack the root causes.
- Following a change management methodology to manage changes in the infrastructure using standardized methods and procedures. This provides an assurance that the changes will be made per previously identified schedule while reducing any reworking or duplication of efforts.
- Ensuring that the IT infrastructure is available based on service and cost expectations that organizations are willing to pay.
- Release of new changes to IT infrastructure software and hardware without disruptions.
- Qualification and quantification of IT service management as expected by the customers.
- Continuous communication through reports on performance, trends, assets, and compliance.

 ## WHAT IS SERVICE MANAGEMENT?

In an ideal world, the best-serviced customer is one who receives no service, assuming that the IT infrastructure and systems are seamless, fault free, and high performing. The next best option is where the faults are auto-corrected or a method exists where there is self-sufficiency and customers are IT aware and can resolve problems independent of the service desk. This is probably the reality that most CIOs dream of, but it is certainly a difficult goal to accomplish.

The process of effectively submitting, assigning, approving, solution provision (or resolving), and closure of a request coming into an IT organization can be called *service management*. How effective efforts are depends on the standards of a given organization and the criticality of the service delivery process in line with the organization's business needs. Most organizations measure service on the basis of critical parameters such as call volumes, handle time, resolution rate, and FCR. Other organizations use pure customer experience as the only performance measure.

In reality, it is best to strike a balance between service desk measurement parameters and customer experiences.

The service desk serves as a single point of contact for users across all supported locations for all IT-related incidents, service requests, problem management, and change orders. IT customers typically use one of these channels to log their incidents or support requests:

- Self-service incident-logging e-mail tool
- Telephone call (typically a single internal number across geographies)
- Walk-in (in the case either of the other two options are not possible)

In the introductory paragraph, we mentioned that a lot of best practice scenario and details can be obtained from documented standards. As a result, here we focus on idiosyncrasies with service delivery, pragmatic understanding of real-life scenarios, and how organizations tackle the constant pressures from process management, cost optimization, and customer experience.

Receiving the Call

For the purpose of simplification, we use the terms *service desk tickets* and *service desk calls* interchangeably. It is of utmost importance to ensure that first-level ticket-handling staff members are IT generalists with operational awareness and good communication skills. We strongly emphasize communication skills in order to build a strong, centrally operating global desk. Later in the chapter, we touch on the challenges of dealing with an outsourced and/or remote service desk. With strong IT and communication skills, you will build a greater ability to resolve the call in the first attempt. If it is not resolved, you will ensure that the call is assigned to the right second-level (L2) support staff. Some organizations call the first-level staff L1 and others call them coordinators. Organizations striving for quick turnarounds and higher FCR rates tend to build technically competent L1 support models. The FCR rate of calls attended by L1 will be higher if those calls are relatively simple and routine, such as password resets. Chances of resolution during the first contact with IT have improved over time, based on some of these changes in support models:

- Evolution of technology has made it possible for the L1 staff to access end user workstations remotely and increase the FCR rate.
- Increased sophistication in knowledge management and self-service tools also increases the ability of end users to solve basic IT requests on their own. This does not necessarily increase the FCR. However, it does reduce the need to call for IT assistance in the first place.
- Categorization of tickets by the call coordinators along with an assurance that all pertinent request data are collected up front results in a faster turnaround time.

Figure 21.2 is a graphic representation of one support model that may be employed.

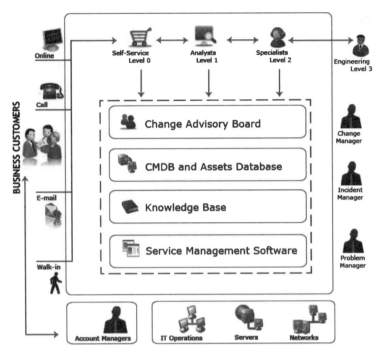

FIGURE 21.2 Service Management

Call Assignment

Once the call has been logged, if it is not resolved by the front-end L1 staff, it needs redirection. Redirection to specialist groups (L2) within the service desk or specialist groups (L3) outside in other departments, such as information security, server infrastructure, or network teams, can be challenging.

Some organizations prefer to have multiskilled L2 specialists within the service desk; others prefer to have L2 specialists purely for services like access provisioning or remote connectivity. In some cases, the L2 layer is relatively thin, and many of these requests are passed on to L3 resources in other departments.

Having a larger L2 population within the service desk can be cost prohibitive. Also, having all access rights for troubleshooting and resolution of tickets may not be possible. As a result, some service requests must be assigned to L3 groups. This certainly impacts on resolution time, as calls are now assigned to other departments.

L3 assignments and resolution depend on two critical factors:

1. The assignment of calls to the correct resolving groups requires L1 and L2 staff with strong technology and business acumen.
2. The operating-level agreements (OLAs) between the specialist delivery organizations and the service desk have to be very strong. A typical service-level agreement is set between the service desk and the customer groups to which the service is provided; OLAs exist between the service desk and the specialist departments that are internal to the IT organization.

Call Resolution

Service delivery organizations strive for a high FCR rate. FCR is measured as a percentage of calls resolved by L1 staff during the first contact compared to the total calls resolved by the service desk in a given period of time.

Measuring resolution time also requires effective tracking of call status. Resolution time is a typical measure of time difference between the time the service was requested and the resolution is provided, minus all the hold time required to obtain pertinent details from the requesting customers.

Modern-day service desk automation systems send out resolution messages (e-mail, Web, or text message–based update) to the serviced customers followed by an acknowledgment from the customers back into IT. The acknowledgment of resolution by end user customers moves a call from Resolved to Closure state.

We touched on what it takes to create a ticket, assign the ticket to various resolving groups, resolve the ticket, and close the ticket with customers. In the next sections, we review other elements of service delivery like call management, service catalog, knowledge management, and asset management.

Call Management

Service requests for password or user management can be managed either using a self-service mechanism or some degree of automation based on employee events. For example, creation of accounts for new hires, closing accounts for terminated employees, and changing access privileges based on job changes are closely tied with the human resources (HR) system. The changes in the HR system should be recognized automatically to ensure quick changes in account privileges. Other service requests that do not require special handling by the L3 organization can be managed within the service desk, and ones that require changes to the infrastructure, such as firewall configurations, network changes, and application changes, are redirected to other support groups.

Categorization of a ticket as a service request or an incident should be managed by the call-handing staff. IT incidents impacting wider customer population often result in a lot of tickets (calls) created for the same problem. Management and closure of these issues can be expensive if not handled appropriately. In such cases, all the individual tickets need to be treated as child tickets and should be closed with a cross-reference to a single parent ticket. The parent ticket typically must be addressed by a specialty L3 organization followed by a root cause analysis of the issue and an update to the knowledge base with relevant resolution details. In addition, in order to reduce the calls coming into the service desk, these situations require a broadcast knowledge of the current situation. Alerts can be provided on plasma screens, dashboards, intranets (web sites), e-mails, and text messages based on the nature of the problem and the organization's approach in communicating such alerts. Also, if these issues are related to outages in the systems or the network, they require close looping with the support organization. There must be a cumulative accounting of outages and assurance that operational-level agreements are managed with supporting functions using these details. In many cases, the problems might not be outages. They can be degradations in system performance from increased usage, increased transactions, or other limitations with infrastructure horsepower or network bandwidth. Issues like these also require close looping with the supporting organizations to track root causes and assessment for ramping up of network bandwidth or infrastructure capacity.

Service Catalog Management

In simple terms, service catalog management is a menu or catalog of services provided by the IT department. It essentially captures different services, categories, approval details, cost information (if applicable), and expected turnaround time for resolution or service. Turnaround time is one of the critical performance parameters for the service delivery organization. It is published to customers being serviced and tightly coupled with the service desk processes and OLAs with other delivery organizations. A typical list of services is illustrated in Table 21.1. A sample entry for e-mail service in the service catalog is illustrated in Table 21.2.

TABLE 21.1 Typical List of Services

Service Type	Provisioning Medium and Processes	Measurement
Communication	Mail, messenger, and broadcast services	Uptime, capacity, and performance
Desktop management	Configuration and upkeep of standard workstation image	Patching, compliance and performance
Productivity tools	Document, spreadsheet, presentation, and process management tools	Patching, integration, and performance
Network access	Access to organization's systems over local, metropolitan, and wide area networks	Uptime and performance
Remote access	Remote access mechanism for troubleshooting, knowledge sharing, and presentation	Authorization, authentication, and availability
Internet/intranet	Restricted and unrestricted access to authenticated and white-listed domains inside and outside of the organization	Uptime and performance
Identity and access management	Managing users, their profiles, personalization, and ease of access to business systems through single-sign-on configuration	Authorization, authentication, availability, and self-service
Threat management	Protecting business systems from vulnerabilities and attacks	Infections, threats, vulnerabilities, patching, and compliance
Backups and archiving	Ensuring high availability of information from disasters and data losses	Backup success, recoverability, and restoration

TABLE 21.2 Sample Entry for E-mail Service in the Service Catalog

Service Name	E-mail
Service Availability	24 hours/7 days a week
Eligibility	Full-time employees and authorized contractors, standard desktop access, and active employment status on corporate HR management system
Service Creation	Automatic creation on the basis of employment entry and inactivation upon termination of employment services as recorded in the HR management system
Service Support	Service desk through published contact mechanisms
Cost	Charge-back component of IT services
Service Availability	99.9% excluding scheduled outages every other Saturday from 12 midnight until 3 a.m.
	Account creation and updates within 48 hours of employment status changes
	Quota/capacity based on designation and specialized needs
	Restoration based on severity of outages

Other services provided in the catalog can include extension to the basic IT services, such as application services (support processes for enterprise resource planning and customer relationship management systems) and specialized services for projects and technology architecture management.

Knowledge Management

Service desk knowledge is not the same as process expertise within L3 groups. Service desk knowledge is built, managed, and accessed using a knowledge database. This database can be a simple collection of files, a repository on the intranet, or a systematic solution that provides a database of known issues/problems along with the resolution steps describing underlying actions. These knowledge tools provide details on IT issues along with resolutions. Organizations seeking customer excellence and process optimization tend to implement high-end knowledge management solutions. Organizations that have cost as the primary driver build rudimentary knowledge bases that are hosted on their intranet.

Sophisticated knowledge management solutions allow creation of structured knowledge with an easy-to-use unstructured search mechanism for service desk staff or end users. In most cases, resolution process/documentation is a narrative presentation that allows easy-to-follow step-by-step instructions for resolution.

Whether a knowledge management solution is bought or a rudimentary knowledge base is built in-house, service desk performance will depend on how the knowledge is maintained in the system. Every time a new call type is logged and resolved, it is imperative that the new knowledge (resolution) is incrementally added to this repository. This discipline will positively impact long-term resolution rates (FCR) and will ease the analysis of root causes.

Asset Management

Many service requests result in allocation of assets to end users in the form of software or hardware. It is essential that when IT analysts serve these requests there is a close tie-in with the software and hardware inventory management. The inventory will certainly tie into the organization's security, data protection, software compliance, and audit policies. Also, it is relatively easy to track and manage inventory of hardware resources as they are physically allocated. If these are devices connected on the network, inventory and desktop management software solutions can easily account for these resources and help you update the inventory automatically. In the case of software installation on desktops, installed units can be maintained as part of the inventory, and new installations can be made using centralized desktop management software with a push mechanism. Desktop management solutions can actually record the number of available licensed software units, track the number of installed software units, and appropriately lock from deployment unauthorized or unlicensed installations. Automating these inventory details improves accuracy of information, reduces the effort required from HR, and protects the organization from licensing violations.

Asset inventory can be managed through a sophisticated asset management tool or a simplified list of assets in the inventory. A typical asset inventory would capture these details:

- Asset identification number (internal to organization)
- Asset name and description
- Asset type (software, desktop, server, etc.)
- Asset location and assigned to user
- Manufacturer's serial number
- Asset make
- Asset model (if applicable)
- License key required
- Asset purchase date
- Asset install date
- Warranty/maintenance period

 ## SERVICE DELIVERY MODELS

Economies of scale, particularly as cost optimization becomes an important driver for many organizations, can be generated by centralizing service delivery organizations in one or two locations. Language, culture, and time-zone differences complicate the centralized service delivery model for those organizations that operate in multiple continents or countries.

Centralized or Decentralized

Centralization gives companies the option to operate the service delivery organization from locations that are business critical, talent rich, and cost effective. It also allows for planning of shadow or backup HR, easy sharing of knowledge, service desk specialists (L2) sitting right next to the L1 service delivery center, and the ability to support multiple time zones from a single location. In addition to offering cost advantages, it also results in tight coupling of IT's people, processes, and technologies.

The next critical success factors should be a focus of service delivery in order to achieve excellence from centralization:

- Greater understanding of the customer organizations' culture by the servicing geography
- Acknowledgment of process, technical, and cultural gaps in the servicing geography
- Continuous improvement road map to bridge gaps periodically
- Strong communication channel and a continuous exchange of knowledge and information

The other opportunity lies in ensuring that there are designated account managers in the major geographies that are being serviced. They provide a continuous communication channel to the service delivery organization with knowledge regarding user expectations, cultural awareness, changes in technology, and other challenges in service delivery.

It is practically impossible for multilocation organizations to have a local service desk at each geographic location. In some cases there may not even be an IT presence at remote or smaller sites, which are typically satellite offices connected to the corporate network but with a small number of employees—sales offices, for example.

Decentralized service desks are built to provide in-person assistance. They are also implemented when support is required in local languages.

Outsourcing

Another popular mechanism of service delivery is a combination of centralized, global, and outsourced service delivery. Outsourcing enables organizations to leverage third parties that have built delivery models and other strengths from years of experience. It also allows scale-up and scale-down of resources and delivery models based on seasonal and other time-sensitive requirements.

Outsourcers bring models, tools, workforce, and processes with a variety of options. Options available with outsourcers may not readily fit into the needs of the organization being serviced. Critical decision points to be considered include:

- Identification of performance measurement metrics. These require fine-tuning over time, as the previously identified measurement parameters based on contractual agreements may not be strongly connected with the real-time customer experience. In an effort to drive process and performance, third parties may dilute the customer experience.
- Tools and processes for ticket management, change management, asset management, and knowledge also require fine-tuning.

- Communication and interaction processes with customers need to be built, validated, tested, and refined over time. Script-based interactions offer a seamless structure but also create a box that might impact customer experience and limit creativity of the service desk staff.
- Outsourcing the service to a third party will require a definite investment to bring the third party closer to the culture of customer organization. If the service is outsourced to a third party in another geography, additional investment and training will be required in building soft skills, customer service etiquettes, and understanding of cultural differences.

Building rapport with customers is yet another piece of the puzzle in real-time interactions. Rapport building can increase the call-handling time and will impact the overall service desk performance. In the case of real-time interactions, to simplify rapport-building conversations with customers, organizations may broadcast updates on events in the customer's location. These broadcasts educate service desk staff about major news, events, weather details, celebrations, and sporting events at the customers' sites.

Service Delivery Medium

Real-time interactions provide a greater customer experience, but they come with their own price tag. Evolution of technology has provided options to increase self-service usage through knowledge bases, IVR, and other tools for account password resets. These are the alternatives, in order of decreasing customer interaction and increasing self-service capabilities:

- Regarding service delivery, the first choice is to have an IT analyst walk to your desk. This method works very well. It allows easy rapport building as well as addressing issues other than your primary request. This is a luxury and not a very pragmatic solution as the cost of doing so is very high.
- The next best option is to make available phone-based support where you still have a remote but real-time conversation. Customers call into a service desk phone queue. For seamless access from any of the offices, it is desirable to have a single extension to call across geographies. Although this is a personalized delivery of service, it does not allow the IT analyst to attend to multiple customers at the same time. In cases when there are multiple queues of servicing organizations, the phone systems are coupled with IVR and computer telephony integration (CTI). IVR allows customers to provide basic information about their query so that the call can be forwarded to an analyst skilled with the specific query type. This increases the probability of FCR. CTI is a simple integration of customer profile information on the service delivery systems with telephony. Customers input a recognizable code during the dial time so that all relevant information about their profile and history of existing reported but unresolved problems is automatically populated. This results in reduced handling time and enhanced customer experience.

- Web-based interaction is the next available option. This is in real time and interactive. It also allows some degree of multitasking for the service delivery organization and makes exchange of information easy. Also, some of the challenges with conversational skills, accent, and language barriers are diluted with this approach.

- With the evolution of the Internet and intranets, knowledge is easily accessible from the workstations. There is no service desk personnel engagement, but this method requires end users to dedicate time. Even though staff engagement does not exist, the content presented to customers can be personalized based on nature of their jobs and queries that they are trying to resolve. When a particular query is searched, the resolution can be in the form of sequential steps to walk end users through the solution. In some cases, solutions are built to detect the problems automatically and fix them based on known solutions.

- In an absolute cost-conscious setup where the volume of requests is very high with a high degree of variation, organizations use e-mail as a medium. Turnaround is not as effective and not as personalized. In these situations, the service is typically outsourced, and it is probably the most inexpensive service delivery option. Customer experience can get compromised with this approach.

 ## CONCLUSION

Organizations can choose from several models and tools for service delivery. To pick the right option, the criticality of providing a certain set of services, nature of the business supported, cost of providing the actual service, and impacts from centralized, offshore, and outsourced approaches must all be considered.

At the same time, organizations should revisit their models to continuously improve service delivery and optimize delivery cost. Emphasis should also be put on consistently reaching out to the customers being served and understanding the softer (human) elements of the services being delivered. Managing and improving internal knowledge will further strengthen the delivery process. Advances in technology must also be introduced to provide the right service at the right time, possibly increasing self-service capabilities in each of the revisions. To repeat, the best-serviced customer is the one who needs no service.

CHAPTER TWENTY-TWO

Balancing IT's Workload

David Blumhorst

M OST CIOs STRUGGLE WITH a common problem: the insatiable demand for IT work from other departments. After all, IT is a service department, providing the underlying and often-strategic technologies that enable many companies to thrive. Considering the rapid pace of business today, those technologies need to keep up with constantly changing requirements.

Thus, we are faced with an overwhelming demand for work against our limited capacity to perform the work. Most strategies for dealing with this overload involve work request intake processes and prioritization schemes. Some may take the extra step of allocating their resources, usually against projects. But if you simply look at the problem statement, the path to a solution becomes more obvious. To balance the load, we must match the incoming demand for work against the supply of resources to perform it.

 IT WORK COMES IN THROUGH MANY CHAOTIC CHANNELS

Incoming demand into IT is not a simple thing. Work can come in through many channels and in many forms. There are tickets flowing through the help desk by the thousands. Some are simple requests for help, such as changing passwords or finding the power button. But many are too complex for Level 1, and require escalation to Level 2 or up to developers. These requests come from all over the company. If there is a centralized support system, most of the requests should come through as tickets.

If not, more than likely problems come into IT via e-mail, phone call, or even drive-by, where users walk over to the cubicle of their favorite IT troubleshooter and ask for help. And as every CIO knows, other executives often turn to them for guidance. I have personally taken more than a few midnight calls from a vice president looking for help with e-mail, VPN connections, or even how to find clip art in PowerPoint. Made me wonder why I had a 24/7 help desk.

Demand for work also comes from within IT, particularly to the operations and infrastructure groups. Here we are looking at routine maintenance of networks, servers, databases, and other core infrastructure pieces. Of course, every new system deployed adds to the ongoing demand for maintenance, and IT is a business department in its own right, requiring systems to help with managing support tickets, networks, data centers, workflow, projects, portfolios, and more.

This demand from within IT can be thought of as base demand—keeping current systems operating in good form (aka keeping the lights on). This type of work is mostly invisible outside of IT—unless, of course, something goes terribly awry. It is, however, the base of the IT workload iceberg, not the tip, and this below-the-surface base keeps growing as IT deploys more technology into more corners of the enterprise.

The more visible tip of the iceberg comes in the form of requests to change existing systems or deploy new ones. The most familiar form is the project request—changes requiring large enough expenditures of funds or resources to require approval and visibility by management. Projects generally require teams of people and follow prescribed methodologies. Since there are approval and visibility requirements, this part of the workload is most understood throughout the company. Projects are usually grouped into portfolios and reported on to the executive team (the subject of another chapter). What is not well understood, however, is that projects are only a minor part of IT's workload. I have worked with many IT departments that track all of their time and have never found projects to consume more than 35 percent. More often projects clock in around 15 to 20 percent of total staff time.

So, what is left? What about the business-requested changes that do not come through the help desk but are too small to be considered projects? Examples include adding a custom field to an order form, adding a new business intelligence report to pull the latest sales data by region, or changing the approval process for purchase orders. Typically the number of these change requests far outweighs the number of project requests. I have heard them called change orders, microprojects, enhancements, and work orders. The most creative term I have run across is "death by a thousand cuts," and this is often how it feels, as this area tends to be the most ungoverned source of incoming work in IT. While support tickets generally flow through a help desk system and projects often require formalized proposals flowing through an approval process, change orders have a way of falling through the governance cracks.

In many IT departments, this work comes into the organization in an ungoverned fashion. Minimally, support work may come in through a help desk system, but sometimes not. When not flowing through a defined process, projects may come in via e-mail, hallway conversations, or direct requests to technical staff. This subjects all staff members to the dreaded death by a thousand cuts as work comes from all directions to just about anyone in IT.

RESOURCE ALLOCATION MYTHS

Let's turn to the capacity for performing all this work—the supply side of the equation. First, though, we need to debunk a couple of myths about resource planning. There is no better way to debunk these myths than by using data gathered from actual time logs of IT employees. Now, I know this is a sensitive topic in many IT groups. IT staff members are generally opposed to logging their time—they have more important work to do. But if all IT staff members do log all of their time, and you analyze that data, some interesting patterns are uncovered.

First is the myth that any person can be allocated to a given project 100 percent of the time—that a person can actually be expected to work 40 hours per week on a given project. This is a common expectation in project management circles, and understandably so. If resources are dedicated to the project, they should have no other work to do, right? Analysis of time logs that I have seen at PeopleSoft (where I worked) and at other companies reveals that this is almost never the case. Even dedicated programmers will spend some time in general meetings, reviewing e-mail, logging time, and doing other administrative work. These activities generally consume 15 to 30 percent of even the most dedicated developer's time. Next, these same developers are the ones brought in to resolve support tickets that have been escalated to Level 3. Theoretically they may be dedicated to their project, but when push comes to shove, an urgent ticket will get priority. Firefighting always takes precedence over the long-term project work. The idea is that they can catch up on the project work, which would be fine if there were not always another fire to fight. As this "support" work shows up in time logs, it must be accounted for.

Myth 2 is that managers do not do project work. Based on time logs I have analyzed, even IT directors can get involved in project work. Indeed, in some IT groups, line managers take on the role of project managers. As I have noted, I have even seen CIOs get involved in troubleshooting.

Finally, myth 3 is that IT is a project-driven organization. As stated earlier, I have yet to analyze an IT group's time logs where project work rises to over 35 percent of the total effort. Most groups report project time in the 15 to 20 percent range. This, of course, is hugely dependent on how a "project" is defined. Different organizations define different thresholds of budget, effort, and risk to cross that project line. Even so, the data clearly show that IT is not a project-driven organization, and simply looking to balance resources against project demand would miss the vast majority of the workload.

What is the lesson learned from these myths? To understand IT capacity, we need to look at all work done by all IT staff. It is simply not possible to segregate the work by one specific IT area or one type of work, no matter how the department is organized.

Given these facts, let's take care of two easier-to-plan areas before turning to more complex matters.

First is the help desk. Here, measuring the volume of tickets and the average effort to resolve each ticket leads to a quick answer as to how much staff is needed. Doing this requires, however, that both those items are actively measured. I can still remember the conversation with my help desk supervisor asking for more staff. When I asked for justification, he responded, "We're just overwhelmed with work—we need more people or we're going to drown!" When I asked how many, he responded that two or three would be good. "How do you know?" I asked. "How do you know it's two or three, and not one or five?"

I continue to be amazed at how many hiring decisions are taken this way. If Level 1 and 2 support simply log their time spent working tickets, and we know the number of tickets resolved, we have help desk capacity in terms of tickets per staff member. Take the incoming flow of tickets and divide by capacity per person, and we have the staff required to "balance" this area's workload. And do not forget to reduce their overall capacity by their own administrative overhead!

The next group, at least in larger IT organizations, is management and administration. Generally, director-level executives on up do very little "productive" work—just ask them. Generally administrative staff—executive assistants, vendor management, IT finance, and so on—are pretty much dedicated to running IT, not doing the technical work that is the source of demand complexities. So we can safely allocate these IT positions to a management or administration bucket. But they still need to log their time as we want to catch any trends that might show otherwise.

This leaves the rest of the IT organization, whose job is to turn business needs and problems into delivered results via technology. As it turns out, their workload is the most complex.

ORGANIZING DEMAND FOR WORK BY SCALE

One way to deal with this complexity is to break the workload into several groupings by scale. Why by scale? Because each of these groupings is governed in a different fashion, each ideally comes through its own intake process, and therefore each needs to have resource allocations planned differently. The categories generally used are:

- Tickets
- Maintenance
- Enhancements
- Projects

Tickets are the support issues flowing through the help desk. These should all flow through a centralized support system. At smaller firms, this may be a simple Access database or a system based on software as a service (SaaS). The point is, all tickets are logged and tracked so that this stream of work can be measured and balanced. Balancing the ticket load for the support group is a simple matter of knowing the ticket capacity per person and adjusting the staff accordingly. It is also important to anticipate peak loads that be caused by new systems coming online or major projects being deployed. For the rest of IT, the demand coming through the ticket stream needs to be balanced against the rest of the demand streams. We will get to this a bit later.

Maintenance work is all the routine tasks required to keep IT systems up and running. Examples include database maintenance, backups, and network monitoring. Most of this work is performed by technical staff that will also be involved in project deployments and ticket escalations in their areas. So, to balance this work stream, we first need to measure it using time logs and then reserve that percentage of time against capacity.

Enhancements are all those changes coming through the door that are smaller than a project but not a ticket. As these do not usually go through a formal approval process, it is again best to first measure this bucket using time logs and then reserve a percentage of capacity. The next trick is determining which enhancement requests will be fulfilled using that capacity. The most successful method I have seen is for business relationship managers (if the department has them) to keep an ongoing list of requests and work with their business counterparts to prioritize those requests.

Finally, there are projects. To delineate this category from the others, it is important to define what meets the criteria for a project. These criteria usually revolve around the costs, effort, duration, and risk of the project. As an example, at PeopleSoft, an effort needed to be over $50,000 in incremental (noninternal labor) cost, or over 90 person-days of effort, or over 30 days' duration to qualify as a project. Anything less was not considered a project and was not subject to our project management methodology or approval processes. Projects require case-by-case analysis and allocation of capacity, as is described in the last section of this chapter.

For projects, it is also important to plan them into capacity before the initiation phase. Project intake, when properly done, is actually a cyclical portfolio process—not part of the formal project management methodology. In this way, requests are considered as a slate on a monthly or quarterly basis. They can be analyzed based on strategic alignment and viewed against capacity. Since they are not being approved ad hoc, there is less chance of a later, more important, project trumping an already in-flight project, which produces extremely inefficient churn. A good way to look at this is illustrated in Figure 22.1.

In this diagram, we see that capacity planning is aligned with intake. This is not the end of the resource planning process; it is the beginning. Any given project's resource plan will continue to be refined during its life cycle, and the traditional role allocation and resource assignment exercises still occur. They are just front-ended by high-level

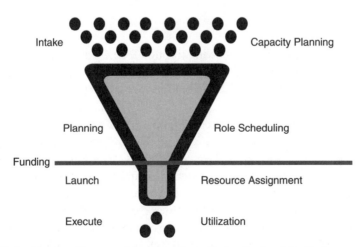

FIGURE 22.1 Aligning Resource Management with the Project Life Cycle

capacity planning, thus increasing the chance that projects will successfully find the resources they need.

PLANNING IT LIKE A MANUFACTURING FLOOR

IT is, fundamentally, a service department. Its job is to provide information technology that supports and enables the achievement of business strategies and goals. There is no doubt that IT can be a very strategic player for an organization, and done well it provides a competitive advantage to the firm. Still, the bulk of IT's work is delivered to other business units and external customers.

Further, as we have seen from our analysis of the types of demand, this work can be very diverse. IT is not like finance or human resources, providing a relatively homogenous set of services. Instead, IT uses very different sets of technologies, such as network connectivity, telecommunications, e-mail, Web, and enterprise applications to pursue very different business goals. And these technologies change and evolve very rapidly.

One way to look at this diverse work is as a continual incoming stream of work requests. These requests, whether they are tickets, minor enhancements, or projects, get prioritized and queued up for execution. The way most IT departments work today, when these requests are ready, they go looking for people to perform the work.

Now, if you were running a manufacturing plant and had more incoming sales orders than capacity, would you wait until those orders hit the floor before looking for equipment to produce them? And if you sold many types of products—say, diverse auto parts such as brakes, mufflers, and wheels—would you wait for the orders to hit the floor before deciding which manufacturing line to send them down? Of course not. Yet this is how we treat our requests for diverse technology work all the time.

Like any other department that produces tangible product—in our case, various technologies—a little planning is in order. Like any smooth-running plant, that starts with capacity planning. Capacity planning is the science and art of aligning all those incoming requests with the proper work teams and deciding which ones hit the floor when to make the most efficient use of available capacity.

DIFFERENT TECHNIQUES FOR DIFFERENT-SIZE DEPARTMENTS

The techniques used to perform capacity planning vary greatly by the size of the IT organization.

Smaller organizations up to approximately 50 total IT staff plan by the person. At this level there is no overlap between functions, and indeed many people perform several jobs. The project manager is likely to also be the business analyst. There may be only one network engineer, and he may also be the network administrator and perhaps even the e-mail guru. The Web developer handles design, HTML coding, and Java scripting. So, for a smaller department, it makes no sense to think of resource pools. It is much more practical to plan by individual resource.

Still, some basic planning elements are necessary. Help desk demand, even if the area is made up only of a couple of people, should still come through a centralized system—even if it is a simple ticketing system. It should be queued and prioritized, and the volume should be monitored, and the help desk staffers must log their time to show just how busy they are. This way, when they complain of being overloaded, they will have the evidence to back it up—and will have a much better chance of obtaining some relief.

Small organizations should also collect their demand for enhancements and projects in a central location, even if it is just a spreadsheet or Access database. Demand for development time can then be prioritized and queued, then fed into the various developers based on their availability. Most small organizations that do this successfully keep a spreadsheet or database with rows for each staff member, with detail on which projects/enhancements they are working on spread over columns of time, usually in weekly increments. Some small IT departments have taken to using low-cost SaaS project and portfolio management systems. Again, members should log their time to gather feedback from their planning, which greatly improves accuracy.

Medium-size IT departments of between 50 and 200 staff members differently. They often contain multiple people doing the same, more specialized jobs. Network engineers and network administrators are different people. The programmer does not do database administrator (DBA) work. And usually there are multiple programmers and DBAs.

Further, while in a small department enhancements and projects often are executed by one person or at most a small team, with midsize departments, larger teams (over five people) often are involved.

Because of the greater size, overlap, and complexity of spreadsheets, it no longer makes sense to plan by individual. Midsize IT departments that successfully balance their workloads start using resource pools or teams—groups of people who typically do similar functions and/or work on similar endeavors. For enhancements and projects, the demand still should be collected and centralized, but it will not be governed and planned in the same way.

For these departments, it works best to allocate time at the pool level and to allocate certain percentages of time for different scales of work. So, for example, we might allocate programmers to work 40 percent of the time on enhancements, 30 percent on projects, 20 percent on ticket escalations, and 10 percent on administrative work. Network administrator's allocations would be more weighted to tickets and less to projects. Of course, the help desk would be almost entirely ticket driven.

How the work is planned changes in midsize groups. Ticket work still follows the normal help desk queuing and escalation scenarios. Enhancements are usually prioritized and gated by an IT business relationship manager working in conjunction with a business-side colleague. This work is then fed into the development area by priority but only up to the allocated percentage.

The most successful way to handle project work is to gather the requests cyclically, either monthly or quarterly. The requests are then reviewed and prioritized by a steering committee. This steering committee reviews the upcoming availability of the resource pools and slots requests into time frames based on availability. If there is insufficient capacity to handle all the requests (and there always is), the steering committee decides which requests to approve and which to deny.

The steering committee is an important piece of project governance, of course. Ideally it is a cross-functional body comprising executives from around the company. As representatives of the company, it is their job to make prioritization and approval decisions that best align with corporate objectives. Making these decisions is most decidedly *not* IT's job. When IT takes on prioritization and approval role, plenty of blame and finger-pointing from the other business units ensues. As these decisions have a profound impact on the company, they should be made by the company's leaders.

Large IT organizations typically contain well over 200 staff members. These organizations are characterized by a high degree of both overlap and specialization. There may be whole departments of Web developers, network engineers, DBAs, and so forth. At this size, even measuring capacity by resource pool breaks down. Why?

Let's look at the type of work coming into IT again. A typical network upgrade project will employ several resource pools. There will be a network project manager (PM), network analyst, network engineer, and operations staff to implement the project into production. There may be seven or eight resource pools involved in this one project. Other projects will also employ several resource pools (see Figure 22.2).

If we are looking to measure capacity for projects, which resource pools do we look at? When looking at slates of 50-plus project requests, it is very difficult to queue them up by resource pool when they all involve multiple pools. Yet simply looking at total IT capacity for, say, 500 people is way too broad. This method could lead to the approval of too many application projects, leaving network engineers twiddling their thumbs, or vice versa. How, then, to look at and plan capacity in a meaningful way?

Just as manufacturing lines use many sets of equipment, IT projects use many sets of resource pools. And, just as those sets of equipment are organized into a manufacturing line, we can organize resource pools into virtual production lines based on project type (see Figure 22.3).

Enterprise resource planning (ERP) projects will use the app project manager pool, app programmer pool, and the app DBA pool. A network rollout will use the network project managers, network engineers, and network operations. If we can find an alignment of resource pools that lines up with types of projects, we can measure capacity for each of these virtual production tracks and make capacity-planning decisions based on those tracks.

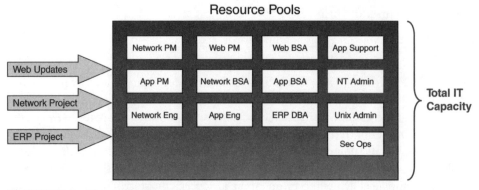

FIGURE 22.2 Classic Resource Pools

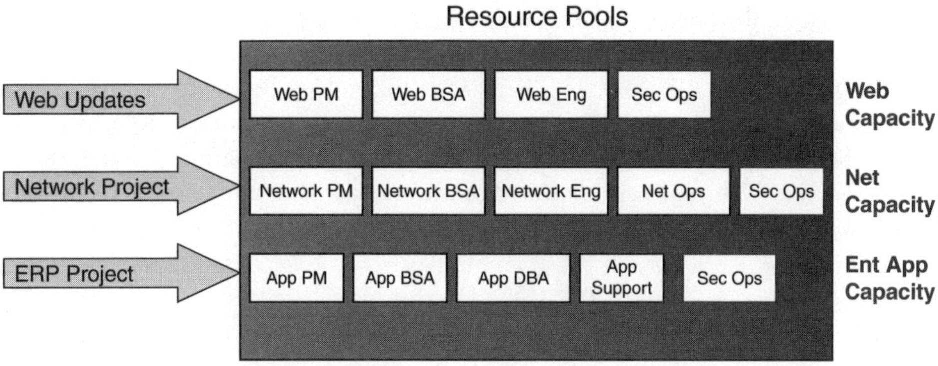

Resource Pools

FIGURE 22.3 Virtual Resource Tracks

We can even look for resource pool bottlenecks. Again, the manufacturing floor model is a good analogy. Equipment type 1 might process 100 items/hour, while type 2 processes 200. We therefore need two pieces of type 1 for each of one of type 2. Likewise, we may need more programmers for an enterprise app project than DBAs, and can adjust our staffing levels accordingly.

Of course, analyzing time logs so that we know how much each pool can process is critical to finding these bottlenecks.

KEYS TO SUCCESS

There are four keys to successfully balancing IT's often overwhelming workload:

1. **Consider all of IT's work and staff, not just projects and programmers.** As everyone in IT may get involved in the various types of work IT does, narrowing in on just one aspect will not solve the problem.
2. **Govern the workload by scale.** Tickets are governed by help desk queues, enhancements by targeted percentage policies, and projects by a formal intake funnel.
3. **Plan capacity early.** Just as in manufacturing, capacity planning must be done long before projects are launched. Done properly, planning capacity early reduces the scramble for resources and minimizes conflicting priorities. It also allows more work to be completed without interruption, reducing inefficiencies caused by churn.
4. **Track all time.** To truly understand the workload in IT, everyone from the CIO on down must log their time. At a minimum, they must log time to the different scales and types of work and to individual projects. Without this critical feedback, even the best planning process is just guesswork.

CONCLUSION

IT is one of the most demanded resources in a modern corporation. No matter the size, the idea of a balanced workload may seem like a pipe dream. The natural reaction to simply work harder often results in burnout and costly errors. As is obvious from the analysis in this chapter, tackling resource allocation on a project-by-project basis or through individual IT departments will not solve the problem. But once this overload is seen as a fundamental IT-wide supply/demand problem, the answers become much clearer. IT still will not be able to do all of the work asked of the department, but it will be able to analyze, plan, and gain control of that workload. The result is a more efficient, more motivated, and ultimately better-regarded IT organization.

CHAPTER TWENTY-THREE

Outsourcing and Offshoring

Jeff Richards

I N TODAY'S HIGHLY COMPETITIVE global environment, many companies are asking the question: "Is outsourcing right for me?" The short answer is probably a qualified yes. Some part of almost every organization could undoubtedly benefit from an outsourcing assessment, but "which part" and "why" are the hard questions.

What exactly is outsourcing? First, outsourcing is always a service. Second, outsourcing differs from the purchase of normal services in three material ways:

1. The service is performed to a service level that is managed by the service provider.
2. Some kind of time commitment exists (e.g., fixed term or continues until terminated).
3. The buyer usually has some personnel offset.

Some examples may help clarify the idea. Some things that are not outsourcing are: purchasing and implementing an enterprise resource planning system (it is a product with installation services), FedEx delivery services (no time commitment), and staff augmentation (you manage the resource, not the provider).

Some things that are clearly outsourcing include HP/EDS operating the IT infrastructure, using Laidlaw to operate the school district's buses, or ADP handling payroll processing.

Services that can be defined either way include tax preparation and application maintenance. Each is outsourcing if the work is ongoing (has a fixed term) and the provider manages the personnel resources.

REASONS TO OUTSOURCE

There are hundreds of reasons why companies outsource. Most companies have multiple objectives targeted. The most common reasons fall into three main categories, including finance, operations, and labor. A list would include:

- Improve quality, process, or customer satisfaction
- Access difficult-to-source skills
- Reduce capital requirements
- Improve cost efficiency or facilitate low-cost entry
- Provide disaster recovery and business continuity
- Improve technology
- Level resources during peaks and troughs of demand
- Leverage international time zones
- Focus on core business

The best reason to outsource a service is to focus on your core business (the reason you have customers, profits, and market share) and minimize the distractions. By far, the most common reason companies investigate outsourcing is the promise of financial reward.

Some of the more common financial rewards are lower cost, reduced capital requirements, improved cash flow, investment avoidance, and turning assets into cash. In the final analysis, there are not many (if any) outsourcing deals that do not have some form of financial advantage. Executive management would be neglecting fiduciary responsibilities if they outsourced a function that cost more. In the few cases where outsourcing appears to cost more, an in-depth analysis shows the cost to be less than the internal cost to obtain the same quality, functionality, or growth ability that the provider is promising.

A word of caution: Focusing on lower cost alone is usually a recipe for disaster. This is because any function can be delivered at a lower cost if quality, functionality, and quantity of service are ignored. The best outsourcing strategies focus on the non-financial reasons to outsource and use financial rewards as the ultimate tie-breaker.

The final category is labor. Common reasons to outsource are access to difficult-to-source skills, the need to scale labor, reducing human resources overhead, and gaining additional points of view and industry experience. The last point is perhaps the most important for growing companies that are focused on core business and lack the time or resources to take full advantage of advances or technology in the common business processes.

 WHAT TO OUTSOURCE

"How do you decide what to outsource?" is one of the most commonly asked questions. One approach is to place processes/functions in the matrix in Figure 23.1. The horizontal axis is the organization's current competency (poor on the far left and

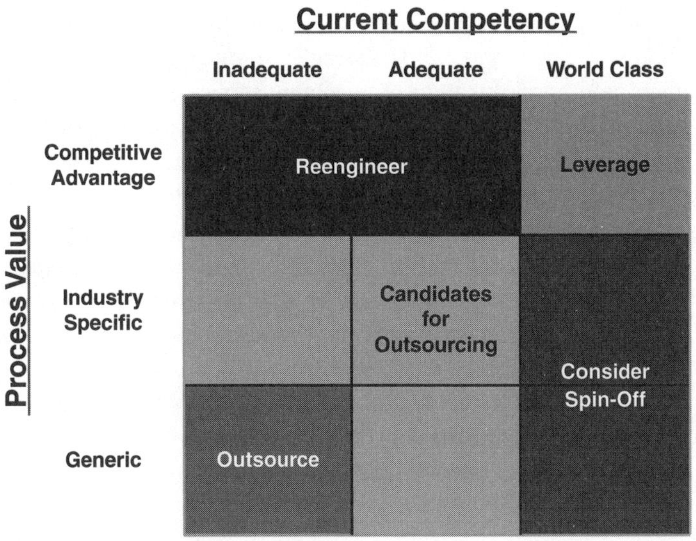

Current Competency

FIGURE 23.1   Current Competency versus Value of the Process

outstanding on the far right). The vertical axis is process value (generic on the bottom and competitive advantage on the top).

Matrix Structure

Current competency (the horizontal axis) is usually well understood and is simply a rating of an organization's competency when benchmarked with service providers. Process value (the vertical axis) is slightly more complex. Essentially, business functions that are common to all businesses are in the bottom row (i.e., telephone services, payroll administration, IT operations, etc.). If a function is specific, but common, to an industry, then it falls about halfway up (i.e., fleet management for the transportation industry). Things that are unique to an individual organization that are perceived to add significant competitive advantage and are not commonly available in the industry are high on the scale. These are reasons a company has a market share and loyal customers.

Cells in the Matrix

Things in the bottom left cell are "no-brainer" outsourcing targets. Plainly put, an organization is not very good at them, and every business needs the function. It is easy to find a provider that can do it better and usually cheaper. The cells surrounding the bottom left corner need to be evaluated on the merits of the function and the corporate direction. The top row and right-hand column generally are not good outsourcing candidates. If there are performance issues with the processes in these cells, they probably should be fixed internally and leveraged, even spun off as business units.

Services, such as telephone management services, data center management, or other back-office functions, might appear in the lower left-hand corner. The organization performs these tasks poorly when compared to similar service providers, and they are generic to all industries. This means that managing telephone services should be considered an outsourcing target. Is it any wonder many organizations have outsourced the management and administration of telephone services?

In contrast, a customer loyalty program is unique and not generally available. If a company were to perfect such a program, become competent at delivery, and attain positive results, it would be placed in the upper right of the matrix. Outsourcing the application would probably reduce the amount of time the company holds a unique competitive advantage and could easily offset any potential cost savings.

IT application development tied to new product introduction for an organization may reside in any of the cells in the matrix. It depends on how strategic it is viewed and how well it is performed.

Finally, based on the matrix, collections should probably be evaluated for outsourcing. Some of the factors that might play into a decision are the collection rate, cost of collection, and the community service policy.

STRATEGIC FRAMEWORK FOR GLOBAL SOURCING

Several alternatives exist as to the method and location for performing business processes. Subject to certain constraints, these processes may be located anywhere in the world, and can be performed internally by the company or by other organizations. Simply put, business processes do not have to be performed by the company in the United States.

Global sourcing is a term that describes how goods and services may be obtained anywhere in the world, and also expands on the type of services that may be procured. A succinct strategic framework should be used to illustrate the alternatives for global sourcing.

Sourcing Types: In-House, Contract, Outsource

One dimension to consider is to identify who performs the work. The main alternatives include in-house, contract, or outsource. These sourcing types form the columns in the strategic framework.

In-House

In-house is the traditional, do-it-yourself work. The company maintains complete expertise in all parts of this work; the people working in the area or process are full-time or part-time employees. These employees may have a full range of benefits, including pension plans. The assets used for in-house activities may be owned by the company. Alternatively, the assets may be rented or leased. Assets that are owned must be on the balance sheet, which means that they must be financed. All standard metrics are impacted, including the analysts' use of return on investment, sales per employee, assets per employee, and so on.

Contract

For some businesses, contracting is an alternative. For example, many companies hire temporary workers as 1099 contractors. These contractors may include U.S. citizens, permanent residents, or H-1B visa workers. In any case, a company is buying labor capacity. The company is still responsible for the management and direction of the contractor's efforts. In many cases, a company may still have provisioning expenses, such as personal computers and telephones.

Outsource

Another alternative is to outsource. Outsourcing can be structured in a number of ways with the objective of having an external party take responsibility not just for the required tasks but also for results. Depending on the agreement, outsourcers are generally self-managed and use their own assets to perform the work. This is the area where the greatest possibility exists for cost savings.

Sourcing Locations: Onshore, Nearshore, and Offshore

At one time, most manufacturing by U.S. companies was done in the United States. That changed as Mexico, Japan, Taiwan, and other countries increased their abilities to manufacture based on preset specifications more consistently and as U.S.-based businesses could manage those third-party relationships more effectively. Now manufacturing is performed worldwide to take advantage of lower labor costs, proximity to markets, and other factors. Business processes, such as manufacturing, now can also be performed anywhere in the world due to advances in enabling technologies.

We segment geographic locations into three categories relative to the United States: onshore, nearshore, and offshore. These geographic locations form the rows in the strategic framework.

Onshore

Onshore refers to locations in the United States using domestic resources.

Nearshore

Nearshore can refer to two types of locations. One definition is locations in the same time zone, perhaps with a different language involved. Examples include Mexico, Costa Rica, Panama, and Canada. It can also mean relative proximity to the United States; again, Canada and Mexico are good examples. In some cases, locations outside U.S. time zones, where the language and culture are similar to those of the United States, such as Northern Ireland and Australia, are also considered nearshore.

Although the cost of nearshore alternatives may be higher, using them has advantages. The benefits of nearshore alternatives include easier access by U.S. companies due to geographic proximity and fewer perceived risks (e.g., language and cultural barriers, more familiar and similar laws).

Many companies accept the trade-off between less cost savings and less risk with nearshore locations because they are willing to pay for the risk mitigation.

Offshore

Offshore sites include India, China, Russia, and other countries in different time zones, where different languages are spoken, with different cultures and considerable geographic separation. These countries may be developing countries.

 ## USING THE STRATEGIC FRAMEWORK FOR GLOBAL SOURCING

Assembling the sourcing types as columns and the sourcing locations as rows yields a 3×3 matrix that can be used to segment who performs processes and where those processes are performed.

In-house processes can be performed onshore, nearshore, or offshore. In addition, onshore processes can be performed in-house, under contract, or outsourced. The completed matrix is set out in Figure 23.2.

This 3×3 matrix provides a concise way to illustrate the relationships between a company and its service providers as well as to identify where the work is being performed. Using this framework allows situations to be described quickly and also shows how changes in an organization's capabilities may be needed.

If the sourcing strategy and agreements work as planned, every cell in the 3×3 matrix is a legitimate sourcing strategy. A common problem is for companies that intend, for example, to enter into an outsourcing agreement with an offshore service provider and, in fact, end up with an offshore contract agreement. In these situations, the companies spend more time managing the offshore service provider than originally anticipated, eroding much of the planned cost savings.

You also need to remember that movement among the cells is possible. Relationships with a service provider should be flexible, either by design from the outset or by evolution.

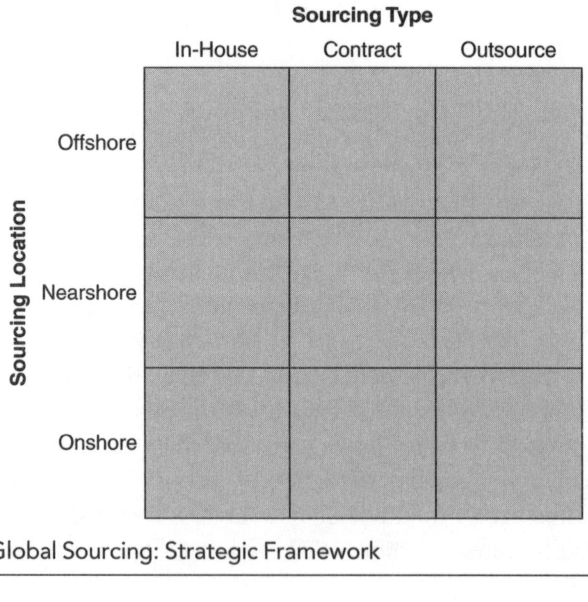

Sourcing Type

	In-House	Contract	Outsource
Offshore			
Nearshore			
Onshore			

Sourcing Location

FIGURE 23.2 Global Sourcing: Strategic Framework

THE OUTSOURCING PROCESS

By now you have determined *if* you need to outsource and, if so, where and under what structure. This section is intended to lay out how to conduct an outsourcing transaction. If this is your first time outsourcing, we suggest that you retain a professional outsourcing transaction advisor.

A suggested methodology for the life cycle for outsourcing services is laid out in Figure 23.3. It is comprised of five phases and a total of 12 distinct and separate stages.

Based on your organization's maturity, changing business conditions, or new information, it is possible to enter or exit the life cycle at any point in the process. Each entry or exit point has associated risks, costs, and benefits. What follows is an overview, rather than a detailed explanation. Each of these phases and the stages within are outlined in more detail in later in the chapter.

Phase I: Assess and Document Outsourcing Opportunities

Stages in Phase I include:

- Organize the effort.
- Assess outsourcing opportunities.
- Develop strategy and requirements.

This is the preparatory phase where you look across your organization to determine what you are doing well and efficiently and what you are not, or what is not core to your business. This is where you will develop your overarching outsourcing strategy and process or geographically specific business cases for outsourcing. You can use that framework to prioritize your efforts and generate executive awareness. From there you can create detailed requirements that along with the strategy feed into the next phase.

Perhaps the largest source of value leakage in the outsourcing process is failing to articulate a clear outsourcing strategy. Why? Because most companies do not state or even understand what their "real" objectives are from outsourcing. Outsourcing usually starts as a way to reduce cost.

Much has been written that suggests focusing strictly on the financial aspects of outsourcing leads to problems. Our experience corroborates this. Outsourcing offers many nonfinancial benefits. However, frequently companies do not understand or articulate their nonfinancial objectives when working with and evaluating service providers.

Whether you elect to formalize your outsourcing strategy as a separate deliverable or not, ensure that the requirements and request for proposal (RFP) in Phase II are predicated on a clear strategy that is evident through the contents of the RFP.

FIGURE 23.3 Phase I: Assess and Document Outsourcing Opportunities

FIGURE 23.4 Phase II: Evaluate and Select Service Provider

It is not uncommon in this phase to find improvement opportunities, either short- or long-term, that do not require outsourcing to generate process improvement, efficiency gain, and cost reduction. You may even stop here and not proceed to outsourcing. In any case, we recommend that you have this information available so you know where the low-hanging fruit are before you open a dialog with an outsourcing service provider.

Phase II: Evaluate and Select Service Provider

This phase starts with the creation of a request for information/proposal (RFI/RFP) and concludes with the selection of a service provider (see Figure 23.4).

Stages in Phase II are:

- Prepare and issue RFP.
- Service provider proposal development.
- Proposal evaluation and service provider selection.

Using the outsourcing strategy and requirements developed in the previous phase, it is time to open discussions with the outsourcing service providers. As previously noted, we believe that articulating your outsourcing strategy prior to preparing the requirements/RFP will provide the touchstone for the entire effort.

By articulating an outsourcing strategy that ties to the overall business and IT strategy, you will be able to significantly reduce the uncertainty and have a guiding document for the RFP and subsequent evaluation of responses and the service provider negotiation. Tactically, an explicit outsourcing strategy improves the usefulness of the RFP document both for you and the responding service providers.

If you have an understanding of the service provider community relative to your needs, you can move directly to a RFP with a small set (we recommend three to no more than five) of qualified service providers. Your RFP should be a well-thought-out representation of the detail developed in Phase I.

We will not go into the specific contents of an RFP in this chapter. However, you should use the RFP development stage to think through the scoring techniques before you issue it. If these techniques are not designed up front, you run the risk of losing time in the evaluation stage by trying to compare apples to oranges when reviewing submitted proposals.

If you need to develop familiarity with the service provider community, you can issue a request for information (RFI), which is just a request for capability based on a high-level requirements document. However, be advised that you will receive generic responses and put yourself on the lead tracking radar screen of every service provider to which you submit your RFI. If you go with the RFI to narrow the field of prospective bidders, you will need to iterate through the RFP to get to Phase III.

Then comes the quiet time before you evaluate the responses. This is when service providers are developing their proposals for your consideration. They will need your assistance to prepare their responses despite all of the thought and preparation that went into the RFP. Your procurement team will need to manage all interaction with the service providers for clarification questions, bidders' conferences, and so on. In the interest of fair procurement practices, we recommend that you share any question-and-answer exchanges you have with one specific bidder with all bidders.

Last, you will review the service providers' proposals, conduct site visits, and complete reference checks in order to select a service provider with which you can enter into contract negotiations. If you have done your homework properly and developed an effective RFP, it should not be overly difficult to normalize submitted proposals for comparison purposes.

We suggest three separate segments for scoring:

1. **Objective.** The capability is scored based on quantified facts, such as process skills, hours of coverage, technology, and the like.
2. **Subjective.** The capabilities are scored based on opinions and impressions, such as feedback from reference checks, meetings with service providers, executives, and so on.
3. **Pricing.** We recommend that service providers' pricing information be submitted separately or in a format that can be cleanly extracted from the proposals. Pricing should be reviewed only after the first two criteria are evaluated. This method will avoid contaminating the evaluation team's initial recommendations and allow them to better understand the value prior to being exposed to the cost information.

Before exiting this phase, we suggest that you advise your second-choice service provider to stand by in the event that you are unable to come to agreement with the selected service provider in the next phase.

All other service providers should be thanked for their efforts, released, and afforded the opportunity for a postmortem or loss review with a member of your evaluation team and a representative from procurement.

Phase III: Contract Development and Service Provider Negotiations

Next comes Phase III, where a contract is developed through negotiations with the service provider(s). (See Figure 23.5.)

Stages in this phase include:

- Develop initial contract positions.
- Negotiate contract.

FIGURE 23.5 Phase III: Contract Development and Service Provider Negotiation

This is the phase in which you develop the framework for your relationship with your new business partner—yes, business partner. If you allow your procurement or legal departments to go into the contract negotiations with a customer versus vendor attitude (us versus them) position, you will end up with a contract that focuses on you gaining an advantage and driving down unit cost. You should avoid this by focusing on life of the contract cost and not putting your service provider in a defensive position where they will work to the letter of the contract (and make it up in change orders), not the spirit of the contract.

This does not mean that you do not need a solid, detailed contractual vehicle, but it has to have mutual benefit and responsibility spelled out in addition to all of the customary terms and conditions.

Service providers have specialized teams that exclusively negotiate contracts, which gives them a substantial advantage over companies that attempt to do negotiate themselves. Moreover, service providers' draft contracts are carefully structured to give the service providers a better deal.

The best way to nullify a service provider's advantage is for you to provide the first-draft contract and to go to the table with an equally experienced team. (If you have not outsourced before or have not retained an outside advisor, it is critical to do so at this juncture.) However, an effective contract foundation is set long before contract negotiation begins.

By articulating your outsourcing strategy early on, you will know what points are important to you and what you can use as bargaining chips. For purposes of contract management in the operational phase, when the service provider is providing the contracted services, you will need to document all of these points in service-level agreements (SLAs).

SLAs are the objective means by which both parties articulate and manage their respective expectations, responsibilities, and contributions. Basic components of an SLA are: service definitions, performance metrics, upper and lower transaction volume or full-time-equivalent parameters, reporting formats and frequencies, and exception management procedures. This is not an exhaustive list but provides some insight into the purpose of an SLA.

Hopefully you have managed to get through this process without alienating the service provider, your executive team, or staff. If so, you are ready to sign on the dotted line and move to the next phase.

Phase IV: Service Transition

Phase IV is the phase in which preparations are made to transfer actual work and then performance of work by the service provider begins (see Figure 23.6).

Plan Service Transition ⟩ Execute Transition ⟩

FIGURE 23.6 Phase IV: Service Transition

Stages in this phase include:

- Plan service transition.
- Execute transition.

Although this phase has only two stages, it is where all of your and the service provider's efforts either come to fruition or go off the track. If the latter occurs, both parties will spend inordinate amounts of time trying to regain their credibility and repair the relationship for months to come, if not for the life of the contract. This risk can be mitigated by proper planning, process design, and skills transfer.

Service transition is another area where there is no replacement for experience. This fact should be weighted heavily in your evaluation and reference checks of service providers. Have they done this before, in your industry, using these specific processes or technologies? Do not be impatient with this stage; preparing for a service cutover takes a significant amount of time. Have contingency plans and additional resources standing by to deal with the difficulties that will unfailingly appear with the inception of services.

Phase V: Ongoing Management

Phase V indicates that the service provider is firmly in place and performing work. The task at this point is to manage the relationship with the vendor and also to manage any SLAs that have been put in place (see Figure 23.7).

Stages in this phase include:

- Manage SLAs.
- Manage the service provider relationship.

Just because you have outsourced a process or function does not relieve you of the responsibility of managing that process. Ongoing proactive management of performance to SLAs and the overall relationship between you and your service provider is the only thing standing between you and service degradations, dissatisfaction, executive escalations, unplanned change orders, and early renegotiation or termination of the contract.

Depending on the scope and scale of what you have outsourced, you will need to assign full-time resources or a team to manage your contribution and the service provider's performance. If this relationship is treated as a partnership and if the issues that invariably arise are addressed quickly, it is likely that your contract will run its term and you will renew or begin this process again. This is an ongoing process or cycle, as shown in Figure 23.8.

FIGURE 23.7   Phase V: Ongoing Management

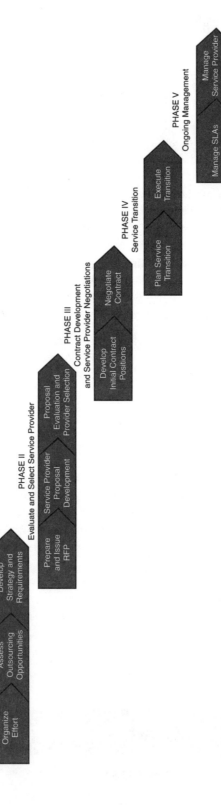

FIGURE 23.8 Outsourcing Life Cycle: A Phased Approach

As always, we believe that a methodology is a guide to thinking, not a replacement for thinking. This chapter is an overview of the journey you need to navigate. In the interest of brevity, we have left out several branches and tributaries to the route. We hope you will find it helpful.

 ## CONCLUSION

Some important points to keep in mind when undertaking an outsourcing/offshoring endeavor are:

- Just because you have outsourced a process or function, you are not relieved of the responsibility of managing that process.
- Outsourcing something does not mean it is inflexible.
- Successful relationships require proactive management on both sides.
- Evaluating outsourcing nearly always leads to improved business processes, either through internal improvements or outsourcing.
- Although outsourcing is not for every company, nearly all companies will benefit from periodically asking, "Is outsourcing right for me?"

PART THREE

Technology

CHAPTER TWENTY-FOUR

Information Technology Portfolio Management

Louis Carr, Jr.

O NE OF THE MOST common dilemmas of information technology management is properly and adequately measuring the value of IT for an organization. In years past, many IT departments were considered cost centers. That is to say, many in management believed that funding IT was a necessary expense that had some operational (and nonstrategic) benefit. Many managers believed IT was similar to a utility—for example, water or electrical service: It was necessary but did not really offer any strategic value.

Today, most would agree that a certain portion of an IT department's service catalog is operational, but there is a portion of the department that must be strategic and align itself with the business objectives and strategies of the organization. At the highest level, IT governance is the broad discipline and framework that can help integrate business decisions and strategy with IT decisions and strategy. One of the concepts supporting IT governance is IT portfolio management.

Most technology managers and directors would define IT portfolio management as "the management of IT projects where all IT project resources, funding and tasks are managed in a prioritized, systematic manner across the enterprise." Although portfolio management of *software applications* can be construed as IT portfolio management, it is more common for *IT projects* to be the object of portfolio management. It is more common because IT projects can include more than just software application projects. IT projects include hardware projects such as server upgrades, telephone/VoIP (Voice over Internet Protocol) initiatives, and so on—not just software applications.

WHY IS IT PORTFOLIO MANAGEMENT NECESSARY?

IT departments receive requests for projects and services daily. Unless an IT department has unlimited resources and unlimited budget, choices have to be made as to which projects will be placed on hold or in a queue and which projects will be implemented right away. If an organization is facing challenges, such as having limited IT resources that need to be managed, wanting to ensure IT's alignment with business priorities, or wanting to maximize the IT investment, IT portfolio management is one methodology that will pay tremendous dividends when implemented properly. One function of IT portfolio management is to establish an objective method for scoring or rating projects. From this scoring process, a priority can be established that will help the CIO better understand which projects should be implemented and which should be placed in the queue.

IT portfolio management is necessary because IT departments have limited resources that need to be managed. In most IT organizations, those resources are in high demand; establishing which IT project will receive which services is key to delivering services to customers in a consistent and timely manner. For example, a database administrator may be needed for three different projects at the same time. IT portfolio management helps determine a priority for each project and therefore can determine which project would receive the database administrator's time now and which projects would receive the database administrator's time later.

IT portfolio management can be used to show the need for additional resources too. Using the previous example about a database administrator needed for three different projects at the same time, the IT department could solicit the sponsors of the lower-ranked projects for additional funding for contract resources in order to get those projects completed in a shorter time frame. Good CIOs will give their clients options, not edicts. Giving the sponsor the option of providing more funding to accelerate a project's timeline or allowing the project to fall in the queue based on an agreed-on calculation/formula puts the control partially in the sponsor's hands, which is a good thing.

IT portfolio management can also help ensure IT's alignment with business priorities. If the scoring/rating of projects includes questions such as "Does this project support a council or commission priority?" or "How many council or commission priorities does this project support?" one can see how higher-scoring projects should reflect stronger alignment with city council or county commission priorities. The real value of IT is shown when it can not only support a business's operational objectives as a "utility service" but when it can be a driver and a change agent for strategic objectives.

Another benefit of an organization having an IT portfolio management strategy is that the organization can better maximize its IT investment. Companies typically spend anywhere from 3 percent to 8 percent of their budget on IT. For large companies, that can be tens of millions of dollars. It obviously makes sense to spend those dollars as wisely as possible. The concept of maximizing one's IT investment is simple in principle but more difficult in practice. An organization can spend its IT dollars on any number of technology initiatives, but selecting which projects provide the most value to the organization is tricky. To start, "value" has to be defined by the business units. IT systems that lower the cost of producing widgets might be considered valuable; IT systems that improve communications might be considered valuable; IT systems that increase the reliability and consistency of providing emergency services might be considered valuable. As mentioned before, a scoring system is one way of objectively separating the value of IT projects. Scoring questions that inquire about proposed systems' ability to integrate to existing systems or proposed systems that build on existing technologies (like enterprise resource planning [ERP]) help maximize IT investment by providing new capability for a fraction of the staff training and ongoing operation and maintenance (O&M) costs as compared to a stand-alone system.

Other criteria to show the value of an IT project might be how much this proposed IT project transforms the organization. Here the definition of *transforming technology* is a technology that forever changes the way a business process works. For example, in the 1990s, e-mail and the World Wide Web forever changed the way businesses communicate. In the twenty-first century, a transforming technology might be social networks that increase corporate presence, brand recognition, and ultimately sales or leveraging mobile computing (over commercial carrier's infrastructure) to drive service delivery costs down and efficiency up. A project like that may be a better investment of IT staff time and budget than other proposed projects in the portfolio. One of the scoring questions could address the likelihood of this project transforming the organization. Depending on the type of organization, this criterion could be very important. A high-tech company might find this criterion very important; a city or county government agency might find this criterion less important because government agencies typically *adopt* transforming technology, not create it.

The other "consequence" of using IT portfolio management is that business units are forced to think more about corporate goals and less about individual department goals. Addressing this concern may be one of the biggest hurdles a CIO will have to face. Each department head has a set of goals or performance metrics to meet. If IT resources are limited, how can everyone get everything they want? The answer is that *they cannot*. Using a portfolio strategy forces each department head to examine what his priority and focus should be as it relates to the corporate goals and priorities and compare that to other departments' goals and priorities. Using an objective scoring model, it may be that one department has more priority-1 IT projects than another department. It is likely that each department will not get an equal share of the IT resource pool for its projects.

However, this can present an opportunity for departments that may not have aligned their projects to corporate goals and priorities in the past to do so with the help of a project scoring system. For example, in local government, agencies such as parks and library departments have to compete for funding and IT resources along with police and fire departments. Since citizens almost always list personal and property safety as one of their primary needs from local government, parks and library departments tend not to get the lion's share of resources (money, IT resources, or people). If these departments can focus on closely aligning their IT needs to corporate goals—leverage existing IT systems, such as geographic information systems and ERP, have funding for acquisition and O&M, document their existing business processes so that upgrading or converting to new systems is less time consuming, and have a resource (business analyst or application administrator) outside of IT to help manage the daily operation of the system—it is highly likely that such a project could rank higher than one from the police or fire department whose scope, budget, and resource needs are not well defined.

IMPLEMENTING IT PORTFOLIO MANAGEMENT

Implementing and maintaining an IT portfolio management program is one of the key indicators of success for a CIO. As discussed in the previous section, some sort of methodology must exist for prioritizing IT projects and the resources that support those projects because IT resources and money are both finite. If a CIO wants to implement IT portfolio management, four steps must be taken:

1. Review and document strategic business objectives.
2. Develop a scoring system to rank each project.
3. Conduct an inventory of all IT projects.
4. Apply the ranking formula to those projects.

The purpose of reviewing and documenting strategic business objectives is to fully understand the focus of the organization and to help establish what questions will be most appropriate in order to rank the IT projects according to that focus. If there are multiple strategic goals or objectives, projects that meet or support all those goals should generally be more appealing than projects that support none of those goals. Also, knowing those strategic goals will help a CIO align internal projects (like server upgrades or UPS replacement) to those strategic goals, since internal projects compete for IT resources too.

For the twenty-first-century CIO, understanding business objectives is even more important than understanding network protocols and C++ code snippets. Forward-looking organizations can leverage technology to improve delivery of services or improve the overall experience of customers when interacting through web sites or telephone. Unlike other department heads, CIOs must know a lot about technology, but they must also learn a lot about every other business unit. For example, the director of marketing does not have to understand network protocols or active directory security schemes, but the CIO should understand concepts such as branding, marketing mix, and the fit of one's product in the marketplace. CIOs must have a broad understanding of business in general so that as they review and document strategic business objectives, they understand those objectives and create synergy between them and the technology projects.

The next step in implementing IT portfolio management is to develop a scoring system to rank each project. Every organization will have different criteria, but most can start with a basic set of criteria that transcends organizational size and corporate construct (i.e., government versus for profit versus nonprofit). Those criteria are strategic alignment, business process impact, technical architecture, direct payback, risk, and mandatory changes. Those criteria are defined as described next.

- **Alignment to corporate strategy:** The alignment of IT investment strategy with the organization's business goals and objectives
- **Business process and cultural impact:** The impact on the requirement for the company to redesign business processes and culture (too much change too quickly is very difficult)

- **Technical architecture:** The integration, scalability, and reliability of system components (databases, operating systems, applications, and/or networks) for the project
- **Direct payback:** The financial benefits that a project can deliver, such as cost savings and better information
- **Risk:** The identification of the proposed investment's exposure to failure or underachievement
- **Mandatory changes:** The determination of the necessity to change because of a change in law, rules, or regulations

A spreadsheet can store and sum each criterion and the scores for the supporting questions. Tables 24.1, 24.2, 24.3, and 24.4 show how the supporting questions could look and total possible scores. For the "strategic alignment" criterion, projects that support multiple strategic objectives would naturally receive a higher score than projects that support none or one strategic objective. This technique would be used for each subsequent criterion.

TABLE 24.1 Alignment to Corporate Strategy

0–5	This project supports one strategic objective
0–5	This project supports two strategic objectives
0–5	This project supports three strategic objectives
0–5	. . .
0–20	TOTAL

TABLE 24.2 Business Process and Cultural Impact

0–5	Ability of technology to cope with changing business processes
0–5	Support for industry best practices
0–5	Ability of technology to measure process performance
0–5	. . .
0–20	TOTAL

TABLE 24.3 Technical Architecture

0–5	Level of compatibility with preferred server environment
0–5	Level of compatibility with preferred database standard
0–5	Level of compatibility with preferred networking standard
0–5	. . .
0–20	TOTAL

TABLE 24.4 Project's Weighted Score

Raw Score	Weighting Factor	Criterion
20	2.0	Alignment to corporate strategy
20	1.0	Business process and cultural impact
20	0.7	Technical architecture
	64.0	TOTAL

Naturally, the supporting questions and the range of scores for each question can be customized based on the organization's needs. The range of scores, 0 up to 5 or higher, will be based on the importance of each question relative to that criterion. Optionally, a weighting factor can be added to each criterion.

Weighting factors are a good way to allow the organization's IT steering committee to help determine which criterion is most important to the organization. An IT steering committee should be formed of department heads of various backgrounds and responsibilities. A credible IT steering committee represents a cross section of the business and has the influence and authority to affirm or deny the CIO's decisions on the strategic direction of IT.

In government, "direct payback" probably would not receive the highest weighting factor. It would probably receive 0.5 or 0.6. That would place less emphasis on IT projects that focus on direct payback. By its very nature, government initiates many programs that do not make money. Maintaining public parks or public streets in neighborhoods are not revenue-generating programs but are high on the list of government programs in many cities.

After the scoring sheets have been developed, the next step is for the IT department to conduct an inventory of all IT projects and apply the ranking/scoring formulas to all those projects. This will give the CIO a good picture of the relative importance of each project. The list of projects can be sorted and distributed to the organization's IT steering committee for review and discussion. Depending on the complexity of each criterion and the supporting questions, completing the rating spreadsheet for one project may take only 30 minutes. However, questions should be developed in most criteria that require some input from the business units. IT can answer the technical architectural questions, but the business unit should have supporting questions that give them input into rating the importance of the project from its perspective.

MEASURING EFFECTIVENESS OF IT PORTFOLIO MANAGEMENT

For any program to be considered a success, there must be a way to measure it and objectively define what constitutes success. CIOs who embark on this type of initiative should define clear parameters and metrics for what constitutes success or at least what constitutes acceptable effectiveness.

One metric that can be used to determine the effectiveness of an organization's IT portfolio management program is on-time and on-budget percentages of projects. Another measure is the project management office's ability to match documented requirements to actual functionality in systems it has deployed. The CIO suggests to the IT steering committee an acceptable percentage of on-time and on-budget projects, say 80 percent. This would mean that if at least 80 percent of the projects in the portfolio are completed on time and on budget, the CIO would meet the measure of effectiveness. The CIO could also suggest that at least 85 percent of documented requirements match actual functionality from each priority-1 project. This measure is especially useful at determining how well IT (and the business unit) did in terms of implementing a solution that closely matched the requirements gathered during the initiation and planning phases of the project.

 ## CONCLUSION

In summary, IT portfolio management is one of several tools CIOs can use to track internal performance measures of the project management office and, to some degree, the entire IT organization. Techniques such as measuring effectiveness of an organization's IT portfolio management program using on-time and on-budget percentages of projects or the project management office's ability to match documented requirements to actual functionality can be good performance measures. The other more strategic use of IT portfolio management is to help the organization prioritize IT projects so that limited resources can be managed, ensuring IT's alignment with business priorities and maximizing IT investment.

CHAPTER TWENTY-FIVE

Strategic Information Security Management

David Finnis

NFORMATION SECURITY IS THE protection of confidentiality, integrity, and availability of data. In addition to the technology, it includes the people and processes that use and protect that data. Information is a business asset that helps drive revenues and increase competitive advantage in the global marketplace. Protecting information is a worthwhile investment: It protects your investment in the development of your organization's intellectual property; ensures that adequate controls are in place within your environment to protect employee data and customer data considered personally identifiable information (PII), such as Social Security numbers and credit card data; and ensures compliance with regulatory requirements that your organization may be subjected to.

 ## INFORMATION SECURITY BUSINESS ALIGNMENT

Information security can be a business enabler as long as an organization adopts information security frameworks and management practices that balance investment with data protection. It is important that the information security framework and practices are aligned with the business strategy, the supporting IT strategy, regulatory requirements, the security objectives of the organization's management, and culture of the organization.

Unfortunately, in many organizations, it is common to perceive information security as a roadblock or "business disabler;" this is due, for the most part, to the fact that information security is not considered when business and IT decisions are being made. The source of this problem is usually a lack of awareness around data protection and the lack of communication between information security resources and business representatives.

Today's business strategies are placing significantly more demands on IT to reduce cost, which is leading to projects that involve offshoring, outsourcing, and the variety of outsourced service offerings, such as software as a service, infrastructure as a service, and storage as a service. These types of IT projects are increasingly presenting your information security organizations with new and unique challenges for protecting data. The establishment of an information security framework that supports these business and IT strategies is recommended; it should include data protection criteria, such as vendor selection security criteria, information security service levels, contractual agreements that contain data protection clauses, the ability to validate providers' security controls (right to audit capabilities), and up-front security architecture reviews. By doing this you are establishing your organization's risk acceptance level and introducing an information security reference framework that can be used over and over again. Over time, this process will introduce information security standards to your processes, technology deployments, and workforce habits. The introduction of standards early on in the decision-making process will over time enable the business to conduct its processes in a secure manner.

Introducing information security within either manual or automated business processes early on can have a dramatic downstream effect on protecting data, saving costs in the future, and presenting an image of integrity to customers, vendors, suppliers, and other third parties. Presenting a sense of security with regard to your business in itself is a competitive advantage.

There are several ways that information security can be introduced early on in business and IT decision-making processes: Raising awareness and utilizing an enterprise architecture framework are two effective ways.

Raising Awareness

Information security is only as good as the weakest link. Your workforce's information security awareness and data protection training are critical in any information security program and are probably the most effective ways to enhance your organization's security posture. In general, information security awareness can be increased with a fairly low investment when compared to other information security controls.

You may be wondering how to raise awareness surrounding information security and how important data protection is to your business. There are many ways of increasing awareness; for example, a simple e-mail to your employees from an executive member of staff about the importance of protecting data could have a good effect. Some of the many other ways to raise awareness within your organization include:

- Awareness campaigns
- Regular information security training
- Electronic screen messaging
- Contests, games, giveaways
- Relate data protection to your employees' personal lives and data
- Policy awareness and acknowledgment
- Information security days

Raising awareness is an important first step to reducing risks associated with data protection. As mentioned, raising security awareness can take many forms. It is important that people are trained in information security practices and that they have access to tools, documents, and resources that allow them to execute their business objectives in a secure manner. Make security as easy to use as possible. Security by its very nature can be an obstruction, but often the less obtrusive information security controls will be adopted. Find your organization's risk acceptance level, communicate to your employees regarding the importance of security, and deploy information security solutions that are usable and effective. Your employees are your first line of defense in your information security infrastructure. By making it easy for them to protect data and making them aware of the information threats, you will have a made a significant step forward in maintaining the confidentiality and integrity of your organization's data.

Enterprise Architecture

Establishing an enterprise architecture framework helps align IT with business process and strategy. One example of enterprise architecture framework, TOGAF 9 (www .opengroup.org/togaf/), outlines a framework and methodology for establishing an enterprise architecture. Enterprise architecture is a way of ensuring information security standards and controls are considered as the business and IT makes decisions regarding the portfolio and resulting projects.

Information security is somewhat unique within an enterprise architecture as it generally touches all layers within the architecture. Information security "slices" through these architectural layers:

- User interface
- Application layer
- Services layer
- Information/data layer
- Infrastructure layer

Understanding the security elements at each of these layers and building an information security architecture that is supported by people, process, and technology will encourage more usable information security reference architectures, help centralize information security solutions, and enable the business by providing usable security architectures.

Communication and collaboration with the business is key. Your information security management team should be appropriately aligned with IT management to ensure that, when necessary, information security can add value to the discussions as business decisions are being made. In doing this, it is likely that information security controls or at the very least provides advice early on in the decision process. Information security architectures, existing security infrastructure, and applications and services that already exist in your environment may be utilized by the business. Obviously, utilizing existing information security technology, processes, and related information security services will contribute to saving costs within your organization while at the same time maintaining a good information security posture.

Establishing an information governance committee or board can help collaboration between information security representatives and others from within your organization.

Information Governance

Cross-functional organizational management level support is a key element for protecting data. It is common for enterprise organizations to establish a data protection board. This board is often called different names in different companies, but the charter and board members are the same. A common name is the information governance board (IGB). An IGB helps raise the visibility of the importance of data protection within an organization. An IGB may help sponsor and approve corporate policies such as data classification and sponsor programs to help your workforce resources become compliant with new and existing policies. Data classification policies and supporting documents (guidelines, standards, and procedures) are necessary to help implement controls for protecting data that is shared outside your organization. IGB-supported programs and policies help the data custodians (those responsible for protecting data) implement and maintain technical and process-level security controls that in turn help protect an organization's sensitive data.

Forming an Information Governance Board

An IGB is usually made up of vice president–level or at least director-level representatives from those departments shown in Figure 25.1, plus any other business unit

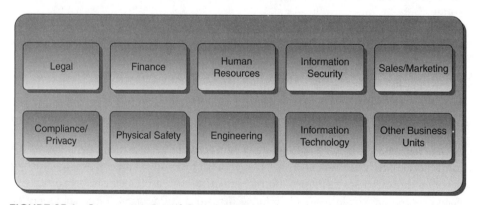

FIGURE 25.1 Governance Board Constituents

heads that you would consider key stakeholders for data protection within your organization.

When forming your IGB, you must first define its charter, mission, and information security guiding principles. It is usual for this board to meet at least quarterly to discuss items such as data protection initiatives, company policy, and strategic business objectives that benefit from information security.

Typically, a chairperson would be elected, and this person would be supported by the chief information security officer.

The IGB usually reports to the executive management team, the audit committee, and the board of directors. Subcommittees may also be established within the various cross-functional units that would be responsible for program-level initiatives as required by the IGB.

 DATA PROTECTION

Most data are at risk from information security threats and, for that reason, should be appropriately protected. Your organization's data that is shared with remote parties (customers, vendors, service providers, business partners, outsourcing providers, etc.) generally are susceptible to significantly more information security threats due to the typically decentralized nature of the security controls framework that may or may not be in place within your company and the remote environments. Understanding your remote data risks, process, and technological control frameworks is an important step in reducing your company's exposure to remote security threats. This section discusses some common risks and remediation activities related to data protection of different organizational domains; it is not a comprehensive data protection work plan.

Why Worry? What Is the Value?

Protecting data is important for many reasons, some of which may be known only to your organization. Some common reasons are:

- Maintaining competitive advantage, for example, protecting your intellectual property
- Protecting the integrity of your brand
- Compliance with legal and regulatory requirements
- Protecting your employees' personal data
- Protecting your customers' data

In a 2009 survey by the Ponemon Institute (www.ponemon.org/data-security), it is reported that data breaches cost enterprise organizations an average of $6.6 million per year with an average of $202 per record compromised in a breach; these data reflect a 2.5 percent increase in data breach–related costs since 2007 and an 11 percent increase in the same costs since 2006.

Different vertical markets have different (and sometimes overlapping) regulatory, privacy, and legal requirements that organizations must comply with, and every organization should understand its own unique requirements. Regulations such as the Data Security Standard, the Gramm-Leach-Bliley Act, state laws such as California SB1386, and many others require varying levels of data protection for sensitive data types such as customer data, PII, and other regulated data like financial and healthcare records. Not all regulations or standards may have specific requirements related to remote data; however, as company boundaries merge and outsourced and managed service providers are adopted, it is important to understand where data protection responsibilities reside not only from an information security perspective but also from a legal and compliance perspective.

Getting Started

Sometimes the most difficult task is taking that first step. A logical sequence is needed. This section presents one such sequence.

Inventory Your Business Processes and Related Data

It is critical that you understand current business processes; the data that are utilized; and how those data are stored and flow in and out of an organization, in both electronic and physical forms, before attempting to reduce the risks associated with your organization's data. Usually there are also manual business processes that occur without the interaction of the IT environment. For example, there may be processes that include only a single business unit, such as legal or human resources, that involves sensitive data in hardcopy or even in technology environments that are not under IT's purview. Understanding the various process initiators, inputs, and outputs across all of your organization's departments can take time; however from an information security perspective, it is useful to understand these flows so that you can develop an appropriate information security strategy and identify any potential gaps, to reduce your overall data risk.

Ensuring that the business has the tools and awareness to ask the important security-related questions is paramount to protecting company data.

Understand Your Data

Obviously, in order to protect your company data, you first need to understand your data. Inventorying all data types and records within an enterprise environment is usually a lengthy if not impossible task (without sophisticated tools). Sometimes inventory and data classification efforts have already been performed for certain data subsets—for example, compliance, financial, and employee data, or certain patent data or intellectual property that is particularly important to your organization. These data types may already be appropriately recorded and controlled. In addition, structured data versus unstructured data may be more easily identifiable within your environment. Data shared with remote parties or outside of your organization's perimeter could be considered a subset of your overall data landscape. It is important to gain some understanding of the types of external data flows that support your business processes. (There are methods and tools that can help this process.) From here one can start evaluating the risks associated with those data assets.

Inventorying your data may seem a daunting task. Choose a business unit, an important data set, or some other criterion for selection and begin the process of understanding the information security controls. In doing this, you are starting the process of data protection rather than ignoring it.

Information Risk Management

One common exercise for understanding the risks associated with data is to undertake an information security risk assessment. These types of assessments (there are many risk assessment standards and widely used methodologies[1]) vary in size, scope, and methodology.

Quantitative assessments focus on the asset risk in terms of the perceived value of the asset to the organization, usually in the form of high, medium, and low risk; the vulnerability; the likelihood of an threat event; the controls in place; and the resulting residual risk. Qualitative assessments generally focus on the asset's monetary value and the resulting potential monetary loss should an information security threat be realized for the asset.

Experience shows that qualitative types of assessments are usually easier to perform than quantitative ones, as it is often difficult to determine the value of a digital asset until a loss or threat has occurred. The quantitative methodology generally produces faster risk analysis results; they can be used to form and implement remediation plans sooner rather than later, lowering the information threat exposure window. Once the risks have been assessed and in-place controls are evaluated, it is time to plan and prioritize remediation activities. Remediation activities are designed to reduce information risks to a level that is acceptable to your organization; this is known as information security risk management. Typically remediation efforts require that projects, programs, and other types of tasks are initiated, funded if necessary, and implemented.

The IGB would likely be informed of risk assessment results so that executive support could be secured and appropriate projects and programs could be funded to implement the desired information security controls.

Reducing Data Risks

There is a trade-off between risk and cost when discussing the reduction of risk associated with data. You should also consider the value of the data itself and whether it is even worthy of stringent protection. Some points to think about when reducing data risk are discussed next.

Information Security Controls

As there are many options available, I will not attempt to discuss in detail all the various process and technology controls that may be associated with protecting data. Many technologies can help enforce the security of data at rest and data that traverse your organization's perimeter, such as data loss prevention technology, controlled documents, rights management software, and others. The degree of implementation or adoption of information security controls is often determined by many unique factors, including the organization's ability to accept and/or consume significant process or technology changes, the funding available, the ability to implement technology that prevents and detects events that are not compliant with policy, and the level of security needed for certain data types.

Process Controls

As important as technology controls are process controls. As mentioned, understanding your business processes ensures that appropriate information security controls can be embedded within those processes to protect your data.

An example that is becoming increasingly important is data that will traverse your organization's perimeter as part of a vendor partnership, software as a service (SaaS), or other cloud-based initiative. As mentioned, vendor selection processes for these initiatives should consider data protection and your information security requirements. Organizations must establish processes that measure the security controls for data that are outside the organizations. As part of the outsourced vendor selection criteria, it is important to include data protection clauses in the services contracts and agreements. Some of the types of clauses that may be considered include:

- **Data security:** Clauses related to policies and general data security practices.
- **Data transmission:** How your organization's data must be transmitted, both hardcopy and electronic transmissions as appropriate.
- **Data storage:** How the data must be stored. (Do you need your sensitive data encrypted at rest?) Consider also terms regarding data stored on removable media, backup tapes, and the like.
- **Data encryption:** If encryption is required, outline in the agreement acceptable encryption technologies and any associated requirements you may have for data that is stored globally, especially where there may be government requirements about export laws related to encryption.
- **Data reuse:** Affidavits that address data reuse.
- **End-of-agreement data handling:** How data must be returned.
- **Data destruction:** Outline controls on how electronic and hardcopy data that is no longer required must be destroyed so that it can no longer be used.
- **Right to audit:** Legal terms that permit your organization the right to audit the environment(s) and systems associated with your data.

Other process artifacts, such as procedures, flows, checklists, and report templates, also help streamline the process and ensure consistent results. Consider automating processes with workflows—for example, request and approval processes to ensure security and other controls or requirements are in place before confidential data leaves your company. A well-defined process also ensures that the appropriate departments are involved (e.g., legal, human resources, IT, security). Defining and communicating processes raises visibility and accountability, and supports future data security audit requirements. It is also important to define your organization's security requirements for external party compliance when initiating new relationships or reviewing older ones.

Review and Audit

Unfortunately, once new process and/or technology controls are implemented, you are not done. You must put all of that effort to good use as it has established a baseline against which you can now measure future success and also better protect data going forward. Establishing process and technology metrics and key performance indicators specific to data protection enable you to understand where improvements or additional investments have to be made. Implement a review and audit program to ensure that security controls are monitored and maintained throughout the life cycle of the business need. Review and audit processes may consist of performing process walkthroughs; reviewing process documentation, inputs, and outputs; and ensuring that records and artifacts are consistent as stated in procedures.

 INFORMATION SECURITY MANAGEMENT SYSTEMS

There are many information security frameworks, controls references, and standards available to organizations. Many of them articulate similar practices for data protection.

The International Standards Organization maintains a family of standards under ISO27000 that address various components of information security management. The main standards within the family are:

- **ISO/IEC 27000: 2009**, Information Security Management Systems—Overview and Vocabulary
- **ISO/IEC 27001: 2005**, Information Security Management Systems—Requirements
- **ISO/IEC 27002: 2005**, Code of Practice for Information Security Management
- **ISO/IEC 27003**, Information Security Management System Implementation Guidance[2]
- **ISO/IEC 27004**, Information Security Management—Measurement
- **ISO/IEC 27005: 2008**, Information Security Risk Management[3]
- **ISO/IEC 27006: 2007**, Requirements for Bodies Providing Audit and Certification of Information Security Management Systems
- **ISO/IEC 27007**, Guidelines for Information Security Management Systems Auditing

An information management system provides a framework by which organizations can assess data risk and establish, implement, and measure information security process and technology controls.

ISO27001 Information Security Management System

The ISO27001 Information Security Management System (ISMS) standard details a management system for information security. It defines a management process that organizations can adopt to identify data assets that are important, assess the information risks associated with the assets, and implement controls and a plan to reduce the risks.

Once in place, the ISMS provides a living management process. It requires various data inputs and outputs that enable those charged with information security management to make data-driven decisions so as to continually manage data risks. The ISMS establishes processes for monitoring information security controls and for improving them when metrics or other measurements are not being met within the environment. ISO27001 is comprised of two parts: the first part is related to the management system itself and the second part (Annex A) contains the recommended security controls.

ISO27001: Annex A

Annex A contains 11 domains that detail recommended control security controls to be considered as part of an information security framework.

1. Security policy
2. Organization of information security
3. Asset management
4. Human resources security
5. Physical security
6. Communications and operations
7. Access control
8. Systems acquisition, development, and maintenance
9. Security incident management
10. Business continuity management
11. Compliance

ISO27002, the Code of Practice for Information Security Management, provides detailed information and standards for the controls contained within ISO27001: Annex A.

Information Security Framework

An information security framework brings together many of the concepts and recommendations that have been discussed in this chapter. Figure 25.2 provides a conceptual overview of the types of processes and attributes that typically make up an information security framework.

This conceptual framework outlines some example processes or services offerings that a typical enterprise organization would establish. These processes support the organization's information security policy as defined by the IGB. Procedures, standards, guidelines, and other forms of documentation provide further details on how to perform the processes, how processes are related, and the roles and responsibilities required to ensure that processes are performed as desired.

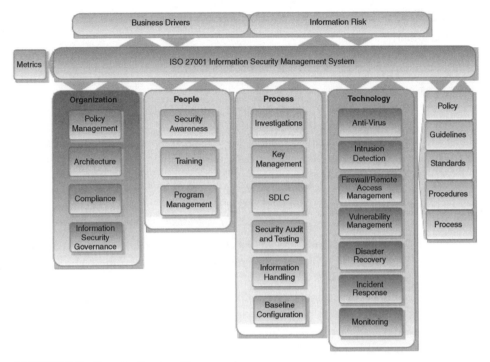

FIGURE 25.2 Security Services Framework

Business drivers, strategic objectives, and the identified information risks provide input to the management system. Metrics provide management the ability to monitor the controls to ensure that business strategies are being met while at the same time reducing risks related to information security.

ISMS Benefits

There are many benefits to implementing an ISO27001-based ISMS. These benefits include:

- Generating immediate customer confidence when asked about information security
- Streamlining regulatory compliance processes (SOX, HIPAA, GLBA, CFR, PCI, privacy laws, etc.) by adopting a common security controls framework
- Investing in information security technology and resources based on information risks that matter to your business
- Involving the business in the assessment of information risks and quickly determining where to focus your resources
- Efficient security and IT processes that saves resource time and increases productivity; this leads to better operational efficiency
- Providing measurable process and technology output so that you can make more informed management and security decisions

- The ability to provide certified documentation regarding information security to global markets
- Involvement of all levels of management in information security and the protection of information assets.
- Increased information security visibility and awareness.

Organizations may also become certified against the ISO27001 management standard, which is increasingly becoming the accepted standard for measuring the information security posture of an organization, especially in the global marketplace.

 ## SUMMARY

This chapter provides ideas and strategies related to data protection and how to align your information security program with your organization's business strategy and objectives.

Understanding your business processes and its associated data and flows and collaborating with a cross-functional board dedicated to data protection that is supported by an information security management framework will enable you to better manage risks related to information security within your organization.

By raising security awareness and integrating information security into your enterprise architecture framework, you will enable a more secure and competitive business.

 ## NOTES

1. ISO27005: Risk Management Standard: http://en.wikipedia.org/wiki/ISO/IEC_27005; National Institute of Standards and Technology: http://csrc.nist.gov/groups/SMA/fisma/framework.html.
2. Publication of ISO/IEC 27003 was approved by ISO/IEC JTC1/SC27 despite significant concern from some national bodies who submitted hundreds of pages of comments in the closing stages of the standards development process. It was agreed that parties would carry forward significant comments to a revision of the standard after it is published.
3. Supports the general concepts specified in ISO/IEC 27001 and is designed to assist the satisfactory implementation of information security based on a risk management approach.

CHAPTER TWENTY-SIX

From Vision to Reality: Implementing Information Security

John M. Millican

I N ORDER TO BE effectively aligned with the enterprise's objectives, the information security (IS) function must be implemented from a top-down basis. Unfortunately, IS is an afterthought for too many organizations. This leads to a patchwork approach prone to significant gaps and ineffective controls. If the enterprise information security (EIS) team is treated merely as the final gate check in the development of new processes and technologies in the organization, insecurities within the process and technologies end up forcing the EIS to block it from implementation. This leads to EIS being perceived as a barrier to accomplishment that in turn reinforces the tendency to avoid involving the team in the development of the next initiative. Additionally, controls that are bolted on at the end are generally less effective and more burdensome than those that are built in from the inception.

ENTERPRISE INFORMATION SECURITY ARCHITECTURE: BRIDGING THE CONCEPTUAL TO THE ACTUAL

How do you take the high-level goals and strategies described in the previous chapter and make them real in your organization? That is the role of the enterprise information security architecture (EISA). Its purpose is to bridge the high-level vision of executive managers with the tools available to frontline contributors responsible for actually implementing the IS function.

The EISA is the framework that takes the high-level vision and strategies defined by senior management out into the day-to-day activities of the organization.

As described by Tom Scholtz of Gartner Research,[1] the EISA has two dimensions: levels and viewpoints.

The architectural levels range from conceptual to implementation:

- The **conceptual level** represents the intent and goals of the EISA. It encompasses the security services framework plus the various models and frameworks, such as the roles and responsibility model and the security policy framework.
- The **logical level** provides more detailed requirements and models to guide solution development.
- The **implementation level** defines the tools that will be used to implement the conceptual and logical designs.

Viewpoints provide an additional dimension to each of the levels:

- The **business viewpoint** defines how the information security function will be carried out and how it will relate to the rest of the enterprise. It includes items such as the process model or the roles and responsibility model.
- The **information viewpoint** defines the information required to perform the IS function, such as the security policy framework and the information classification inventory.
- The **technical viewpoint** translates the various models into guidance for required hardware and software configurations.

 ## TOOLS OF INFORMATION SECURITY

Information systems are compromised of computers, networks, applications, data, and users. It is the function of the EIS to ensure that the enterprise can successfully meet its responsibility to ensure that its information assets are available to authorized users when required and that the integrity of the information can be relied on for effective decision making or transaction processing all while managing who has the right to use the information.

Developing the EISA provides the IS function with the primary tool to guide its activities and to ensure their alignment with the organization's strategic objectives. It aids in the selection of the components needed to protect the organization's information assets.

An effective IS function is based on a layered defense-in-depth design. It is comprised of processes supported by tools that allow individuals to identify themselves to the information systems and provides a means for the systems to verify or authenticate that people are who they claim to be. After users have been identified and authenticated, controls are required to ensure that users have access to only those systems, applications, and data necessary to perform their jobs. Additionally, controls are required to make sure that no changes are made to the data that make them unreliable for further use or allow them to be disclosed to unauthorized individuals.

Security Awareness Training

Effective IS relies on each member of the enterprise recognizing his or her responsibility for maintaining the confidentiality, integrity, and availability of the organization's information assets. The purpose of the EIS team is to assist the enterprise in fulfilling this responsibility. In other words, the EIS does not own the responsibility for IS; everyone in the organization does. This is the foundation of a successful IS program because it makes everyone a member of the IS team.

Support from the highest executive levels is required if there is to be any hope of getting everyone to take their IS responsibility seriously. Selling security up to management is performed by developing and leveraging relationships with key business leaders. In the best of all possible worlds, the CEO is fully committed to the cause, but the reality of the position usually makes that unlikely. Most of the time CEOs are under pressure from the board to increase shareholder value by increasing profits and revenues while decreasing costs. Usually the only time the board ever asks about IS is when it is too late and a costly, embarrassing breach has already occurred. The best way to obtain the CEO's support is to garner the support of the executives whom the CEO relies on. These executives have many concerns that are shared with the EIS team. For the chief financial officer, it is usually Sarbanes-Oxley compliance. For the general counsel, it is protecting the enterprise from legal liability. For the human resources executive, it is keeping track of the status of all the employees and protecting personally identifiable information, such as employee Social Security data and records. Developing relationships based on these mutual concerns can lead to a better executive understanding of the issues to be addressed and the resources that the EIS team can provide. With any luck, as these leaders become aware of the value that the EIS team provides, good things will be conveyed to the CEO.

In addition to developing support from the executive team, it is necessary to raise the security awareness of everyone else in the organization. Many activities, ranging from picking strong passwords to properly handling e-mail, appear innocent but can have a serious impact on the organization's security posture. This is where the security awareness program comes in. Its objective is to bring these issues to everyone's attention.

Not every topic is a good candidate for the security awareness program. Therefore, it should focus on high-value initiatives tailored to the enterprise. For instance, a retail business might focus on loss prevention, a research organization may address intellectual property protection, and a bank might concentrate on data privacy. Other good candidates are enterprise policy education, threat awareness recognition for threats such as e-mail–borne malware or phishing attacks, and good security practices such as not sharing login information with coworkers.

Several tools exist for use in a security awareness program:

- Classroom or online training is effective when a large number of people need to be educated at the same time or if the same material needs to be presented on an ongoing basis, such as new employee orientation.

- E-mail/newsletters are also effective in reaching a wide audience. These methods lend themselves to covering a wide range of topics that change over time. For example, they are effective tools for communicating new or evolving threats.
- Slide presentations can be presented by the EIS team or distributed to managers for use through the organization.
- EIS involvement in company events, such all-hands meetings or departmental sessions like brown-bag meetings, raises awareness by showing management's commitment to IS in addition to conveying the presentation subject matter.
- The corporate intranet can be an excellent location not only to publish security awareness material but also to act as a single location that employees can go to for any security-related question.

Once a security awareness program has been put in place, it is important to measure its effectiveness to learn what is working and what needs to be changed to make it more effective. This feedback loop is also helpful in identifying who may need additional training. Creative organizations have employed quizzes, games, and contests in an effort to make it fun. Others periodically require employees to correctly answer security-related questions during the login process in order to gain access to the system.

User Identification, Authentication, and Access Control

While it would be nice to have a security awareness program in place, and it is a best practice to provide some IS and policy training before a person is given access to the enterprise information systems, this is not always not possible. But, assuming that this has been done, the next issue that needs to be addressed is user identification and authentication.

User identification is how individuals identify themselves to the system. Generally, people are assigned usernames that they are prompted for by the various systems and applications that they need to access. In some cases a token such as a smart card or key card may be used.

User authentication is the more difficult task. Authentication is based on something that the person knows, has, or is, or in some cases the person's location. Passwords are the best-known instances of something a person knows. Security tokens, smart cards, and digital certificates are examples of something a person has. Fingerprints, retinal scans, and voice prints are considered something that is an integral characteristic of who the person is. Finally, as GPS-enabled devices become more prevalent, some organizations, such as the U.S. military, are using GPS coordinates provided during login to verify that users are connecting from their expected location.

Authentication systems are also characterized by how many additional means or factors they use to verify the person's identity. For example, if an individual needs to provide a password in addition to the login name, authentication is considered single-factor authentication. Dual-factor authentication requires additional proof to establish identity. The additional proof could be a security token or a digital certificate that resides on their workstation or a USB (Universal Serial Bus) flash drive. Some security tokens are designed to provide a response to a challenge from the system. For instance, a key fob could display a value that individuals enter along with their username and password. The display value could change based on the login time, or it could be the next value in a preestablished series of responses. Time-based responses sometimes introduce problems associated with time synchronization drift between the host system and the security token while sequential responses can get out of sync if the individual inadvertently advances the token's display value. In spite of these complications, security tokens generally provide a higher level of assurance that people are who they claim to be. These methods are recommended whenever access is granted to more sensitive systems, such as payment processing systems, or data, such as credit card information. Requiring biometric matches in addition to a security token is an example of three-factor authentication. Generally, using more factors for identification leads to better authentication.

Keeping track of multiple usernames, passwords, and how many factors are required for access can be a difficult task. Add that to issues such as password aging, which requires users to pick new passwords periodically, and password history requirements that keep them from reusing old passwords, and system users could quickly revolt. In order to meet security requirements yet still be able to remember their login credentials, people often resort to poor practices, such as weak, easily guessed passwords or new passwords that are closely related to previously used ones.

Two basic approaches have been developed to make things easier for users and system administrators: single-sign on and password synchronization.

Single-sign on (SSO) systems allow people to remember one password and provide authentication credentials to all the systems that they can access. Integrated Windows Authentication and Kerberos are examples of SSO. Web-based third-party systems are available too. SSO has the advantage that it can replace the disparate login authentication mechanisms of different operating systems with a single authentication protocol. Therefore, a user authenticated by Windows Active Directory services can access a Linux server without having to go through the Linux system's login process. By accommodating these different operating environments, SSO eliminates the need for users to remember multiple usernames and/or passwords.

Password synchronization also allows for people to use a single password, but it synchronizes that password across all the systems. Password synchronization is considered easier to implement than SSO because it does not require the installation of client software. Critics of password synchronization say it suffers from the fact that if the password becomes known for one system, it becomes known for all systems the person has access to. Proponents state that SSO suffers from the same flaw if the primary password is cracked on the authentication server. The difference is that with password synchronization if one server is compromised, all related servers are cracked; with SSO, if a system other than the authentication server is cracked, the threat is isolated to that system. In either case, both SSO and password synchronization require that the single password be strong and remain confidential to the user or system.

Infrastructure-Based Controls

Once users have been successfully authenticated, they have access to the enterprise's information resources. A defense-in-depth approach provides for multiple controls limiting what networks, systems, applications, and data they can access and what they can do with those resources.

A defense-in-depth strategy can be implemented in various ways, but essentially it consists of complementary security layers that continue to provide protection even if one layer is breached. Defense in depth reflects the OSI Network model[2] in many respects as it is implemented on the physical resource, such as routers, firewalls, and servers, up through the data processed by the information systems applications and finally to the information provided to the end user.

Network Security Tools

The first security layer is the network itself; it provides the physical and logical connections to the organization's information assets. The first objective of network defense should be a well-segmented network. It would be foolish to make all enterprise systems accessible to the world at large. The first obvious step is to segregate or segment the enterprise's internal systems from the public network. Of course, the enterprise is going to need to make some of its servers, such as e-mail or Web servers, accessible to the outside world and to internal users and systems.

The need to provide access to different systems for different classes of users demonstrates the need to compartmentalize or segment the network into a collection of security zones. Firewalls, routers, and switches are the devices used to physically implement the security zones. Network segments that are both segregated and access-controlled are known as screened subnetworks. They are differentiated from non–access controlled subnetworks that can be created for other purposes, such as traffic through-put optimization.

Security zones are established to provide appropriate controls based on several different factors, such as the position of the resource within the network—for example, border routers or Web servers that provide services to external networks. To accommodate these situations, a "demilitarized zone" is established to allow semipublic servers to be accessed in a highly restricted and controlled manner. At other times, segments are created to provide additional protection to strategic IT resources, such as those that serve research and development, human resources, or the enterprise's financial systems. Additionally, devices with low trust levels should be segmented so that additional controls can be placed on them. Wireless access points are an excellent example of low-trust devices in need of additional controls since anyone who can receive or transmit a radio signal to them can potentially establish a connection to the rest of the internal network.

The purpose of network segmentation is to control the flow of data. The next security layer focuses on controlling the content of the data that is moving across the network. The objective of this layer is not only to detect malware but also to identify inappropriate data movement that may be an indication of data leakage. Security is accomplished at this layer through content blocking tools and network monitoring.

Content blocking attempts to stop malware from making it to the target system or user. A common example is antivirus (AV) solutions. AV systems rely heavily on recognizing signatures of known attacks. In response, attackers go to great lengths to change those signatures. In an attempt to identify unknown attacks, antivirus tools also use heuristic techniques, such as emulating a file's activity in a sandbox to determine if malware is present.

Antispam tools attempt to identify and eliminate unsolicited junk e-mail. Many organizations are moving their antispam measures to cloud-based antispam service providers that specialize in spam prevention. Most antispam service providers also perform antivirus services. Additionally, antispam measures provide the benefit of increasing bandwidth to the organization because e-mail is initially routed to the cloud service and only scrubbed traffic is sent to the enterprise. With spam representing 50 percent or more of e-mail traffic, this can be a substantial bandwidth boost.

Phishing attacks attempt to fool users into going to a hostile site and providing sensitive information. E-mail or instant messaging usually delivers these attacks. Therefore, it is closely related to spam, which makes spam prevention techniques useful in protecting users from phishing attacks.

Since many attacks depend on tricking users into visiting malicious sites, tools are available to identify the URLs associated with these sites and to filter them before they can reach end users. Unfortunately, given the speed with which attackers can establish new sites, it is very difficult to maintain the URL blacklists, a fact that diminishes the effectiveness of this approach.

Networking monitoring tools, such as intrusion detection systems (IDSs) or intrusion prevention systems (IPSs), function by analyzing network traffic for attempts to compromise the target systems. IDSs usually have sensors to monitor the traffic, a control console that monitors events generated by the sensors, and an engine that logs and analyzes the events according to a set of rules to generate alerts to security administrators. IDSs evolved to IPSs that go beyond alert generation and attempt to prevent the attack's execution in real time. IPSs can block an attack in various ways, such as by dropping malicious traffic or adding firewall rules to block the offending traffic.

System Hardening

Most attacks rely on either taking advantage of the end users or exploiting vulnerabilities on connected systems. The antivirus, antiphishing, and URL filtering tools attempt to protect against user targeted attacks. IDSs and IPSs do that too, but they also attempt to identify and prevent system targeted attacks.

However, it is impossible to identify all attacks or to react to every attack in time. The best defense ultimately is to eliminate the attacks' target. It is necessary to ensure that each device is properly patched and configured so that it performs its function as intended with no unintended consequences. There are countless examples of major attacks targeted at known vulnerabilities for which fixes had been published; in some cases, the patches were available for years. The announcement of a patch often starts a race among attackers who reverse engineer the fix and then develop attacks for the hole it is plugging. Therefore, it is imperative that patches are applied in a timely manner. However, a perfectly patched system can still be totally exposed it is not configured properly. For example, it does no good to have a firewall perfectly placed in a well-designed, fully patched network if the first rule in its access control list is "allow all."

Every network device, whether a router, firewall, or server, is software driven. In some devices, the software is coded directly into the firmware; in others, it resides on a hard disk. But regardless of where the software resides, it is almost guaranteed to have some vulnerability associated with it. For instance, although Microsoft has made great strides in improving the security of its products, it still regularly posts multiple fixes for critical vulnerabilities on the second Tuesday of each month. Keeping track of vulnerabilities is a burdensome task as there is no single location where all vulnerabilities are identified.

The first step in the vulnerability management process is to create an inventory of all the devices and systems that are attached to the network. One nonsecurity side benefit of doing the inventory is that it can also be used as part of the enterprise's license compliance program.

Automated discovery tools are available to assist. These tools can be categorized as either active tools that scan the network or passive tools that analyze network traffic to identify connected devices. These tools are not bulletproof so it is important to not treat their output as the final word. It strongly recommended that the reports be reviewed for completeness by the appropriate staff. The minimum information that should be collected includes the network address, device name, its purpose, asset owner, installed operating system with its current patch level, installed applications with their current patch level, and network services in use.

Once the inventory has been established, it is vital to make sure that the inventorying tools continue to monitor the network to detect any changes that occur and to alert IT management to any events that they detect. This not only helps to identify whether an unauthorized device is attached to the network; it also helps to alert management to the possible theft of an information asset. Remember, the value of the information on the device might be substantially more than the cost of the device itself. It is also important to properly secure the asset inventory, as it can provide vital information to an attacker.

With the current state of the network inventory known, the next step is to group and prioritize the systems on the network. Doing this will help the system administration team to focus its efforts on the most critical assets first. Grouping can be done on characteristics such as common management control, common function, similar security requirements, a common operating system environment, importance to the organization's operations, importance of the information assets residing on the system, or exposure to external users.

The next step is to develop the means to identify when new vulnerabilities are discovered or when vendors announce patches or updates for their products. This information is available from a variety of sources, including web sites, mailing lists, and databases maintained by vendors, third parties, and commercial entities. Additionally, tools are available to perform automated vulnerability scans and assessments.

When a vulnerability is identified, consideration should be made to determine the significance of the threat, whether known exploits exist for it, and what impact applying the fix might have on the affected systems. This information will provide the basis for prioritizing how remediation will be implemented. The significance of the threat depends on the systems it affects. Because not every system has the same significance to the organization, the impact of an attack on a given system varies. Financial systems warrant greater attention than a personal computer that uses the Web to track shipments. Additionally, how those systems are configured may mitigate the threat altogether. For instance, if a new vulnerability is found for SMPT (simple mail transfer protocol) but no servers run that service, the vulnerability would have no impact and no immediate need for remediation. Conversely, vulnerabilities with known exploits definitely warrant greater attention. However, just because an exploit is not publicly known does not mean that the threat can be ignored. With the growing sophistication of attackers, exploits are being developed and kept secret so that they can be used against selectively targeted systems.

Vulnerability remediation is done by installing a software patch, making a configuration change, or, in extreme cases, removing the affected resource. To guard against production downtime when deploying patches or updates, a remediation test process should be implemented. Centralized patch testing eliminates the need for local system administrators to test each patch, but to be effective, standard system builds are required. Local system administrators would be responsible for testing patches to nonstandard systems. Patch testing should be performed first in nonproduction environments where possible. Ideally, a quality assurance/test environment would be in place for this purpose.

All organizations should be using some form of automation to deploy vulnerability remediations. Only those systems with unique, nonstandard builds should be patched manually. Automated solutions are either agent or non-agent based. Either type of system typically has a central system that acts as a management console and as the repository of all remediations to be applied. A notable exception to this is Microsoft's Windows Update service, which is decentralized and allows local administrators to decide which patches will be applied to which systems.

A non-agent-style system scans the network with administrative access privileges to identify systems in need of patching and then installs the patch. A key disadvantage for non-agent-style systems is that their scans may be blocked by a host-based firewall or systems may be missed because they were not online at the time of the scan. Systems used by telecommuters are especially vulnerable to this issue.

Agent-based deployment systems have a software program installed on each system to be managed. The agent periodically contacts the central repository to determine what patches are available and installs any appropriate patch for the system it resides on. While agent-based systems address many of the shortcomings of non-agent systems, they are more difficult to implement initially and require continuous care to make sure that the agents are installed and running on every system. Also, agent software may not be available for every device on the system.

Data Protection

With the user and infrastructure security layers addressed, it is time to apply a layer of protection directly to the data itself. After all, protecting the information is the whole point. Once again, the process starts with taking an inventory—this time of the organization's information assets. In addition to identifying what information assets exist, it is necessary to categorize each asset according to its value and sensitivity based on the organization's need to protect its confidentiality, integrity, and availability. The information asset inventory is foundational to compliance requirements, such as the PCI Data Security Standard (PCI-DSS), the Health Insurance Portability and Accountability Act, or the Gramm-Leach-Bliley Act. Risk impact for data should take into consideration how long the data must be protected, its business impact, regulatory jurisdictional concerns, and where data resides.

Generally, information is classified into one of four groups, normally defined as:

1. **Public information:** Data that are specifically approved for public release or information otherwise available to the public at large and intended for distribution outside the organization.
2. **For internal use only:** Information intended for use within the organization and, in some cases, within affiliated organizations, such as business partners. This classification also serves as a catchall for information that does not easily fit into any other category.
3. **Confidential information:** Information considered private or otherwise sensitive in nature and restricted to those with a legitimate business need for access.
4. **Secret:** The most sensitive customer and business information intended for restricted use strictly within the enterprise or with partners as approved by executive management.

The information owner—defined as the person responsible for a business process and its related data—is responsible for assigning the initial classification for information assets and determining when an information asset should be reclassified. It is the responsibility of executive management to review and accept the resulting classifications to ensure a global perspective. Once the information has been inventoried and classified, access roles and rules need to be established so that controls can be selected and implemented.

Data at Rest

In broad terms, data are categorized as either at rest or in motion. The term "data at rest" refers to all data stored on systems or devices and not currently in use. These data can be located on the servers of a storage area network, an employee's computer, or off-site backup tapes. Therefore, the biggest problem with data at rest is determining all the locations where a particular piece of information may reside.

Traditionally, protecting data at rest involved techniques similar to those used to protect system infrastructure by segmenting the data storage systems and defining appropriate access controls. However, there has been an explosion of devices that can store data, from employee computers, to USB drives, to smart phones and even iPods. As a result of this explosion, system administrators have lost control over data storage. That responsibility now belongs to end users, who generally lack the professional awareness and skills to handle the task properly.

Since end users cannot be relied on to carry out this essential task, another way had to be adopted to make the data inaccessible for unauthorized use. One approach that is being widely adopted is to encrypt the data. While the files themselves may be accessible, the information within them is not. This makes the files useless to unauthorized viewing. Data encryption can protect data on network storage devices, servers, end-user computers and laptops, USB drives, and offline backup media. Encryption can also protect data as they travel across the network. This is most commonly seen when Web clients communicate with sensitive applications such as online retail web sites via HTTPS (Hypertext Transfer Protocol Secure) or SSL (Secure Sockets Layer) connections.

Encryption is a complex process that requires very careful implementation to be done successfully. Various types of data have differing life cycles ranging from short-duration Web transactions to offsite backups that must be retained for years. Further, various standards, such as PCI-DSS, mandate specific key-handling procedures.

Secure key management is paramount to the security of any process relying on data encryption. Key management becomes even more complex as encryption is used for more and more purposes. Secure Web transactions rely on digital certificates provided to the organization, end user data encryption solutions use another set of keys, encrypted data within a database use their own keys, and offsite backups require yet another set of keys. Therefore, a system is needed to address the complex, sensitive task of key management. A key management system should provide these capabilities:

- Security, tamper resistance, and high availability
- Key generation, rotation, revocation, and deletion to enable encryption and to limit key access to authorized individuals
- Key rotation without requiring re-encryption
- The ability to manage keys for disparate databases, operating systems, and devices
- The ability to manage keys for backup media with extended storage life cycles
- Extensive logging and auditing capabilities

Data in Motion

"Data in motion" refers to the movement of data between the locations where they are stored to the locations where they are used. Data in motion are comprised of data traversing the Internet as well as the internal network. Examples include virtual private network (VPN) connections from mobile workers and secure SSL-based Web transactions. However, merely encrypting external traffic to the trusted network perimeter is insufficient. It is possible for attackers to eavesdrop on internal network traffic if they are able to compromise an internal system. To secure a Web transaction properly, the message needs to be encrypted from the Web client to the external Web server to the back-end application server and finally to the back-end database server. Sending the traffic in the clear at any point makes it vulnerable to disclosure.

Many enterprises have implemented content monitoring of their data in motion to prevent data leakage. Content monitoring applications are more helpful in detecting and preventing accidental data leakage than against deliberate leakage.

Two basic approaches exist to monitoring the data. The most common approach is to monitor the information that is traversing the network. This is the simplest and easiest method to deploy. However, organizations are increasingly attempting to do the monitoring at the point of usage, such as on the user workstation. This approach relies on agents installed on each system and device, which makes its deployment more complex and difficult.

From a practical implementation standpoint, these two approaches form a continuum that organizations progress through as their content monitoring systems mature. Generally, enterprises begin by focusing on the network perimeter where the information leaves its domain. Content such as e-mail, instant messages, and Web traffic is examined as it leaves the organization for keyword or regular expression matches that are signs of sensitive data moving in violation of established policy. Attention shifts from the network border to the internal network as monitoring processes mature. At this level, policy is enforced through a combination of network monitoring and host-based tools.

The most mature end of the content monitoring continuum is managing "data in transition." This term describes data as they go from data at rest to data in motion. It is at this stage that the organization has the best opportunity to identify and prevent malicious user behavior. To illustrate, what if an individual is allowed to access a file that contains a list of individuals and their Social Security numbers, but the person is not authorized to send that data outside the organization. A host-based system would determine that the person was authorized to access the file. A network-based solution would detect and block any attempt to e-mail the file to an external recipient since the user was not authorized to do so. However, a person determined to get the information out of the organization might encrypt the file to hide its content from the monitoring systems. Endpoint solutions attempt to control the actions a user can take with the data. In this case, the user would be prevented from encrypting the file before sending it.

This is an excellent example of defense in depth. Host-based systems protect the file from unauthorized access. Network-based systems prevent the data accessed by authorized users from being sent to unauthorized locations. Finally, endpoint systems prevent authorized users from taking unauthorized actions.

Secure Application Development

Many organizations do not need to concern themselves with secure application development because they rely exclusively on vendor-provided packaged solutions. However, secure development practices should be a primary concern for those that do develop their own applications either for their own use or for resale. After all, most security breaches are based on attacks that target known vulnerabilities with some application. Firewalls are usually viewed as access barriers barring unauthorized persons from accessing unauthorized applications. But conversely, they can be viewed as access enablers granting access to authorized applications. So firewalls are not effective if the authorized application is flawed and allows malicious actions that lead to inappropriate data disclosure. Therefore, developing secure applications addresses one of the major root causes of data compromise; most of the efforts already described in this chapter address the symptoms of application or infrastructure insecurity.

Developers naturally focus on features rather than security for the obvious reason that they are tasked to develop an application that does something aside from just being secure. However, it is just as important to prevent unintended results as it is to produce the intended results. Unfortunately, most of the security efforts in the software development life cycle (SDLC) involve trying to identify vulnerabilities through testing rather than building security throughout the SDLC. This leads to security being patched on at the end of the SDLC process rather than integrated from the beginning. To correct this problem, it is necessary to institute a full application security program.

To a large extent, the process of establishing an application security program mirrors that of establishing an IS program. It begins with the awareness by all developers that it is their responsibility to include security as a specification for all applications they create. Engineering management should create a set of security principles and establish security policies that define how applications will be coded and tested to support those principles. Individual developers need to be trained so that they understand the types of coding practices that are insecure and how to avoid them. Organizations such as the Open Web Application Security Project (www.owasp.org) provide many resources for secure application development. Vendors such as Microsoft or Oracle also publish best practices for use when developing applications based on their technologies.

With a good application security framework in place, building security into the SDLC is usually straightforward. At the design phase, the security principles are included in the design document. During development, the coding practices defined by the secure coding policy are followed. Source code analysis is also performed during this phase to ensure that no unsafe practices have been introduced into the application. Automated tools exist to assist with the analysis, but it is important to also perform manual analysis to catch those practices that only a human can spot. Preliminary security assessments, such as penetration tests, are done during the test phase. Again, tools can help to automate this step, but since they are often weak at recognizing the context of a response, manual testing should also be performed. A final security assessment should be completed during the staging phase to ensure that the application remains secure in its deployed configuration. Finally, once the application is in production, application security should be part of the code change control process, and ongoing compliance audits should be conducted.

CONCLUSION

The objective of the IS system is to protect the confidentiality, integrity, and availability of the enterprise's information assets. At a strategic level, protecting information assets entails aligning the IS program with the organization's objectives, raising awareness within the organization of its responsibilities in protecting its information assets, creating an EIS architecture, establishing an IS governance committee, and implementing an IS management system.

Tactically, an IS program is best accomplished by taking a multilayered, defense-in-depth approach. Since the biggest security vulnerability usually exists with the end user, it is imperative to implement an effective security awareness program as the first layer. The IS architecture is then used to bridge the strategic plan into tactical actions. An effective process needs to be put in place to define who can do what within the system.

This is backed up by a strong user authentication and access control system to identify valid system users and to manage what information resources they can use. The resources themselves should be segmented so that they are made available only to those who have a need for them as part of their job function. System resources should be hardened through well-defined system builds backed by an ongoing vulnerability patching process. Data should be inventoried and classified according to their value to the enterprise and the risk to which they are exposed. Data at rest should be fully identified and segmented in order to develop appropriate protection schemes. Data in motion should be monitored to identify any inadvertent or deliberate data leakage. Encryption should be considered for protecting the organization's most sensitive or valuable information assets. The encryption system should include an effective key management system to ensure that the encryption keys are secure, tamper resistant, and highly available. For those organizations that develop applications for internal use or resale, a secure application development program should be put in place. Software security principles and policies should be developed. Developers should be trained. Security should be a design specification and tested throughout the development cycle, including after the system has been deployed to production.

While it is possible to develop a perfectly secure IS, it is highly unlikely and usually not cost effective to do so. Therefore, the secure, multilayered combination of people, process, and technology best minimizes the risks to the enterprise's information assets to a level acceptable to the enterprise.

 ## NOTES

1. Tom Scholtz, "Structure and Content of an Enterprise Information Security Architecture," Gartner Research, January 23, 2006, http://www.gartner.com/DisplayDocument?ref=g_search&id=488195.
2. The OSI Network model is an abstract description of network architecture that consists of seven layers which, from top to bottom, are the application, presentation, session, transport, network, data link, and physical layers.

CHAPTER TWENTY-SEVEN

Business Continuity Planning

Dave McCandless

S AGE WISDOM TELLS US that "Life is what happens when you're busy making plans." A more recent version of this same sentiment can be politely phrased as "Stuff happens." No matter how it is said, the message is clear: As we go on about our daily business, both personal and professional, disruptive events will take place that have the potential to substantially change what we had planned for our future.

For business, undefined change is very likely a bad thing. Business plans define key objectives that must be met for the business to survive. Deviation from these plans will likely result in higher costs and lower revenues, sometimes to the point where the business must pause or even cease to exist. Stable businesses exist because their leaders are able to understand the nuances of whatever industry they are in—they find the path and navigate the obstacles to success. The good leaders show us everyday how they can manage what they can control.

But what happens when that control is threatened? How do these leaders react to sustain a business when faced with disruptive events? How do they ensure continuity of the business plan to be able to achieve their key objectives? Leaders make this happen by creating a company culture that methodically plans and executes to sustain business operations when faced with disruptive challenges.

Business continuity planning (BCP) is the self-imposed discipline that defines how well a business can sustain operations when faced with disruptive events. As a CIO you will be part of this process, since in the information age a substantial number, if not all, of a company's business processes will rely on IT systems. This chapter will give you insight into how to navigate the journey that is the discipline of BCP.

DEFINING THE NEED FOR BCP

While leaders universally agree that continuity planning is a vital component of strategic business process delivery, they have widely varied opinions on how to define and justify the actual function that is BCP. Successfully defining the problem means creating a crisp yet persuasive value proposition that business leadership will endorse and champion.

Why We Plan

If all went according to plan, we would not need alternatives. No spare batteries for the flashlight. No spare flashlight. No candles for when you cannot find the flashlight. And no matches for the candles, since we no longer use candles. But things do not go according to plan—which means we are stuck with figuring out how to plan for events that happen that we cannot predict.

This gap creates the challenge to create a collection of manageable business processes that can lead a company through the resolution of disruptive events. There is a clear choice of words here: *disruptive* meaning we will know what to do when disruptions happen, but we likely will not know when the disruptions will occur. Words like *unforeseen* and *unexpected* could both be interpreted as events for which the company was not prepared. *Disruptive* means events that change the course of the action, but if planning is complete, the corrective action is defined and methodically initiated. Planning for the continuity of operations becomes the exercise and includes all operational areas of the organization. Any foreseeable disruptions need to be defined and then analyzed for their impact and eventual remediation. When completed, operational procedures are updated to include these new changes. To ensure correctness, recurring testing must take place. As an ongoing process, these changes likely represent a tremendous cost to a business—for many foreseen disruptive events that may never happen.

Which leads to the question: At what cost? How much investment must be funneled into this process to ensure continuity? Answering this fundamental question is the responsibility of senior management, since they ultimately are responsible for the ongoing operation of the business. Management has the final say in what processes are critical to ongoing operations. Through this leadership process, management communicates to the organization what is important and sets the expectation for all business and operations leaders to find sustaining solutions. Without agreement on what is important at the time of the disruption, chaos is the likely outcome.

Taking an example from history, one of our great planned achievements has been to send men to the moon and return them safely to Earth. These two simple objectives drove an unprecedented continuity planning process that sought to uncover every foreseeable disruptive event in NASA's Gemini and Apollo programs. This led to an unfathomable price tag. What percentage of this cost is attributable to contingency planning? Can we make the argument that any of the planning or the subsequent redundant systems deployment was not required to meet the objective? Certainly few of these contingency systems were ever used, but would we ever have sent men into space without them?

Executive strategy requires that a choice be made of what kind of BCP an organization will embrace. It must start at the top.

Expecting the Unexpected

Earthquakes. Hurricanes. Global economic collapse. Loss of network connectivity at a critical call center. These and thousands of other events like them jeopardize delivery of a company's global business every day, all day. With rigorous planning followed by methodical execution, these events will not impact the business—in fact, they may add value. A Thursday afternoon blizzard will not be nearly as well received in Chicago as is will be in Aspen.

The Web has shaped all of us to expect always available, fully functional services. Online shopping available 24/7. Customer support available anytime via a text message, mouse click, or iPhone. Instantaneous e-mail and chat responses. To achieve these service levels, companies are increasingly less tolerant of outages and have expectations that outage durations will be minimal.

Dwight Eisenhower, a master planner, once said: "Plans are nothing; planning is everything." This concept is the basis for BCP: An organization that has taken the time and committed the resources to plan for the unexpected will have a greater chance of surviving than one that has not. An untested strongbox full of backup tapes, user manuals, and contact lists could very well be useless the minute it is opened. Yet in many companies this is exactly the expectation—that some magic "survival package" will be ready when needed at a time of crisis.

Internal expectations for high availability are not unique; requirements are also on the rise for companies to be able to demonstrate externally the *capability of resiliency* in the face of impact events. Each year, more pressure is created from business partners and regulatory agencies to show documented proof of a continuity plan and its subsequent successful test execution. The regulated permission to stay in business may be dependent on a thorough and successful BCP process.

Adding Business Value

Is it reasonable to make a case that a strong BCP process can add business value? Is avoiding unavailability of the business a strong enough argument to gather support for BCP? Or do we also need to make the case for tangible business value?

Risk professionals can demonstrate that, yes, there are sufficient examples of businesses that are severely impacted by business interruption. But for business leaders who require more convincing, there are ways to make a case for how BCP adds tangible business value. The details are not found in widgets sold or expenses reduced; they are accumulated over time via reduced incidents of outages and consistent costs of operation.

 ## PROCESS OF CONTINUITY PLANNING

Many methodologies exist that explain the BCP process. This section covers the basic concepts common to each. Any organization pursuing BCP needs to craft a process that matches its specific business needs.

Commitment to the Process

The first step in BCP is critical—recognition by leadership that the organization needs a BCP strategy and commitment of resources to support it. Executive sponsorship not only ensures the commitment but demonstrates to all employees the importance of the BCP process. Sponsorship means delegating the BCP responsibility to an internal team of professionals that will deliver on the objectives.

How should the BCP team be created? To add the most value, the team should include a mix of journeyman members of both business and services parts of the business. Members should also have previous exposure to a BCP implementation or be provided with formal training. Finally, a team leader with solid project delivery experience is needed, preferably an internal resource with sufficient authority and finesse to make change happen.

Assigning responsibility without proper authority will destine the process to languish with no chance of success. Also assigning "any available resource" demonstrates a lack of commitment to complete the task right the first time through. External experts can assist to make the process happen, but the right internal staffing is crucial to success.

Defining the Objectives

Once BCP oversight is created, the next step engages the BCP leadership team with the company executives to define what are the strategies and priorities for the business. Some examples: Online companies need their commerce web sites available 24/7; grocery stores that survive by just-in-time inventory need the doors open and the supply trucks rolling in; airlines need not just planes and crews readily available but decent weather in which to fly them. Each of these companies has the same goal—to keep the goods and services moving that bring in the revenue. Yet each has vastly different requirements as to what are the priority activities of the company.

The responsibility belongs to the senior management team to define the operations that are important. These are not low-level decisions about e-mail and enterprise resource planning; these are high-level, what-is-important-to-the-business decisions. Once these critical business operations are identified and their priorities of importance are established, the process cascades down the management chain to subsequent levels as details are added. Each business team participates as needed to add depth to the requirements. When finished, the company has a clearly defined business process classification—a target list of business priorities.

Of course, none of this planning can be done in a vacuum—BCP needs to coexist with other risk mitigation processes. Viable organizations will likely have risk management policies in place, so BCP objectives and risk mitigation objectives need to be in alignment. Often businesses already will have recognized this need and will have created a framework to bring similar processes under one objectives-defining umbrella.

Determining Impact

The next step involves the tasks to identify and qualify the impact on the business processes posed by the disruptive events. To begin, the analysis team must determine the various event categories to consider and, for each type of event category, the specific events themselves. For example, in the case of natural disasters, the specific events could be floods and tornados. In the case of malicious attacks to computing systems, the specific events could be denial of service attacks, intrusion attacks, and spam e-mail injection overload attacks. Businesses must assess their own unique requirements to define events and categories.

Once all the event details are fully defined, each event is rated—both for the magnitude of the potential disruption as well as the likelihood of the event actually happening. The smaller the disruptive impact, or the smaller the likelihood of occurrence, or the smaller the importance of the impacted capability means the overall business impact is low.

The common tool used in BCP to facilitate this process is the business impact analysis (BIA). This inspection of each critical business process will identify scenarios where interruptions or failures may happen, the likelihood of them happening, and the damage they will likely do to business operations when they happen. The BIA will also establish how quickly a business process can return to operation (recovery time objective), and what levels of functionality and data availability must exist within the business process (recovery point objective). Once completed, the BIA provides a complete specification of requirements on how to enhance the business processes that will result in the most effective mitigation of impact of disruptive events.

Knowing how to measure impact becomes an interesting exercise. For example, in the area of IT, an interesting paradox has emerged: Just how important is e-mail? Seldom does the process of sending and receiving e-mail account for any substantial amount of revenue, yet it is hard to imagine a company's staff completing useful tasks if e-mail is not available. But now consider business-to-business or business-to-consumer messaging: Any company that relies on its internal e-mail infrastructure for significant communication with customers and partners substantially raises the impact potential of loss of any part of this infrastructure and operation. So now how important is e-mail? This is a good example of the kinds of questions the BIA works to answer.

Creating the BC Strategy

Armed with the management priorities and the business impact findings, the next process is to create a strategy for business continuity that ensures ongoing business operations. Two remediation types are possible: corrective remediation that minimizes impact and restores operations, and preventive remediation that expands operational capabilities to withstand outages. Additionally, multiple strategies can be created that will provide resumption of some aspects of business operations. Equally possible is that the same impact can be resolved by differing recovery solutions. Total cost of the various possibilities will play a significant part in defining the strategy.

A quick analysis of alternate data center strategies is a good example of how to apply these principles. Companies with a single data center that rely on an outsourced provider for an alternate data center have chosen to correct the disruption of the loss of their only site by moving to the alternate site. Companies with multiple data centers with integration of systems and operations across sites have chosen to avoid or prevent disruptions by managing transaction activities through distribution. Which remediation type to choose is driven by a compromise between business needs and available funding.

Creating the BCP strategy also means engaging the various business units to elaborate on their technology dependencies. Many business units may expect IT to own this investigation on their behalf. However, this expectation is flawed, given that IT only provides the platform and is in no position to judge the critical importance of the various capabilities of business systems.

Once the importance of all critical systems and their outage impact are established, the final steps in creation of the strategy are to define which systems are selected for operational and technology changes. While simple in concept, this process defines where the investments in the business should be made to fulfill the requirements of the strategy.

Implementing the BC Strategy

The implementation process is the execution of the details described in the strategy. Simply stated, this is the process that implements value changes to existing operations and infrastructure that will result in higher resiliency to impact events. Up until this stage, all previous BCP activity is focused on analysis. BCP implementation forces a change process and creates the potential for disruption to these critical business systems due to the change itself.

Implementation also includes other areas critical to the business: updated emergency response procedures, the creation or upgrade of an emergency operations center capability, updated crisis management capabilities, and updated BCP training and education procedures. A fully-defined BCP testing process must be deployed and validated to ensure the changes are implemented and will deliver the expected results.

Ongoing Plan Maintenance

The final step in the BCP process is to ensure that this strategic planning exercise is not a one-time event but continues on through regular and predictable execution. This ongoing process will provide additional business value if continuous improvement techniques are performed as part of year-to-year program management.

It is very likely that new requirements will emerge as the BCP process is in execution. Like any other large project, scope creep can be assured. Testing with partners and outside agencies? Review of test plans to meet BCP objectives? Review of management objectives for comparison with BCP objectives to ensure they are still in alignment? Adding new lines of business or retiring old ones? Adjusting to substantial changes to the market or customers? Many questions like these will emerge during the execution of the analysis and deployment processes.

Business processes will undergo constant change. New types of disruptive events will emerge to threaten the business. Executive objectives and priorities will change. The BCP process must continue to adapt to these changes to avoid the impacts of disruptive events.

STRATEGIC VALUE OF BCP

Measuring the business value of BCP is tricky. In the classic sense, the question has been *What is peace of mind worth?* But as the process of BCP becomes better understood, organizations discover how the process creates value to distance them from the competition.

Value before a Disruptive Event

In a world where every interconnected organization deploys some amount of BCP, regulatory and certification agencies will continue to require more resiliency capability before granting permission to participate. For companies with strong BCP, this process will prove to be a filter to slow weaker industry competition, creating a competitive advantage.

Having the appropriate BCP processes in place at the right time enables a company to focus on the core business. Having insufficient BCP in place could mean diverting key resources to the BCP process to bring it up to a minimal industry standard. Perhaps the business intends this catch-up as part of the strategic plan—a reasonable business strategy. But it raises an interesting question: Without sufficient investment in the BCP process, how would a company know what is a minimal acceptable level of BCP, and how would it know when it has caught up?

For companies that struggle with tracking the maturity of their various business units and their interactions, a strong BCP process can add management value. Since the basis of BCP is to ensure continuity across the entire business, BCP participation will identify business capabilities in need of improvement. This leads to resiliency across the entire organization to withstand impact events and create a healthier business process environment.

Value after a Disruptive Event

As soon as a substantially disruptive event occurs, the first reaction from all involved will be "Good thing we made the investment in BCP." Of course, if there was minimal or no investment in BCP, the reaction will be much different.

A well-crafted BCP process will go into execution automatically—procedures will be followed and operations teams will execute according to plan. Companies that have planned well will be seen as strategic thinkers and will likely see their brand value and possibly their financial position improve due to their ability to sustain operations. Their immediate and well-honed messages to customer, partners, and the general public will instill a sense of respect and feeling that "I want to be in business with this company." Not only will the company sustain its current business, but in all likelihood it will generate new business.

But the added value does not stop there. Disasters as impact events may put businesses in various market segments or geographic regions temporarily or permanently out of action. Companies designed to adapt quickly can aggressively take on a greater share of an existing market or get a foothold in a new one. BCP in this case becomes an enabler of business opportunity—what would have been lost opportunity is now possible because of a previous commitment to BCP.

WHAT BCP IS NOT

Now that we have talked a bit about what BCP is, it is worthwhile to spend some time on what it is not. There is often confusion in the business world on the value of BCP. Those companies that do not recognize the value will not understand the discipline and will perpetuate the misconceptions.

BCP Is Not Disaster Recovery

One aspect of BCP is the ability to recover from disasters, or disaster recovery (DR). While the exact numbers will vary, the industry consensus is that fewer than one in five business-disruptive events are caused by disasters, such as hurricanes, floods, and earthquakes. With 80 percent of the impact posed by nondisasters, wouldn't a company be better off spending time on nondisaster recovery (NDR)?

Ironically, no one ever asks about an NDR plan, nor do any CIO peer-level discussions ever address the value of an NDR plan. Even a recent Google search found zero results for "nondisaster recovery plan" but over 400,000 results for "disaster recovery plan."

This one area creates so much confusion in the industry that it is worth addressing in detail: Disaster recovery is not business continuity. Years ago in a less mature IT world, the methodology was called DR. DR may be an integral part of BCP, but only a small part, and depending on the nature of the business, it may be a minor part of the BCP process. A future CIO's best approach is to learn to use the terms *BCP* and *DR* correctly. And when faced with a DR-centric organization, it will make for quite an education challenge.

BCP Is Not Insurance

As a business discipline, insurance is the end result of defining a monetary value to an asset such that in the loss of that asset, your insurance partner will pay you the agreed value of that asset. The process of obtaining the insurance includes the process for assigning value to the assets—which in turn implies some discovery process for identifying of all the company's assets, followed by the determination on which assets are worthy of a declared a value.

While insurance may be part of contingency planning, the BCP process is too important to the survival of the business to relegate to another annual finish-and-forget-it process. Insurance is normally a process the finance team uses to mitigate the cost to replace key assets without incurring the costs of the replacement.

True business leaders understand that BCP is not a loss mitigation computation but a strategic business-sustaining process that needs ongoing attention. They recognize that business operations will have continuity procedures interwoven into daily activities. They are willing to accept the cost of BCP beyond that of simple asset replacement.

BCP Is Not a Part-Time IT Job

Companies that expect to stay in business when faced with disruptive events understand the need for BCP. Those that do not understand the value will often do just enough to get by—and that means doing what is minimally required to pass the many audits imposed across the company's administrative functions.

Take an example of a company with a web site as its primary platform for business transactions that is suddenly faced with a disruptive event. Most likely the IT team has created a solution with the appropriate alternate site capabilities and 24/7 on-call procedures for systems administration. But is the same true for the customer service teams that support the customers: Do they have alternate plans for e-mail, phone, chat, and other tools—even a place to go to work—to execute their jobs? Are the communications and marketing teams coordinated in advance to be able to quickly and effectively get the word out about the disruptive event? Does senior management have confidence that the entire process will be put into motion with the same effectiveness as normal daily operations?

Most small and many medium-size businesses choose not to allocate sufficient funding to sustain an enterprise-wide BCP process. Instead these companies may choose to have a minimal few members of the IT team keep a current DR plan. This of course creates BCP only if all your problems are planned disasters and if the only impact to the business will be to IT.

EMERGING TECHNOLOGIES AND BCP

Each tick of the technology evolution clock brings IT planners a variety of solutions available to them with the potential to change the nature of systems recovery. BCP experts who for decades practiced the concept of backup tape creation, off-site media management, and emergency data center failure now have a range of modern alternatives that will rewrite industry best practices. Years from now even these cutting-edge capabilities will seem archaic, but today they represent potential for substantial value.

Virtualization

Enterprises large and small are reaping the benefits of using tens or hundreds of standard computers to run thousands of server images. This concept—creating fully encapsulated application environments that are transient and adaptive across hardware infrastructures—makes the process ideal to support rapid recovery from the disruptive nature of impactful events.

Which is a better way to re-create a server: Spend hours installing operating systems, then patches, the applications, then more patches, then adjust configuration, or in minutes instantiate another instance of the same server? And do so anywhere in the global infrastructure? IT plans that incorporate virtualization into daily operations will find that minor changes to the process will simplify how the process expands to allow fail-over and fail-back recovery operation activities between multiple hot sites.

Systems management tools already exist that simplify the rapid migration of workloads across data centers. Need to move processing out of a data center threatened by a hurricane? Very easy to accomplish if the enterprise core infrastructure is already enabled for this capability.

As virtualization technologies mature, the product extensions seen as unique to BCP will likely become transparent features within product offerings. Planners will be able to use configurations in the standard solutions to enable preventive and corrective actions that kick in once disruptive events are discovered—or, even better, anticipated.

Supernetworks

Gone are the days of high-cost, low-bandwidth networks. Innovative communications technologies are driving new methods for moving large quantities of data to multiple global locations. Increasingly more intelligent data routing and caching technologies allow for critical data to be replicated as part of common business process to facilitate rapid remote site recovery. As the concepts of "local" and "remote" blend, planners will change the decision processes that have traditionally defined global operations.

Cloud Computing

Cloud computing by its nature has the potential to change the face of BCP for IT. The ability for business to quickly move its computing resources across infrastructure capabilities the way business travelers switch hotels creates massive flexibility unheard of in the current world of event recovery.

Consider the current model for popular recovery services used by the large providers. BC planners contract for emergency services that match existing corporate infrastructures, with the expectation that when the event happens, the corrective recovery process goes into action. The actions taken are those defined by the contract—an agreement that is infrequently tested and comes with a specification that is very likely a distant reflection of the company's current and ever-changing production infrastructure.

The infrastructure-as-a-service and platform-as-a-service models of cloud computing provide organizations new opportunities for innovative partnerships that can be kept current with the rate of change of the business needs. BC planners will see an end to the countless hours focused on network and server provisioning and will instead focus on how to build application management and recovery solutions that span a multitude of diverse service offerings.

As is the case with all disruptive technologies, early adopters will be the guinea pigs that will flush out the problems for everyone else. Cloud is no different—and in the world of BCP where resiliency is everything, the evolution will take many years.

De-duplication

The massive glut of information—what we have and what we have yet to create—has the potential to overwhelm organizations that need this information to feed systems critical to always-on business operations. Increased demand to push data efficiently to distributed global locations has forced companies to rethink how to manage the movement and quantities of this data.

Fortunately, the data storage industry has within the past few years created substantial innovation in data de-duplication, or the process of removing duplicate bytes of data of images for storage and transfer. These new duplicate-free image files become a more efficient way to manage data copies—fewer bytes to save to disk, copy to tape, or move across networks.

The value of de-duplication solutions will be recognized in the efficiency of backup operations: Full backups that now take days to complete are reduced to hours, and incremental backups that take hours to complete are reduced to minutes. This creates recovery scenarios such that site-to-site image copies will complete in fractions of historical times, enabling remote-site activities to start with reduced delay time. Coupling this capability with other technologies like virtualization and cloud computing, de-duplication provides BC planners the chance to apply new thinking to process of solving recovery challenges.

 ## SUMMARY

BCP has become synonymous with emergency response—the ability of an organization to withstand the unexpected. BCP creates a process that documents two critical capabilities of a company:

1. The essential business processes that sustain ongoing operations
2. The automatic response activities that will sustain these business processes when the unexpected happens

BCP becomes the backbone process that breaks this knowledge down until preparedness becomes just another brick in the foundation for everyday operations.

Because companies will continue to build business solutions based on IT technologies, CIOs will continue to be called on to impart greater influence in their companies' BCP strategy.

CHAPTER TWENTY-EIGHT

Overcoming the "Computer Guy" Stigma

A Perspective on Why Being Involved in Your Web Strategy Matters

Kevin L. Soohoo

O PPORTUNITIES FOR IT LEADERS to be involved in the company's customer online engagement initiatives are sometimes few and far between. Instead, some IT leaders are content with handing off the opportunity to the sales and marketing group, stating that they have no budget or resources to support another project. Arguably, this was one of the precursors to what we know today as *rogue IT* because of the hands-off approach many IT organizations have taken to such initiatives.

Yet among all the other projects IT can undertake, this is one of the few that can really show how IT can be a key player within the business, a way for your peers to recognize that you, the CIO or IT leader, truly understand the company's *customers, competitive landscape*, and the *industry* within which you operate.

Being involved in the company's online strategy can be an eye-opening experience on many levels. If you already understand the company's customers, competitive landscape, and industry, you have an excellent opportunity to apply your knowledge and make it known among your executive peers that you understand the business challenges at hand; you are a business partner and can think on their level. For those CIOs who do not fully understand the three dynamics, this is a superb opportunity to engage your peers and take a major step toward shedding the "computer guy" stigma. In either case, understanding the three dynamics will open business engagement opportunities that we as CIOs so very much welcome.

In paraphrasing one of my esteemed business partners over lunch one day, "Everyone has to have a good web site; it's a sign of *credibility* and *forward thinking*. An old, outdated, or poorly constructed web site can be a reflection of the company's quality as well as identify it as a company afraid of change." That says a lot, but it is true on so many levels, from prospective and current employees, to vendors, business partners, and of course customers alike: Your web site, especially in today's connected economy, is a reflection of your company.

This chapter outlines a basic framework and various nontechnical considerations a CIO, along with sales and marketing peers, should contemplate before formulating (or reformulating) a web site strategy. While the question of outsourcing the execution is open (i.e., third-party Web professional versus in-house), the fact remains that a hands-on approach has several thought-provoking and career-enhancing benefits.

 PURPOSE

An important component of your strategy will be to define the purpose and ultimately the desired outcome. A web site whose purpose is solely to inform or educate (think google.com) will have a much different definition of success from a classic company selling widgets. What is the purpose of your web site? In the case of a google.com, its purpose is to "organize the world's information and make it universally accessible and useful"; to boil the purpose down to simpler terms, success may be to return results very rapidly and to have what the user is looking for somewhere on the first page of the search results (not considering pay-per-click or sponsored ads).

Conversely, companies selling goods and/or services will have a much different purpose and idea of success, most commonly tied to increases in sales in one form or another. Despite this rather generic and lofty goal, there needs to be some definition of how exactly success will occur. What specifically will a well-designed web site yield? Obviously, the purpose of your web site is to inform and motivate prospective customers to make contact with you. If you know that your lead-to-sales conversion rate is 25 percent and you are looking to increase sales transactions by 25 every month, a reasonable definition of success would be to attract at least 100 "qualified" leads (meaning visitors who are specifically in the market for your goods or services) to your web site. This is a very simplified example, but as you can see, expectations should be put into a context in which sales are positively affected and that executive management can understand.

Engaging Customers through Layout

Prospective customers will spend no more than perhaps a minute exploring your web site. If they cannot find what they need, you have lost an opportunity, as they will likely move on to your competitors' web sites. How your web site is organized is a key factor in retaining visitors once they happen upon your page, perhaps through Google or another search service (more on that later).

If prospective customers are highly technical, perhaps you should consider a functional type of layout where your goods or services are laid out in a manner that technically oriented visitors would understand. For example, if your business is facilities engineering, you may choose to have your web site organized by technical services, such as "High Purity Process Piping" or "Architectural Metal," terms that have no meaning to outsiders yet are very applicable because you understand that your visitors are technically oriented and will key in on such terms when perusing your web site.

If your customers are not necessarily technically oriented, consider using an applications-type layout. For the same facilities engineering company, organize the web site by applications, such as "Manufacturing—Chemical and Gas Piping Systems" or "Commercial Buildings—Sheetmetal Roofing and Siding," terms that most people would understand. Note that these services correspond to the two services cited in the last paragraph; one is viewed from a technical perspective while the other is not.

The question remains: Who are your customers and what, *in their minds*, are they likely to be looking for? Put yourself in their shoes. In other words, the underlying theme of your web site should be "what can we do *for you*," not "what we do." These are two very distinct thought processes, with the former arguably being more customer-oriented than the latter.

This is not to say that you cannot create two distinct landing pages or segments, one for technical visitors and the other for nontechnical visitors, with links to common information. This method would be especially pertinent if you have both technical and nontechnical customers; by using this method, you incorporate a degree of flexibility that will provide value to all kinds of visitors.

Design Tip: Try to avoid excessive page (vertical) scrolling, as this can cause visitors to lose interest. Remember, you have less than one minute to capture them.

Engaging Customers with Localized Keywords

To further build on the customer-oriented theme, you should also consider using localized keywords throughout your web site to help attract and retain visitors. Is your intended audience local, national, or global? Employing keywords that are location oriented (i.e., "Facilities Engineering San Francisco" or "Global Logistics Services") can boost the applicability of your web site to visitors. Residential services, such as home repair or plumbing, are typically local; in these cases, employing keywords to communicate your operating area(s) would be advantageous. A homeowner living in Houston looking online for a plumber would have no need for someone in Chicago. Conversely, business-to-business services, such as logistics and distribution, can operate at any, but not necessarily all, geographic levels; matching with the appropriate provider would not be clear unless some geographic references are noted (i.e., "APAC Logistics Services" or "Eastern US Logistics Service").

Within the context of your customer engagement approach, be sure to explore these considerations for your web site. By having a keen understanding of these engagement dynamics, you take a step toward being more in tune with your customers and, perhaps more importantly, being recognized as a business partner among your peers.

KEYWORD CAPITALIZATION AND COMPETITIVE LANDSCAPE

Understanding the competitive landscape on the Web is another key component to formulating an effective Web strategy. Keywords that describe your company, such as "IT Consulting"—the keywords customers ideally input into the Googles, Bings, and Yahoos of the world—may already be "owned" by your competition, especially if you are late to the game. Known as search engine optimization (SEO), capitalizing on the right keywords (appropriately used throughout your web site), which directly affects your position on a Web search, is a critical component for driving visitors to your site. While SEO itself is a relatively technical topic, this chapter focuses more on the business considerations rather than the technicalities.

Consider these realities of today's online world:

- Search engines, like Google, Bing, and Yahoo, are the primary sources for prospective customers to find key industry-related information and reach related web sites.
- Visitors who happen on your web site via a search engine are actively looking for services your company provides. They are in essence "self-qualified" visitors; otherwise, they would not have any need to explore your web site.
- High rankings in search engine results establish stronger brand awareness and credibility, much like other marketing avenues such as print ads, billboards, and other visible media.

If you are late to the game and your competition has already staked their cyberterritory, you may find that many of the essential keywords that describe your company are already being used to describe your competition. There are rare instances, particularly in those industries that do not necessarily embrace technology or where the competition does not fully grasp the strategic impact a web site can have, where being late to the game makes no difference. In such cases, you still can realize a sort of first-mover advantage.

Say your company is in the business of providing commercial banking services and operates only in California. It would be logical to assume that potential customers would type in the keywords "bank loans." As such, you would hope the search results would list your bank somewhere in the first page, ideally in the top 10 results. Whether they actually do depends on many technical variables, but by intelligently using and placing descriptive words for your business within your site, you can provide the right foundation to progress from. Think page, section and header titles/footers, service offerings, perhaps articles or newsworthy announcements that contain your desired set of keywords and use them liberally throughout your web site.

Another variable, outside of your control, takes into account the level of competition for these same keyword(s). Google's keyword tool (search "Google Keyword Tool") can provide valuable insight as to whether your competitors are already capitalizing on the same keywords that describe your offerings. A lot of competition for the same keywords can mean difficulties achieving a first-page listing. In that case, consider a more artificial approach, which is equally effective but more expensive; more on that later.

If your first-choice keywords have a relatively high degree of competition, you will have an uphill battle in achieving a first-page listing. Instead consider using alternate or additional keywords (i.e., locality-type keywords) that could better define your business, such as "commercial loans in San Francisco" or "residential electrical contractor serving the San Francisco area."

The actual ranking a search engine bestows to your web site can be achieved organically or artificially (aka "pay per click," or PPC). The intent is not to give a detailed analysis of the PPC model in this chapter, but rather to define a process by which to determine which approach, organic or artificial, makes more sense. If your competitors do not fully understand the strategic impact or you have first-mover advantage, with very little competition for your keywords of choice, an organic strategy may be the best choice, as your ability to capture first-page listings will be notably easier and cheaper, albeit somewhat slower. Latecomers, or those in a market with much competition, may choose to artificially capture first-page rankings through a PPC strategy or to hybridize the methods until organic efforts gain momentum. By understanding the competitive landscape, you can better approach your SEO strategy. Note, however, that it is generally easier to capture new keywords than to overtake ones that your competition uses.

A quick side note: If you pursue an organic approach, you will also need to consider other SEO components that lead to higher rankings, such as quality links and keeping content updated or posting new content, something that a Web development professional can expand upon.

To gain a full technical understanding about SEO and its various implications, consult a Web development professional.

SOCIAL MEDIA

The social media era is one of the latest game changers that will affect your Web strategy, also known as the era in which the customer's voice is louder than ever before. Through social media web sites, customers can have a significant impact on your company's reputation, regardless of how well your site may be designed, linked, optimized, and so on. Conversely, your company can respond directly in kind and better connect to your customers. Companies that have a business-to-consumer focus will certainly want to pay attention to this movement, whereas business-to-business companies can still be impacted indirectly. Remember, there is always some cost to designing a web site but there is practically no cost for customers to post their opinions. CIOs and their marketing counterparts cannot afford to ignore this reality; rather they must embrace it as a means to improve customer service.

Companies big and small are formally incorporating this outlet into their customer service programs, dedicating teams and funneling customer support activities through social media tools. How close your company chooses to keep in touch with such outlets will vary, but keep in mind that by embracing social media, you will have another means with which to promote, and even protect, your company's online strategic goals.

Some of the more popular web sites that can be leveraged, in terms of company promotion, are linkedin.com, yelp.com, and Google's "local business center." All these sites have both a free and a premium (paid) element that, if effectively managed, can enhance your company's visibility in a positive way.

 ## CONCLUSION

Being hands-on in the formulation of your company's online marketing strategy and subsequent success in expanding your company's visibility can open the eyes of your executive peers. By demonstrating insight into the company's customers, competitive landscape, and industry, your image as a business partner rather than just the "computer guy" is enhanced. This topic has many technical considerations, which you should discuss with a Web development professional; however, there are as many and equally important business considerations that a CIO can and should weigh in on.

About the Editor

Dean Lane, founder of The Office of the CIO®, (www.oocio.com) has 30 years of hands-on experience in the IT industry, having been a practitioner CIO at four different companies: Honeywell Aerospace, ATK (Alliant Techsystems), Plantronics, and Masters Institute of Technology. Additionally, he held the senior IT director position at Symantec and was the corporate director of materials for Honeywell. Dean has also been a consultant for Ernst & Young, AT&T, and the Gartner Group. His experience is global, and he is considered an expert on corporate alignment. Dean has served as the CEO for VariTRAK Inc., a company that provides compliance software. He is currently serving as the interim CIO for the Northern California Golf Association, Henley-Putnam University, American Casting Company, and three other smaller firms.

Dean obtained his undergraduate degree from the University of California Los Angeles and his MBA from National University. He is Certified in the Governance of Enterprise IT (CGEIT). Dean serves on the advisory boards of Sparta Consulting, Search CIO, Droisys, Inc., and San Francisco State University. He is well known in Silicon Valley. Aside from founding the Office of the CIO Community, he cofounded the Consortium of Information Systems Executives, is a member of the Institute of Management Consultants and the CIO Collective, and is former president of SIM's Silicon Valley chapter. His first book, *CIO Wisdom*, is a Prentice Hall best seller, and a sequel, *CIO Perspectives*, was published by Kendall-Hunt. During a Hi-Tech Economic Mission to Israel, he consulted with former Israeli Prime Minister Ehud Barach. Dean is a highly decorated U.S. Naval Officer. Dean may be contacted at dlane@oocio.com.

About the Contributors

Walter Bacon is a San Francisco–based senior business development manager for Harvey Nash, an international executive search and IT talent solutions firm with offices throughout the United States, Europe, and Southeast Asia. His successful career of selling technology solutions and products to CIOs for the past 16 years has been achieved through innovative marketing strategies and a passion for adding value to his clients and the IT community. He can be reached at walter.bacon@harveynashusa.com.

David Blumhorst is currently the vice president of professional services for Daptiv, the leading PPM SaaS provider. He is a seasoned executive who has run IT, professional services, and finance departments. He has served as a controller and CFO for small to midsize companies, served as CIO at midsize companies, and was the senior director of the IT-PMO at PeopleSoft. Dave has also provided advice and consulting in IT and PMO management to many Fortune 1000 companies. Throughout his 30-plus-year career, he has always found innovative ways to use technology to create business value.

Tim Campos is a business-oriented technical leader with an emphasis in enterprise systems and application hosting services. With over 19 years of industry experience in both software engineering and information technology, Tim has unique understanding of the challenges in both developing and applying IT.

Tim currently is the CIO at Facebook, the world's largest social network. Prior to Facebook, he served as CIO and vice president of IT at KLA-Tencor.

Tim has held engineering leadership roles at Silicon Graphics, Sybase, and Portera Systems. He holds an MBA from Columbia University and a BS in electrical engineering and computer science from the University of California at Berkeley. He is on the board of directors for the Fisher IT Center at the Haas School of Business at UC Berkeley as well as the advisory board for several Silicon Valley start-ups.

Louis Carr, Jr., has worked for the City of Arlington, Texas, since February 2007. During his short tenure, he has helped the IT department gain a more prominent role in budgeting and planning for future city technology needs. He has established a new IT governance structure, established a project management office, successfully lobbied for funding to update about one-third of the city's server and network infrastructure, and brought technology project portfolio management concepts to the IT department and the City of Arlington.

Prior to working with the City of Arlington, Louis worked for the City of Las Vegas, most recently as the deputy director of information technologies. His responsibilities included managing daily operations for the department of approximately 100 people. His accomplishments included installing the first online interactive mapping system in the state of Nevada and orchestrating Nevada's first state-wide government services portal. In September 2006, Louis and the Department of Information Technologies was awarded fourth place in the Digital Cities "Best of the Web" contest.

Louis has a master's degree in business administration and a bachelor's degree in electrical engineering, with a minor in computer science. Before working at the City of Las Vegas, he worked with the Department of Energy (Nevada Test Site), SRI International (Menlo Park, CA), and Computer Sciences Corporation (Las Vegas Office).

Sam Chughtai is a senior industry leader in cloud computing information risk management and regulatory compliance advisory to Fortune 100 board of directors and C-level management. He has over 18 years of consulting experience in information risk management, cloud computing technology marketing, consulting practice development, and regulatory compliance with PricewaterhouseCoopers, KPMG, and Microsoft Corporation. Sam has provided risk management advisory to congressional committees for Economic Recovery Reform legislation in 2009 and is currently leading cloud computing technology strategy and governance, risk management, and compliance programs at a global software development company.

Baron Concors is chief information and digital officer for Pizza Hut, Inc., with responsibility for all aspects of Pizza Hut's digital business and IT including store technologies, e-commerce, m-commerce, business intelligence, and call centers. Under his direction, the IT department serves as a valued business partner focused on accelerating Pizza Hut's business through technology that delivers a competitive advantage and profitable growth. He brings extensive experience in business process design, operations, and marketing with an emphasis in retail, hospitality, and consumer goods. In 2009, *Forbes* named the Pizza Hut iPhone application the number-one branded mobile application of the year. Prior to joining Pizza Hut, he was vice president of global retail technology for FedEx and held a variety of leadership positions at Deloitte and Touche LLP and at Ernst and Young LLP.

Rossella Derickson, principal of www.Corporate-Wisdom.com, has translated her business and organizational experience into Wisdom in the Workplace consulting, training, and coaching modules that support healthy group and company dynamics.

Her classes to build business and leadership skills have been taught to CEOs, executives, and entrepreneurs in high-tech, biotech, insurance, and many other industries including leading universities.

Connecting CSR to individual, team, and organizational purpose at work is a passionate focus area. She is an author of *Awakening Social Responsibility: A Call to Action* (www.CSRAction.com).

Rossella is a director of the South Bay Organizational Development Network (www.SBODN.com), a leading-edge forum focused on making a difference in how organizations are run in Silicon Valley.

William (Liam) Durbin joined Heinz North America in 2008 as chief information officer. Prior to his work at Heinz, Liam spent nine years with GE companies. His most recent role was CIO at GE Fanuc Automation, a $1 billion division of GE Enterprise Solutions, where he led the IT team through a challenging period of multiple acquisitions. Earlier, Liam was CIO of supply chain systems at GE Consumer & Industrial, where he led the supply chain that included over 150 manufacturing plants, $2 billion globally in purchased direct materials, and $14.0 billion in annual sales. He started his career with GE at GE Appliances, where he held several technology management positions, including director of information technology–sales force automation, master black belt, and was then promoted to vice president–technology systems.

Prior to his corporate career, Liam enjoyed 12 rewarding and successful years as an officer in the United States Navy with a final rank of lieutenant commander. In the navy, he achieved success in a wide array of roles, including squadron staff, operations, logistics, and engineering.

Liam earned his MBA from William and Mary while in the navy; his MS in the Naval Postgraduate School; and his BA from the University of Mississippi.

Liam was honored as the 2010 CIO of the Year by the Pittsburgh Technology Council.

Mark Egan leads VMware's global information technology group. Under Mark's leadership, VMware's IT department is focused on the effective use of IT to bring improved agility and cost savings to the business. Mark brings more than 30 years of experience in IT to VMware, most recently serving as partner of the StrataFusion Group, an executive-level consultancy. Mark served as CIO at Symantec Corporation for six years during the company's rapid growth from a consumer publisher with $600 million revenue to the market leader of security with $5 billion revenue. During his tenure at Symantec, Mark led the IT integration through 28 acquisitions, including a $13 billion acquisition of Veritas Software. Prior to Symantec, Mark held senior-level positions at Sun Microsystems, Price Waterhouse, Atlantic Richfield Corporation, Martin Marietta Data Systems, Walden International Investment Group, and Wells Fargo Bank. Mark is coauthor of *Executive Guide to Information Security: Threats, Challenges, and Solutions* (Addison-Wesley, 2004) and was a contributing author of *CIO Wisdom* (Prentice Hall, 2003) and *CIO Perspectives*. Mark holds a master's degree in finance and international business from the University of San Diego and a bachelor's degree in computer sciences from the University of Clarion.

David Finnis is an information security subject matter expert. His information security and IT background originated in IT network engineering, and his career has spanned the past 18 years. He has worked extensively with enterprise-level clients in the United States and internationally, implementing strategic information security programs that help organizations protect their employees and critical information assets.

David has performed enterprise information security audits and is a security expert in all architectural IT layers; this has enabled him to work and communicate with large cross-functional IT teams that ensure all aspects of information security are considered.

David holds numerous information security–related certifications, such as CISSP, CISA, QDSP, and CGEIT, and is an active member in the Silicon Valley information security associations and communities.

Charles Follett is a partner with the Stratam Group. Charles combines his engineering background with his work as a pioneer in the development of commitment process analysis and design to produce breakthrough process redesigns. His work is known for the elegance and simplicity with which he transforms complicated working arrangements into aligned, purposeful, and efficient processes.

Jeff Goldberg is the chief architect for the Stratam Group. Jeff has been an architect and developer of software for more than 20 years. For the last six years, he has focused on process analysis and design, delivering working software that embodies the theory of commitment-based management. As part of this work, he has developed new techniques for implementing process improvements in software in a fraction of the time earlier methodologies entailed—typically months rather than years.

Gary Kelly is currently a senior manager of finance at Motorola Mobility in Sunnyvale, California. He has previously held managerial positions with the Boeing Corporation, Seagate Technologies, Honeywell Corporation, and Travelers Insurance. He is licensed as a certified public accountant in both California and Utah, is an avid yacht sailor, and does regular travel blogs about North American tourist attractions for a Norwegian-based web site.

Art Klein has been a technology and leadership expert for 18 years. Early in his career, Art served as a senior UNIX and TCP/IP expert, with a focus on heterogeneous networks and high-availability systems and performance tuning. At Pricewaterhouse-Coopers, Art advised one of the first Fortune 50 companies that complied with the Sarbanes-Oxley Act of 2004 and led controls design and testing efforts. Art has advised executives, served as CIO, and worked with and within companies both large and small. Some of the companies Art has worked with include Charles Schwab, Safeway, Visa, Ericsson, Kaiser Permanente, Microsoft, and Capgemini. Currently Art is an executive director at Kaiser Permanente, where he leads its Availability Program Office and governs its problem management process enterprise-wide. Art graduated from Northwestern University with a bachelor's of science degree in mechanical engineering and lives in San Francisco with his wife.

Dave McCandless, CISA, is the director of IT for Navis/Cargotec, the world's leading provider of cargo-handling solutions. He has 30 years of experience in systems development and operations for companies large and small including AT&T/Bell Labs, Oracle, Bank of America, Chevron, Zebra, and HedgeStreet. He serves on many advisory boards, both emerging companies and major universities. Dave holds BS and MS degrees in computer science from Washington State University and the University of Wisconsin–Madison.

Allyn McGillicuddy has IT leadership experience with large-scale, high-technology solution delivery spanning more than two decades. Most recently she was CIO at Golden Gate University in San Francisco, California. There she led her teams to establish the university's private cloud computing environment including a wide area network based on Cisco's MPLS network architecture. In addition, she implemented the institution's first VoIP telephone system, installed comprehensive classroom technology, and launched its enterprise content management system.

In various software engineering executive roles at Filenet Corporation; Delta Dental (Dentegra); and Prudential Real Estate of California, Nevada, and Texas, Allyn successfully led the design and development of a wide range of products and solutions including financial systems based on Oracle Applications; a dynamic web site architecture to support more than 10,000 unique, real estate agent web sites; CRM systems, and enterprise content management systems.

As director for Scient Corporation, she led the teams that designed and delivered Wells Fargo Bank's corporate electronic office, the first commercial banking system offered via the Internet in the United States. This achievement followed her successful delivery, as IBM Global Services Project Executive, of Washington Mutual Bank's Internet retail banking system at wamu.com.

A certified Project Management Professional and a certified IBM Project Executive, Allyn earned her bachelor's degree at Case Western Reserve University, her master's in information technology at the University of San Francisco, and her master's certificate in project management from George Washington University.

John M. Millican is a business-first manager with strong experience in driving value to the enterprise through IT and information security. His experience is divided between positions in both industry and third-party IT service and information security provision.

John developed and led the global information security team for Expedia Inc. as its chief information security officer and was VP of IT operations for Hotwire.com. He also founded and led a 12-person independent IT/information security service provider. Clients and employers have ranged from small wholesale/distributors to regional financial institutions and Fortune 1000 Internet-based companies.

John is a Certified Information Systems Security Professional and was the first person to be certified by the SANS Institute for its core security programs: Windows Security, UNIX Security, Intrusion Detection Analyst, Incident Handling, and Firewall Analyst. Additionally, he is coauthor of the *SANS Security Essentials Toolkit* (Que, 2002).

John has a BS in business administration degree from the University of Akron.

John Moran has achieved recognition as a bridge between the academic communities and industry, blending more than 35 years experience in industry as an executive, product developer, and project manager and in academia as a course developer/instructor. John's courses at the University of Nevada–Reno, Notre Dame de Namur University, UC Berkeley Extension, and San Jose State Professional Development program reflect the real-life business situations derived from his work in developing IT communities of practice with Silicon Valley companies. Additionally, his academic experience contributes to his ability to create unique collaborative environments that facilitate learning, sustainable growth, and increased productivity for his industry and academic clients.

John's educational background includes a BA in computer science from UC Berkeley, an MBA from Golden Gate University, and a PhD in educational psychology with an emphasis in IT in education from the University of Nevada, Reno.

Subbu Murthy, PhD, is a senior IT executive with a strong technical background who has managed IT in consumer-packaged goods, electronics, healthcare, and professional services companies. He is currently CIO (Consultant) at QuickLogic and CTO at CPM Systems, where he provides on-demand CIO/CTO services. He leads the Los Angeles chapter for The Office of the CIO.

Throughout his career, Subbu has innovated, developed, and marketed technology in a number of fields, including software-enabled medical devices. As CIO and head of a business unit, Subbu helped QTC grow to over $100 million in revenues and helped sell the technology to portfolio investors. He helped asset management companies acquire small to medium-size businesses by providing an in-depth assessment of the target company's business processes and technology. His IT due diligence framework became the standard for comprehensive assessments leading to quick acquisition and merger decisions. He has helped companies productize technology and sell to both privately held and publicly traded investment firms. He developed the first reuse library in 1984, the first global delivery model for IT services in 1985, the first SaaS-based ERP and CRM systems for claims processing in 2003, and the first SaaS fuzzy logic system in 2006.

Subbu earned his bachelor's degree in electronics and his master's in computer science from the University of Southern California. He earned his doctorate in information systems from Claremont Graduate University, where he pioneered the use of metrics and analytics in managing information technology. His interests include building products for IT governance and pragmatic outsourcing that embrace quality principles drawn from his expertise in FDA GMP practices, CCE (Malcolm Baldrige criteria for excellence), ISO-9001, ITIL, CMM, and Six Sigma. Subbu is considered an expert in Indian classical music and enjoys solving Sudoku puzzles, playing bridge, and keeping up with his twin son and daughter.

Jeff Richards, managing partner, The Office of the CIO Professional Services, is an inspirational leader with the ability to develop the big-picture strategy, then drive it down to executable tactics for implementation. He has over 25 years of experience developing business strategy and aligning the supporting IT and associated organizational changes to deliver the results. He developed his global perspective during significant profit and loss management-level positions in Asia and Europe.

He focuses his in-depth knowledge of supply chain, after-sale service, IT, and outsourcing to help his clients grapple with sourcing and operational issues on a global basis. His varied and diverse assignments have helped him to develop a broad depth of knowledge across multiple industry verticals including high technology, manufacturing, financial services, energy and utilities, software, telecommunications, and aerospace and defense.

A sample list of recent clients includes ACE, Agilent Technologies, Hewlett-Packard, Juniper Networks, Mitsubishi Motors, Motorola, NetScreen, Pacific Ethanol, Palm, PGP, Simons Petroleum, Southern California Edison, Sun Microsystems, Valeant Pharmaceuticals, and Wipro.

His past employers include Computer Sciences Corporation, Tatum, Cap Gemini, Ernst & Young, Boeing, Dresser, and Baker/Hughes.

Jeff has a bachelor's of science in business administration in management science from Shippensburg University in Pennsylvania.

Stuart Robbins is a Silicon Valley veteran, author, speaker, and business coach who has provided executive-level guidance to a broad list of institutions in the public and private sector. He specializes in turnaround efforts for projects, teams, and individuals.

As the founder and executive director of The CIO Collective (www.cio-collective .com), a nonprofit professional association of senior IT executives, Stuart has consulted for Cisco/WebEx, Yahoo, Macromedia, the World Bank and the International Monetary Fund, Bessemer Trust, and Morgan Stanley from 1999 to 2006. Most recently, Stuart provided senior-level guidance to the IT organization at TriNet HR, Inc., a leading human resources outsourcing firm where he brought numerous best practices to the company and served as the company's interim CIO during its merger with Gevity in 2009. Previously Stuart served as the CIO for Jamcracker, a leader in cloud computing platforms and, before that, held senior IT positions at Documentum, Synopsys, and Cadence Design Systems.

Author of the critically acclaimed *The System Is a Mirror* (John Wiley & Sons, 2006), Stuart has published dozens of articles on IT and knowledge management throughout his career. He was awarded a master's degree in fine arts from Warren Wilson College in 1986 and earned his bachelor's degree from Oberlin College in 1975.

Himanshu Shah is the director of global IT at MSC Software. He is an established leader with experience in managing global engineering and IT functions of high technology, telecommunications, and consulting organizations. Early in his career, Himanshu managed global business systems, technology infrastructure, and service delivery functions at Symantec. Throughout his career, he has built offshoring, outsourcing, and cosourcing models that significantly reduced costs and increased business effectiveness. Himanshu has a bachelor's degree in computer science from Mumbai University and a master's degree in organization management from the University of Phoenix.

Robert Slepin is an experienced healthcare CIO and certified Project Management Professional who gets things done. His 28-year IT career includes CIO and IT executive roles at some of the nation's most admired healthcare, health insurance, and health improvement organizations, including Sutter Health, Delta Dental of California, and LifeMasters Supported SelfCare. Robert builds teams and leads the planning and execution of IT projects that deliver measurable business value. His extensive experience includes IT assessment, strategic IT planning, IT organization restructuring, electronic health records, health data exchange and analytics, call center and technology infrastructure, software development and implementation, information security, outsourcing, and IT process improvement. He received his bachelor's degree from Duke University and holds certificates in IT service management (ITIL) and IT governance (COBiT).

Michael Skaff is the CIO of the San Francisco Symphony, where he oversees the enterprise-wide technology strategy for one of the Bay Area's largest nonprofit organizations. From start-ups to multibillion-dollar enterprises, Michael has a distinguished record of building high-performing teams in strategy, development, operations, IT, and consulting across an array of industries including retail, high tech, consulting, and nonprofit. With over 18 years of experience that ranges from the data center to the board room, he built a solid reputation as a leader in the industry and as an expert in identifying and executing business-driven technology strategy that delivers quantifiable value. Michael is a published author and has served on the advisory boards of a number of organizations including Everything Channel, *eWEEK* magazine, the Marin County Bicycle Coalition's Technology Board, and several software companies. He is a regular speaker, panelist, and judge at technology and music industry events, such as the RSA Conference, CTIA Wireless, Frost & Sullivan's GIL Global 2010, Network World, and XChange Americas. Michael holds a bachelor's degree in psychology from the University of California, Davis.

Kevin L. Soohoo is the director of IT for Air Systems, Inc., a San Francisco–based construction subcontractor focused on designing, building, and servicing energy-efficient facilities from campuses to offices to critical facilities such as data centers and labs. Additionally, Kevin is involved in the company's business development initiatives relating to green IT within data centers. Through this, Kevin is actively engaged in developing strategic relationships with external partners and customers to promote energy efficiency awareness within data center environments. Prior to joining Air Systems, Kevin held several progressive IT management roles, from regional IT manager to global infrastructure manager for Volex, Inc., a global cable manufacturer and supplier.

Kevin holds a master's degree in information systems management from the University of San Francisco and a bachelor's degree in business/MIS from San Jose State University.

Makarand Utpat is an award-winning executive and a proven IT leader with a track record of delivering vision, pragmatic strategies, and sustainable value growth. Makarand has spearheaded change, turnaround, and business transformation initiatives for global corporations such as IBM, Johnson & Johnson, Merck, Hoffmann-La Roche, Chubb, and Prudential Financial. Makarand is adept at nurturing initiatives from concept to completion. He is equally at ease defining holistic strategies or guiding day-to-day technology implementations. He has also led large-scale vendor procurement efforts to drive standardization and cost improvements. Makarand's areas of expertise are strategic planning; application portfolio management and rationalization; business process management, enterprise architecture; project and program management; information integration; data warehousing and business intelligence; enterprise capabilities areas such as portals, content management, and collaboration; Agile software development; and service-oriented architectures. Makarand is a master problem solver, is highly respected by his peers, and is consistently recognized for improving the IT infrastructure performance and for enhanced decision-making capabilities that achieve significant cost savings and accelerated/improved alignment of IT with business objectives.

Makarand holds certifications in project management discipline such as PMP and enterprise architecture discipline such as TOGAF (The Open Group Architecture Framework) and Zachman. Additionally, he is a trained specialist in Six Sigma Green Belt and Black Belt. Makarand holds an undergraduate degree in production engineering, a diploma in computer management, and a master's degree in computer sciences. He resides in central New Jersey and can be reached at makarandutpat@yahoo.com.

Mark Wayman is the founder and CEO of The Foundation, an executive placement firm focused on gaming and high tech. Mark was previously with two technology companies; one went public on the NASDAQ and the other was acquired by IBM. He is an active supporter of Las Vegas community, participating in Make-A-Wish, Three Square, and the Arthritis Foundation. For more information, go to www.godfatherlv.com.

Pamela Vaughan is a business-focused, high-energy, proactive IT executive. Her first CIO role was 17 years ago with Hub Group Distribution Services, a third-party logistics provider and four-time Inc. 500 company during her tenure. Pamela has also held IT executive positions with Ariat International, The SAK, American Century Investments, and The Dialog Corporation. In 2009 she became a partner at the Office of the CIO. Pamela is now the president and CEO at Advance Management, a management consulting business providing interim CIO, supply chain, and project management services.

Pamela excels at transforming underperforming IT departments to strategic high-performance teams focused on aligning with the corporate goals. She is experienced leading the ERP selection, implementation, and support of SAP, Oracle, PeopleSoft, Microsoft, and Workday. At numerous companies Pamela has implemented business intelligence solutions providing a "single version of the truth" and significant improvement and efficiency in reporting and analysis.

She is a contributing author of *CIO Perspectives* (Kendall-Hunt, 2007), a book covering best practices from Silicon Valley's leading CIOs. Pamela is the chairperson of the Northern California IBM Cognos User Group. She is an active member of both the Office of the CIO and the Consortium of Information Systems Executives and former membership chair for the San Francisco Bay Area Society of Information Management.

Pamela holds both an undergraduate degree and a postgraduate degree, in applied statistics and computing, from the University of Wales.

Index